# History
## for CCEA GCSE

# History
## for CCEA GCSE
### Second Edition

Finbar Madden

HODDER
EDUCATION
AN HACHETTE UK COMPANY

The following questions are © CCEA 2013, reprinted with the permission of the Northern Ireland
Council for the Curriculum, Examinations and Assessment: p.27 Foundation 1(b), (c) & (d);
p.47 Foundation 1(b) & (d); p.56 Foundation 1(b) & (d); p.76 Foundation 1(b) & (c);
p.91 Higher 1(a), (b) & (c); p.116 Foundation 1(b) & (c); p.128 Higher 1(a)(i) & (ii), (b) & (c);
p.189 Foundation 1(a); p.190 Higher 1(a), (b) & (d). All other questions are written by the author.

Although every effort has been made to ensure that website addresses are correct at time of going to press,
Hodder Education cannot be held responsible for the content of any website mentioned in this book. It is
sometimes possible to find a relocated web page by typing in the address of the home page for a website in the
URL window of your browser.

Hachette UK's policy is to use papers that are natural, renewable and recyclable products and made from
wood grown in sustainable forests. The logging and manufacturing processes are expected to conform to the
environmental regulations of the country of origin.

Orders: please contact Bookpoint Ltd, 130 Milton Park, Abingdon, Oxon OX14 4SB.
Telephone: +44 (0)1235 827720. Fax: +44 (0)1235 400454. Lines are open 9.00 a.m. – 5.00 p.m., Monday to
Saturday, with a 24-hour message answering service. Visit our website at www.hoddereducation.co.uk.

© Finbar Madden 2004, 2009
First edition 2004
Second edition published in 2009 by
Hodder Education,
An Hachette UK company
338 Euston Road
London NW1 3BH

Reprinted with revisions 2014

Impression number     10
Year                  2015

Cover photo © Peter Kemp/AP/PA Photos; MPI/Getty Images; AKG-images
Typeset in Goudy 12/13pt and produced by Gray Publishing, Tunbridge Wells
Printed in Italy

A catalogue record for this title is available from the British Library.

ISBN: 978 0340 984 109

# CONTENTS

## CHAPTER 1 Germany c1918–39

**The Aftermath of the First World War and the Weimar Republic**    1
Germany before 1918    1
Impact of the War    2
The Treaty of Versailles    6
Threats from the Right    8
The 1923 Economic Crisis (I): The Problem    10
The 1923 Economic Crisis (II): The Solution    12
The 'Golden Twenties'    13
Hitler and the Origins of the Nazi Party    14
Nazi Reorganisation and Growth    18
Germany and the Great Depression    19
1932: The Year of Four Elections    22
Hitler's Rise to Power    24
Practice Question (Foundation and Higher)    27

**Nazi Germany 1933–9**    28
Nazi Consolidation of Power (I)    28
Nazi Consolidation of Power (II)    31
Nazi Economic Policy (I): Unions and Unemployment    33
Nazi Economic Policy (II): Stability and Autarky    34
Hitler in Control    36
Youth    37
Religion    39
The Police State    40
Propaganda    42
Anti-Semitism and the Persecution of Minorities    44
Practice Question (Foundation and Higher)    47

**Nazi Policies and Actions in Europe 1933–41**    48
Nazi Foreign Policy    48
Disarmament    49
Rearmament    50
1936–8: Becoming Bolder    51
The Road to War    54
Practice Question (Foundation and Higher)    56

# CHAPTER 2 Peace, War and Neutrality: Britain, Northern Ireland and Ireland 1932–49

**Anglo-Irish Relations Before the Second World War**   **57**
Ireland Before 1932   57
Northern Ireland   60
The Free State under de Valera   62
The Economic War   64
The 1937 Constitution   66
Britain and the Threat of War   68
The Anglo-Irish Agreements   70
Developments in Northern Ireland 1939   72
Declaration of War   74
Practice Question (Foundation)   76

**The Effects of the Second World War on Northern Ireland**   **77**
Ready for War?   77
The Battle of Britain   79
Northern Ireland's War Effort (I): Strategic   80
Northern Ireland's War Effort (II): Economic   83
The Belfast Blitz   84
War and the Free State (I): Military Preparations   86
War and the Free State (II): Assessing Neutrality   87
Practice Question (Higher)   91

**Post-War Social and Political Changes**   **92**
The Welfare State (I): Great Britain   92
The Welfare State (II): Northern Ireland   93
Éire: Post-War Problems   95
Éire Becomes a Republic   97

# CHAPTER 3 Changing Relationships: Britain, Northern Ireland and Ireland c1965–85

## Northern Ireland in the 1960s and its Relations with the Republic of Ireland — **101**

Introduction: The Emergence and Development of Northern Ireland 1920–63 — 101
O'Neill's Policies (I): Economic — 102
O'Neill's Policies (II): Political — 103
Reactions to O'Neill's Policies 1963–7 — 105
Civil Rights to Armalites: Northern Ireland 1967–9 — 108
NICRA's Tactics and O'Neill's Response — 110
The People's Democracy March — 112
People's Democracy: Reactions and Resignations — 114
Practice Question (Foundation) — 116

## Escalation of Political and Civil Unrest — **117**

Countdown to Chaos: Northern Ireland 1969–72 — 117
Reactions (I): Westminster and Stormont — 118
Reactions (II): Military and Paramilitaries — 120
Internment and Bloody Sunday — 123
Stormont: Suspension and Reactions — 125
Practice Question (Higher) — 128

## The Search for a Solution — **129**

A New Political System — 129
Sunningdale — 131
The Executive in Operation — 133
The Strike — 135
Developments 1975–80 — 136
The Hunger Strikes — 137
The Rise of Sinn Féin — 139
The Anglo-Irish Agreement (I): Terms — 140
The Anglo-Irish Agreement (II): Reactions — 142
The Anglo-Irish Agreement (III): Campaign of Opposition — 144

## CHAPTER 4 The Cold War 1945–91

| | |
|---|---|
| **From Allies to Enemies** | **147** |
| A Clash of Ideologies? Communism versus Capitalism before 1945 | 147 |
| Renewing Division: The Events of 1945 | 149 |
| The Expansion of Communism In Eastern Europe | 151 |
| The Spread of Communism in Europe 1945–9 | 154 |
| Confrontation and Containment | 156 |
| Challenges to the Control of the USSR: Hungary and Berlin | 159 |
| Springtime in Europe? The 1968 Czech Rising | 163 |
| *Détente* | 166 |
| The Collapse of Communism and the end of the Cold War | 169 |
| Final Thaw: The USSR and the Satellite States | 171 |
| The Spread of Communism in Asia 1945–75 (I) | 174 |
| The Spread of Communism in Asia 1945–75 (II) | 175 |
| The 1962 Cuban Missile Crisis | 179 |
| The Spread of Communism in Asia 1945–75 (III): The Vietnam War | 183 |
| Practice Question (Foundation and Higher) | 188 |
| | |
| Useful Websites | 191 |
| | |
| Glossary | 192 |
| | |
| Acknowledgements | 197 |
| | |
| Index | 198 |

---

**About the extension activities**

The extension activities throughout the book are designed for high-achieving students. They are questions that challenge the students beyond the level expected at GCSE.

# Germany c1918–39

## CHAPTER 1

## THE AFTERMATH OF THE FIRST WORLD WAR AND THE WEIMAR REPUBLIC

### GERMANY BEFORE 1918

On 18 January 1871 the 39 individual states that made up the region of central Europe known as Germany announced that they were joining together to form a single country with one government. This unification was brought about by the policies of Otto von Bismarck, Chancellor (Prime Minister) of Prussia, which was the most important of these states.

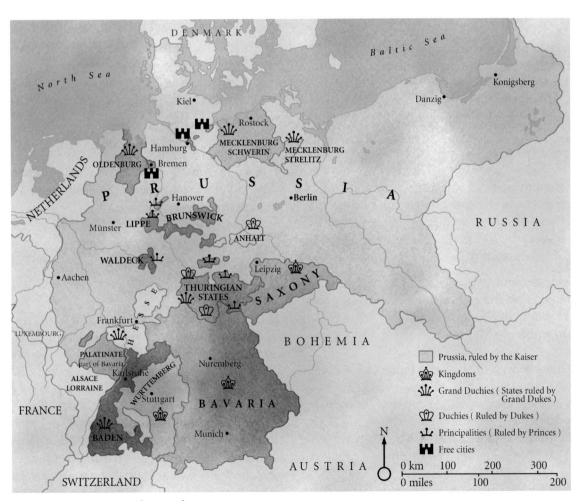

**Figure 1.1** Germany before unification.

### The new German Reich

The new German *Reich* (Empire) was to be dominated by Prussia. For example:

- The new country was to be ruled by the Prussian King who was given the title of Kaiser (Emperor).
- The country's first Chancellor was Prussia's Otto von Bismarck.

At first Bismarck was given the freedom to run the country as he wanted. While modern historians believe that Bismarck was doing a good job, this viewpoint was not shared by Wilhelm II who became Kaiser in 1888. Wilhelm wanted Germany to become the most powerful country in Europe and felt that this would not happen while Bismarck remained as Chancellor.

Wilhelm gave Bismarck the sack and took over the running of the country himself. The Kaiser began to build up the country's military power as well as its political and economic influence. However all of this growth came at a price. Germany's aggressive policies annoyed countries such as France, Russia and Britain. By 1914 war between these powers seemed inevitable; in August of that year it broke out.

## IMPACT OF THE WAR

At first, the outbreak of war was welcomed by most Germans. As the war progressed, however, many became unhappy because of the impact that the war was having on them. There were a number of reasons for this:

- Food was becoming harder and harder to get, mainly because the **Allies'** navies were stopping ships bringing goods to Germany.
- Fuel shortages were becoming more and more common.
- There had been a drop in the value of German money.
- Much of Germany's potato crop was destroyed by the harsh winter of 1917–18 (Source A). That winter became known as the 'turnip winter' as that seemed to be the only available food.
- There was an increase in ill health among ordinary Germans. During 1918 hundreds of thousands of Germans died as the result of a flu pandemic.

Yet due to **propaganda** most Germans still believed that the war was going well. The fact that Germany had defeated Russia by March 1918 seemed to provide evidence to support this belief.

Of course, that was not true and by October 1918 the German government knew that the war had been lost:

- Over six million soldiers had either been killed or wounded.
- The army's most recent military attack had failed.
- Germany's allies (Austria-Hungary, Bulgaria and Turkey) were close to defeat.
- Soldiers were hungry and worn out; more and more of them were deserting.

On top of that there was growing unrest among Germany's working classes.

All of this had an impact on the way in which Germany was governed. In late October 1918 the Kaiser was persuaded by leading generals to make Germany into a **constitutional monarchy**. This was because:

- It was feared that some workers might start a revolution to overthrow the Kaiser. This had already happened in Russia in February 1917.
- The Allies had made it clear that a civilian government would obtain fairer peace terms.
- It was believed that the new government would get the blame for ending the war, allowing the army to accuse it of stabbing them in the back.

As a result Prince Max of Baden became Germany's new Chancellor.

### Abdication

These concessions were not enough for those Germans who wanted the Kaiser removed and Germany made into a **republic**. On 3 November 1918, sailors stationed at Kiel and Wilhelmshaven naval bases staged **mutinies**, refusing to obey orders to go to sea to fight the Royal Navy. Local workers joined in and the protests spread across the country with Russian-style workers' councils (Soviets) being set up. Within a week Berlin had been brought to a standstill by a general strike while **socialist** republics had been set up in two of the country's states, Bavaria and Saxony.

With Germany facing revolution the Kaiser agreed to **abdicate**. He did so on 9 November

## SOURCE A

*Ethel Cooper writing to her sister Adelaide in February 1917, explains what life was like in Germany.*

We have got through a queer week – the worst week the German people has had to face up to the present. No coal, electric light turned off, the gas power turned down … and practically no food … each of us has been given half a pound of what they call potato-flocken … they seem to be the dried parings of potatoes – you have to soak them overnight, then rub them through a sieve.

1918. At the same time Prince Max was replaced by Social Democratic Party (SPD) leader Friedrich Ebert. Ebert soon made the following crucial decisions:

- On 9 December he set up a new government and declared Germany a republic (Source B, page 4).
- On 10 December Ebert made a deal with the head of the German army, General Wilhelm Groener. Under the terms of the Ebert–Groener Pact the Chancellor agreed to maintain the power of the German army and resist the growth of **communism**. Ebert also agreed to leave the influence of the **judiciary**

Crowds queuing outside a potato store in Berlin 1917.

## SOURCE B

*Extract from a declaration by Friedrich Ebert on 11 November 1918.*

To the German people: the government which the revolution has produced, whose political convictions [beliefs] are purely Socialist ... now make the following announcements which will have the force of law ...

1 Censorship ceases to exist ...
2 Opinion, whether by word of mouth or in writing, is free ...
3 Freedom of religion is guaranteed ...
9 The eight-hour day will come into force ...
The housing difficulty will be dealt with by the building of houses. Efforts will be made to secure the regular feeding of the people.

Friedrich Ebert (1871–1925).

and **civil service** untouched. For his part the General agreed to support the new government.

- On 11 November 1918, Germany signed an **armistice** that brought the fighting in the war to an end.

The Kaiser's abdication and the signing of the armistice shocked many ordinary Germans who still believed that the war was going well and could not understand how it had now been lost. With no one else to blame their anger was directed towards the new government – just as the Kaiser and army had wanted.

### Threat from the Left

#### Political Divisions
The terms left wing and right wing are often used to describe different political viewpoints. Put simply, left wing refers to people who want sweeping changes in the way that a country is governed while right wing refers to people who are against any such change. There were plenty of both groups in Germany!

#### The Spartacists
Ebert faced particular opposition from the left-wing Spartacists, led by Rosa Luxemburg and Karl Liebknecht. They believed that Germany should be run by Russian-style workers' councils, not by the *Reichstag* as Ebert wanted. On 6 January 1919

the Spartacists – now calling themselves the German Communist Party (KPD) – launched a *putsch* (rising) against the new SPD government (Source C). The *putsch* was unlikely to succeed though, as the Spartacists were poorly equipped, badly organised and lacked widespread support.

The *putsch* was crushed by the army supported by the Free Corps (*Frei Korps*). This was a right-wing volunteer army that had been formed by Gustav Noske, the Defence Minister, and which was made up mainly of ex-soldiers who were strongly anti-communist. By 15 January 1919 the rising had been crushed and both Spartacist

## SOURCE C

*Spartacist rallying call for revolution.*

Workers! Comrades! The Ebert government is seeking to uphold its power with the bayonet. Your freedom, your future, the fate of the revolution are at stake. Down with the tyranny of Ebert. Long live international socialism!

leaders and many of their followers had been murdered. The whole episode, however, created long-term division between the SPD and KPD which prevented them from ever co-operating together against any threats from the right wing.

## Further Unrest

Over the next few months the left wing posed further challenges to the new state. The two most notable were:

- In March 1919 Berlin was the scene of further communist unrest. Again the Free Corps was called upon to act; again they destroyed the opposition, killing more than 1000 people in the process.
- In the same month a Communist Republic was proclaimed in Bavaria. In response the army, supported by the Free Corps, besieged Munich, the state capital, finally taking control on 1 May.

## A New Constitution

In the meantime Ebert set about organising Germany's new political structures. Elections for the new German Parliament were held in January 1919. The majority of seats were won by the SPD and so, when the new assembly first met in February 1919, Ebert was chosen as the country's new President.

The Parliament's first task was to draw up a **constitution**. As Berlin was too violent, the politicians moved to the quieter town of Weimar. Thus Germany became known as the Weimar Republic.

The constitution was accepted by the Parliament on 31 July 1919 by 262 votes to 75. It made Germany the most democratic country in the world:

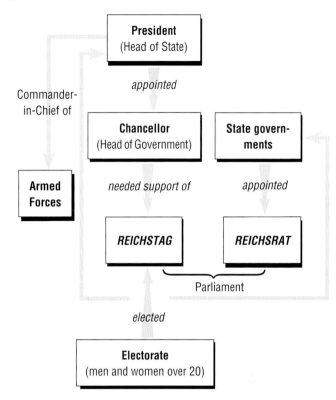

**Figure 1.2** How the Weimar political system operated.

- All citizens (male and female) over the age of 20 could vote.
- Freedom of speech, assembly and movement were guaranteed.
- Freedom of religion was permitted.

However, as Table 1.1 shows, some of the innovations included in the new constitution which were intended to be strengths would also turn out to be weaknesses.

| Part of constitution | Reason why it was a strength | Reasons why it was a weakness |
|---|---|---|
| Proportional representation was used for elections (to be held every four years). | This gave all parties the chance of winning seats in Parliament. | More parties in Parliament made it harder for the bigger parties to win a majority and allowed parties hostile to Weimar to get elected. This usually meant that governments were made up of a number of parties (coalitions) who could fall out quite easily, making laws difficult to pass. This lack of stability – there were 14 different Chancellors 1919–33 – could undermine democracy. |
| In a political crisis when the government could not get enough support from Parliament, Article 48 of the constitution allowed the President to rule using emergency decrees. | This meant that the country could still be governed even in a crisis. | There was no definition of 'emergency'. Using Article 48 meant that the elected government was not running the country, which was undemocratic. Again, if Article 48 was used too much and for too long, democracy would be undermined. |

**Table 1.1** Some of the new constitution's innovations

## Attitudes to the constitution

In addition, the army, civil service and judiciary remained largely unchanged from the old system. These groups wanted a return to what they saw as the good old days of the Kaiser and so remained half-hearted at best and openly hostile at worst in their attitude towards the Weimar Republic.

### ACTIVITIES

1 Why did the Kaiser abdicate in November 1918?
2 Why did the Spartacists try to seize power?
3 Who were the Free Corps? Why did Ebert have to use them instead of the regular army?
4 Why did Germany become known as the Weimar Republic?
5 Explain how the following might damage the Weimar Republic's chances of success:
   • proportional representation
   • Article 48
   • the attitude of the army, civil service and judiciary.
6 How else did communists try to oppose the Weimar Republic in early 1919?

### EXTENSION ACTIVITY

Is it true to say that right from the start the Weimar Republic had little chance of survival?

### REVISION TIP

The origins of the Weimar Republic are very complicated. Not only do you need to understand why the Kaiser abdicated, you also need to understand why there were different left wing groups in Germany. Most importantly, examiners will want you to be able to explain how the Weimar Republic's chances of survival were weakened by its constitution and by the attitudes of some of the groups most important for its survival.

## THE TREATY OF VERSAILLES

The leaders of Britain, France, Italy and the USA spent the early part of 1919 drafting the peace treaties that would officially end the First World War. The German government expected that the settlement would be based on the ideas of the US President, Woodrow Wilson. Towards the end of the war Wilson had made a famous speech in which he had outlined his ideas about how wars could be avoided in the future. His ideas became known as the Fourteen Points. One of the most important points had dealt with the issue of self-determination: people's right to decide which country they wanted to live in.

The German delegation was not allowed to take part in the negotiations and did not see the terms of the Treaty until 7 May 1919. At that point they were allowed to make some suggestions, only a few of which were accepted. The final version of the Treaty was published on 16 June.

### Terms of the Treaty

There were three main parts to the Treaty of Versailles, which are examined in turn below.

### 1. Land

Germany lost territory to France, Belgium and Poland; the latter via the Polish corridor which **partitioned** the country. Any union (known as an *Anschluss*) with Austria was forbidden. Germany also lost all of its overseas colonies. In a number of disputed areas such as Schleswig, Allenstein, Marienwerder and Silesia the Allies organised **plebiscites** to decide who would govern the regions.

In total Germany lost:

- 13 per cent of land area
- 12 per cent of population (about 6 million)
- 15 per cent of agricultural production
- 48 per cent of iron production (similar losses for steel)
- 16 per cent of coal production.

In addition, all profits from the Saar coalfields were to be given to France for a period of 15 years.

### 2. Arms

To prevent Germany going to war again, particularly against France, the Rhineland (the

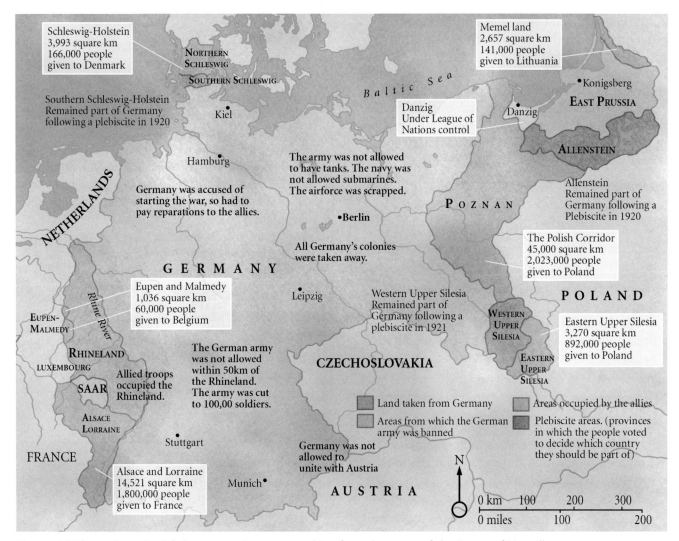

**Figure 1.3** The main territorial changes to Germany resulting from the terms of the Treaty of Versailles.

area of Germany that bordered France) was to be **demilitarised** for 50 km from the French border. To ensure that this happened, the area was to be occupied by Allied troops for 15 years. The German army was limited to 100,000 men and **conscription** was prohibited. The German navy was limited to 15,000 sailors and six battleships while no submarines were to be built. The creation of a German air force was also forbidden.

## 3. War guilt and reparations

According to Article 231 of the Treaty, Germany had to admit that it alone had been responsible for the start of the First World War. On the basis of this guilt, Germany had to compensate the Allies for the damage it had caused during the war (**reparations**). The figure for this would be agreed at a later date.

## Reactions to the Treaty

Given the significant changes that had been made to the way in which Germany was being governed, most Germans had been expecting a just settlement based on Wilson's Fourteen Points. In the eyes of many Germans this Treaty certainly was not fair, as it did not apply the principle of self-determination to areas with German populations. It seemed that the Allies were not doing much to help Germany develop as a newly-emerging democracy. Additional causes of anger were the terms on disarmament (making it more difficult for Germany to defend herself), war guilt and reparations.

Many Germans were outraged by the Treaty, which they christened a diktat (dictated peace) (Source A, page 8). They turned on the Weimar politicians who had signed the armistice in November 1918 that had ended the fighting and had led to the Treaty. They argued that Germany had been betrayed by these politicians and began calling them 'November criminals' (Source B below). Although this charge was untrue, from that point on the new Republic became associated in the eyes of many people with treachery and defeat (Source C).

## SOURCE A

*Headline story from a German newspaper published on the day Germany signed the Treaty of Versailles.*

Today in the Hall of Mirrors [at Versailles] the disgraceful treaty is being signed. Do not forget it! The German people will, with unceasing labour, press forward to reconquer the place among the nations to which they are entitled.

## SOURCE B

*Field Marshal Paul von Hindenburg explains the army's attitude to the loss of the First World War.*

The German army was stabbed in the back. No blame is to be attached to the sound core of the army … It is perfectly clear on whom the blame rests.

## SOURCE C

*Hugo Preuss commenting in 1923 on the impact of the Treaty on the Weimar government.*

The German Republic was born out of … terrible defeat. This … cast from the first a dark shadow on the new political order … The criminal madness of the Versailles diktat was a shameless blow … The *Reich* constitution was born with this curse upon it.

Despite German outrage the Allies refused to change the terms of the settlement. The German government resigned rather than sign the Treaty. However, faced with the threat of renewed war – which the army said they would lose – a new government was formed and Ebert sent two of its ministers to sign the Treaty. They did so in the Palace of Versailles on 28 June 1919.

## ACTIVITIES

1 Explain why many Germans thought that the terms of the peace treaty would not be too harsh.
2 Why did the German government not refuse to sign the Treaty of Versailles?
3 Create a spider diagram showing the main ways in which the Treaty of Versailles had an impact on Germany.
4 How did Germans react to the Treaty of Versailles?
5 Was it unfair to blame the Treaty of Versailles on the leaders of the Weimar Republic?

## EXTENSION ACTIVITY

Do you agree that the Allies undermined the chances of Weimar Germany surviving by making its government accept the Treaty of Versailles?

## REVISION TIP

Obviously examiners will expect you to be familiar with the main terms of the Treaty of Versailles. More importantly they will want you to be able to explain how the Treaty further undermined the new Republic.

# THREATS FROM THE RIGHT

## The Kapp Putsch

Having survived several left-wing attempts to overthrow the government, the Weimar Republic now faced its first challenge from the right. On 13 March 1920 the Free Corps – led by an extreme **nationalist** journalist and politician Wolfgang Kapp – seized key locations in Berlin. The immediate cause was their anger at the reduction in the size of the army as demanded by the Treaty of Versailles.

Ebert ordered the army to take action, but it refused. General Hans von Seeckt, a senior army officer, told Ebert 'The German army does not fire on the German army.' As a result the government was forced to flee. However, workers in Berlin and elsewhere did not support the *putsch*. Rather, they responded to a call from the government and about in terms of the reaction of the military to this threat. Despite this, the government took no action against the army. Indeed, before long von Seeckt had even been promoted to the position of Chief of the Army Command.

## Political Assassinations

The continuing danger from the right wing was also evident from the assassination of Weimar's popular Foreign Minister Walter Rathenau in June 1922. In the eyes of those on the right, Rathenau was one of those responsible for the armistice and the Treaty of Versailles. Even worse, he had also recently agreed the **Treaty of Rapallo** with Communist Russia. As with the perpetrators of many of the 354 murders carried out by elements of the right, during the period 1920–2, the punishment suffered by Rathenau's assassins was insignificant. They were sentenced on average to four years imprisonment (Source B below).

At the same time, as Table 1.2 shows, those responsible for the 22 murders carried out by the left during these years were invariably more harshly dealt with by a legal system that remained strongly right wing in its outlook.

Free Corps on the streets of Berlin during their *putsch* in 1920.

organised a shutdown (Source A below). Within four days the strike had brought Berlin to a standstill. With his *putsch* defeated, Kapp fled the country. In its aftermath the Free Corps were broken up.

While Ebert was undoubtedly pleased with the failure of the *putsch* he had much to be concerned

| Political murders 1919–23 | Left | Right |
|---|---|---|
| Murders committed | 22 | 354 (326 unpunished) |
| Numbers convicted and given death sentences | 10 | 0 |
| Numbers convicted and given severe punishment | 17 | 1 |

Table 1.2 Murders by the left and the right 1919–23

### SOURCE A

*Government proclamation issued to the workers during the Kapp putsch, March 1920.*

Workers, Party comrades! The military *putsch* has started … The achievements of a whole year are to be smashed, your dearly bought freedom to be destroyed. Everything is at stake! No factory must work … Therefore down tools! Come out on strike! … There is only one way against the dictatorship of Wilhelm II: paralysis of all economic life.

### SOURCE B

*Kurt Tucholsky, a left-wing satirist, commenting on the fairness of justice in the Weimar Republic (adapted).*

When the Republic was created, these judges held over from the monarchy found it impossible to transfer their allegiance to the new organisation of the state … They created a private law and undermined the public law of the Republic by refusing to administer justice in an equal manner to all people.

## 'Red Rising'

The Kapp *putsch* might have been over but it was not long before the government was in trouble again. This time the danger came from the Ruhr, Germany's industrial heartland. In reaction to the Kapp *putsch* the Ruhr's workers had responded to the government's pleas for help and had gone on strike. However, even though the *putsch* was over, the communists among the Ruhr's workforce stayed on strike and formed their own **Red Army**. Their aim was to obtain concessions from the government they had just helped save.

However, the government did not show its gratitude in the way that the strikers might have wanted. The so-called 'Red Rising' was crushed by the army supported by some of the same Free Corps who had just tried to overthrow the government.

The events of March 1920 clearly demonstrated the weakness of the Weimar government's position. It had to rely on a group of right-wing extremists to keep it in power, but these same extremists had shown that they were willing to overthrow the government given half a chance.

### ACTIVITIES

1 Explain the reasons for the Kapp *putsch*.
2 Why should the army's reaction to the Kapp *putsch* have worried Ebert so much?
3 How was the *putsch* ended?
4 What was the 'Red Rising'? How did it end?
5 What evidence can you find in this chapter to suggest that right-wing opponents of the Weimar Republic were better treated than those on the left wing?

### EXTENSION ACTIVITY

How secure was the Weimar Republic by the end of 1922?

### REVISION TIP

Examiners will expect you to be aware of the different left- and right-wing attempts to overthrow the Weimar Republic. They will also expect you to be able to explain the differences in the punishments handed out to left- and right-wing opponents.

## THE 1923 ECONOMIC CRISIS (I): THE PROBLEM

### Reparations

The German economy was in trouble long before the 1923 economic crisis. More than three-quarters of the cost of the war had been met by loans that now had to be repaid. Inflation – the situation where prices are rising and the value of money is falling – had been growing in Germany since the time of the war. In the immediate post-war period there was little improvement in the economic situation given the loss of important industrial and agricultural areas as a result of the Treaty of Versailles. In addition, the government made things worse by borrowing and printing more money.

Then the situation deteriorated further. In January 1921 the Allies announced that Germany would have to pay £6600 million in reparations. Germany managed to scrape together the money to pay the first instalment; then in December 1922 it announced that it would not be able to meet the next payment and asked for a break.

Thinking that Germany was trying to get off paying reparations, the French government refused to agree. Instead, the French decided to invade Germany and take what they were owed. In January 1923 French soldiers, supported by members of the Belgian army, entered the Ruhr – Germany's industrial heartland.

The Ruhr occupied by French troops in 1923.

The government responded by ordering the population of the Ruhr to engage in **passive resistance**. This made Germany's economic problems even worse:

- The richest part of the country was not producing anything, thereby reducing the country's income.
- The government had to start importing the goods that were not being produced, costing more money.
- The Ruhr workers still had to be paid even though they were not working.

The policy of non-cooperation also had a more deadly impact. Faced with passive resistance the invading forces killed over 130 people and expelled at least 150,000 Germans from their homes.

## Hyperinflation

The government's solution to its economic problems was to print more and more money and by the autumn of 1923 Germany was experiencing **hyperinflation** (Source A). Particularly affected were:

- the poor who had little or nothing
- those living on a fixed income such as pensioners
- farmers
- owners of small businesses
- the **middle classes** whose savings were rendered worthless by hyperinflation.

| Item | Price in marks in | | |
|---|---|---|---|
| | 1913 | Summer 1923 | November 1923 |
| 1 kg loaf of bread | 0.29 | 1,200 | 32,428,000,000,000 |
| 1 egg | 0.08 | 5,000 | 80,000,000,000 |
| 1 kg of butter | 2.70 | 26,000 | 6,000,000,000,000 |
| 1 kg of beef | 1.75 | 18,800 | 5,600,000,000,000 |
| 1 pair of shoes | 12.00 | 1,000,000 | 32,000,000,000,000 |

Table 1.3 The impact of hyperinflation on everyday goods

With money its worthless, Germany developed into a **barter economy** (Source B).

Not everyone suffered. Those whose wealth was not in money were unaffected, while people with debts or mortgages were able to pay off various kinds of loans (taken out when money was worth much more) cheaply with the devalued currency.

### SOURCE A

*Otto Strasser remembers the impact of hyperinflation on the lives of ordinary Germans.*

Inflation set in. Every month, every week, every day and every hour the value of the mark declined. Our salaries were paid daily, and it was difficult to adjust them to the inflationary landslide. A thing you wanted in the morning you bought at once, because by the afternoon the price might have doubled, trebled or quadruped … Soon the dollar was worth 4200 billion marks. An ordinary postage stamp cost 12,000 million marks … Anger mounted among the people, and the streets re-echoed with noisy demonstrations. Desperation was reflected on every face, desperation of the kind that can lead to outbursts of irreparable violence.

German children were able to find some use for the worthless currency in 1923.

### SOURCE B

*An eyewitness account of the lengths to which Germans went to deal with hyperinflation.*

Bartering became more and more widespread. Professional people … accepted food in preference to cash fees. A haircut cost a couple of eggs, and craftsmen … displayed in their shop windows: 'Repairs carried out in exchange for food'. Once I was asked at the box office of our local fleapit cinema if I could bring some coal as the price of two seats.

# THE 1923 ECONOMIC CRISIS (II): THE SOLUTION

The crisis resulted in the collapse of the government led by Wilhelm Cuno. In August President Ebert used his powers under Article 48 of the constitution to form a new government. The new Chancellor was Gustav Stresemann. He ended the crisis by:

- Ordering an end to passive resistance to start the economy working again.
- Sharply reducing government spending.
- Agreeing to resume paying reparations, realising that this was the only way to get the French and Belgians out of the Ruhr.
- Establishing in November 1923 a new national bank, the *Reichsbank*, and introducing a new currency, the *Rentenmark*.

While Stresemann's actions restored economic stability, the 1923 crisis destroyed the confidence of a significant number of Germans – particularly those in the middle class – in the Weimar Republic.

Gustav Stresemann (1878–1929).

## Recovery

In 1924 Stresemann (now Germany's Foreign Minister following the collapse of his government) and key allied leaders produced the Dawes Plan. This arrangement allowed Germany to pay a reduced amount of reparations for several years with longer to pay overall. However, the overall amount remained the same at £6600 million.

At the same time it was announced that Germany would benefit from the investment of massive amounts of money that would be used to help rebuild the economy. Many of these loans came from US investors.

Further help with reparations came in the shape of the 1929 Young Plan, which was produced at a time of slowdown in the German economy. This agreement reduced the amount Germany would have to pay to £1800 million and gave the German government even longer to pay it.

## ACTIVITIES

1 Why did France and Belgium invade the Ruhr in January 1923?
2 How did the Weimar government react to the invasion?
3 What impact did the occupation of the Ruhr have on the German economy?
4 How did the 1923 economic crisis affect ordinary Germans?
5 How was the crisis ended?
6 What impact did the 1923 crisis have on attitudes to the Weimar Republic?

## EXTENSION ACTIVITY

Not paying reparations caused more problems for the Weimar Republic than paying reparations would have. Do you agree?

## REVISION TIP

The 1923 economic crisis is a very important moment in the history of the Weimar Republic. Examiners will expect you to understand why the economic crisis happened, how it was ended and what impact it had on Germans' attitudes towards the Weimar Republic.

# THE 'GOLDEN TWENTIES'

## The Positive

On the surface it seemed as if Stresemann had returned Germany to prosperity and political stability. Heavy industry had recovered to its pre-1914 levels, exports were rising, wages were increasing, social welfare provision was improving and infrastructure was developing. Moreover, there were no more *putsches*, while the results of the 1928 general election indicated support for moderate rather than extremist parties. That same election resulted in the stable Grand Coalition (so named because it involved so many of Germany's parties) under the leadership of the SPD's Hermann Müller.

Stresemann also enjoyed successes in his foreign policy.

- In 1925 Stresemann signed the Locarno Treaties by which Germany, France and Belgium agreed to accept their common borders. French and Belgian troops withdrew from the Ruhr shortly after.

- In 1926 Germany was finally allowed to join the **League of Nations** (it was refused membership when the League was set up in 1919).
- In 1928 Germany signed up to the Kellogg-Briand Pact, which stated that countries would use diplomacy, not war, to solve disagreements. By signing up to this, Stresemann convinced many that Germany was a country that could be reasoned with.
- In 1930 the last of the Allied soldiers stationed in the Rhineland since the end of the war returned home.

## The Negative

However, much of this stability was misleading. Field Marshall Paul von Hindenburg was elected President in 1925 following the death of Friedrich Ebert. President Hindenburg was not known to be overly enthusiastic about Germany being a democracy. Parties were getting on better because there was nothing important for them to fall out over. Even so, no government lasted for longer than two years. At the same time industry was growing unsteadily, small businesses were under pressure from their larger rivals, agriculture was in a depression, unemployment was on the increase, welfare costs

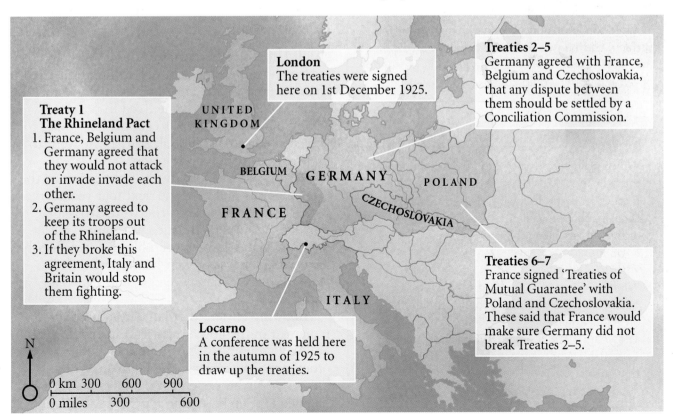

**Treaty 1
The Rhineland Pact**
1. France, Belgium and Germany agreed that they would not attack or invade invade each other.
2. Germany agreed to keep its troops out of the Rhineland.
3. If they broke this agreement, Italy and Britain would stop them fighting.

**London**
The treaties were signed here on 1st December 1925.

**Treaties 2–5**
Germany agreed with France, Belgium and Czechoslovakia, that any dispute between them should be settled by a Conciliation Commission.

**Locarno**
A conference was held here in the autumn of 1925 to draw up the treaties.

**Treaties 6–7**
France signed 'Treaties of Mutual Guarantee' with Poland and Czechoslovakia. These said that France would make sure Germany did not break Treaties 2–5.

UNITED KINGDOM
BELGIUM
GERMANY
POLAND
FRANCE
CZECHOSLOVAKIA
ITALY

N

0 km 300 600 900
0 miles 300 600

**Figure 1.4** The main points of the Locarno Treaties.

were up and the government was spending more than it was making (Source A). Moreover, while Europe seemed more stable, beneath the surface there remained the desire within Germany to reverse the terms of the Treaty of Versailles.

The biggest weakness however was Germany's over-reliance on the loans its was receiving from the USA. Stresemann himself made reference to this when, in early October 1929, he spoke of Germany 'dancing on a volcano' (Source B).

## SOURCE A

*Historian R. Bessel provides an overview of the depth of recovery during the 'Golden Twenties'.*

Even during the years of 'relative stabilisation' all was not well with the Weimar Republic … underlying economic problems remained, and the relative political stability of Weimar's 'golden years' rested on shaky foundations.

## SOURCE B

*Just before his death in October 1929 Stresemann wrote an account of the dangers facing the German economy.*

The economic position is only flourishing on the surface. Germany is in fact dancing on a volcano. If the short-term credits are called in, a large section of our economy would collapse.

## ACTIVITIES

1  Which political position did Stresemann hold for most of the 1920s?
2  Explain how the following helped Germany recover economically:
   • the Dawes Plan
   • US loans
   • the Young Plan.
3  What evidence can you find to show that other countries were beginning to accept Germany as an equal again?
4  The years 1924–9 are known as the 'Golden Twenties'. What evidence can you find to show that this is:
   • an appropriate name?
   • an inappropriate name?

## SOURCE C

*Extract from Stresemann's obituary in* The Times, *October 1929.*

By the death of Stresemann, Germany has lost her ablest statesman.

## EXTENSION ACTIVITY

Did Germany really recover during the Stresemann years?

## REVISION TIP

Examiners will expect you to identify Stresemann's achievements. You will also be expected to be able to explain whether or not Germany really recovered in these years.

# HITLER AND THE ORIGINS OF THE NAZI PARTY

## Early Life

Adolf Hitler was born in Austria in April 1889. At first he did well at school but then he started to underachieve and ended up dropping out. Between 1905 and 1913 he lived in poverty, selling his own paintings to get by, but failing to be accepted into art school. In 1913 he went to Germany to avoid conscription.

When war broke out in 1914 Hitler joined the German army and over the next four years served with distinction, winning the **Iron Cross** for bravery. When the armistice was signed, Hitler was in hospital, having been blinded in a British gas attack. He was broken-hearted when he learned that Germany's leaders had signed an armistice.

Following Hitler's discharge from hospital he remained in the army investigating extremist political groupings. One group that Hitler was ordered to infiltrate was the German Workers' Party (DAP), an extreme nationalist party that had been set up by Anton Drexler. After attending a meeting Hitler joined the party.

Adolf Hitler (1889–1945) (seated right – marked by an X) posing with some of his army comrades during the First World War.

## The Nazi Party

Hitler's influence over the party was immediate. In February 1920 the party launched a new manifesto, the 25-Point Programme (Source A below). The programme – most of which was Hitler's work – outlined a range of key ideas:

- The desire to unite all Germans, with the exception of any Germans who were Jewish.
- Destruction of the Treaty of Versailles.
- The need for *lebensraum* (living space).
- The need for strong government.

Some parts of the 25-Point Programme were somewhat more left wing in their aims. In particular, there was a focus on dealing with the power and influence of Germany's wealthy industrialists and financiers. It is probable that these ideas were more to do with Drexler than Hitler.

Soon after the publication of the 25-Point Programme, the DAP was renamed as the National Socialist German Workers' Party (NSDAP or Nazi for short). The party also adopted the swastika as its symbol.

The party soon increased its membership, attracting people from the lower and middle classes in particular with its new policies, and because of Hitler's abilities as a public speaker. The party's purchase of its own newspaper, the *Völkischer Beobachter*, in December 1920 provided it with even more opportunities to spread its ideas.

In July 1921 Hitler replaced Drexler as Nazi leader after threatening to resign from the party. In November 1921 the *Sturmabteilung* (SA) was set up as the Nazis' military wing. Many of its recruits were former members of the now-dissolved Free Corps. Members of the SA were better known as the Brownshirts because of the colour of their uniforms. Just over a year later the SA could boast 15,000 members.

At the same time Hitler was building up the party's strength, making use of donations from individuals such as Fritz Thyssen, Germany's leading industrialist. By 1923 it was estimated that the party could boast a membership of 55,000. At the same time though the NSDAP still remained a regional party with no real influence beyond the state of Bavaria.

## The Munich Putsch

### Plans

Hitler was outraged at the economic and political mess that Germany was in by late 1923. He had been particularly angered at Stresemann's decision to call off passive resistance. He saw this as yet another example of the kind of cowardice that had led to the signing of the armistice in November 1918. The Nazis' leader believed that the crisis provided him with the ideal opportunity to exploit the Republic's problems. He decided, therefore, to stage a *putsch* in Munich and then lead an attack on Berlin.

On 8 November 1923, Hitler discovered that the heads of the Bavarian government, police and army, Gustav von Kahr, Hans von Seisser and Otto von Lossow, were addressing a public meeting in the *Bürgerbräukeller* in Munich. Hitler interrupted the meeting and forced the leaders to announce their support for his planned rising. Hitler also revealed that the intended *putsch* had the support of General Erich von Ludendorff, one

> ### SOURCE B
>
> *An eyewitness account of the Munich putsch, written by Rudolf Olsen in 1923.*
>
> The police force was ... barring the way and brandishing truncheons. It is not known who fired the first shot. The procession did not halt. Commands rang out; a National Socialist went ahead and warned the police: 'Here comes Ludendorff.' The police shot. Fourteen men fell ... Göring was wounded and fled abroad. Ludendorff went straight on, right through the sharpshooters, was arrested, and let go on parole ... At the first shot Hitler had flung himself to the ground. He sprained his arm, but this did not prevent him from running. He found his car and drove into the mountains.

of the most prominent First World War leaders. Ludendorff had entered the hall by this stage and supported this disclosure. Hitler believed that Ludendorff's backing would secure the backing of both the Bavarian army and the Munich police.

### Failure

However, Hitler's plans went badly wrong. Once free von Kahr, von Seisser and von Lossow organised the army to stop the intended *putsch*. They all believed that the rising had absolutely no chance of succeeding. On the morning of

Nazi forces preparing to seize power in Munich in 1923.

Hitler (fourth from the right) pictured before the start of his trial in 1924. Also pictured is Erich von Ludendorff (1865–1937) (centre).

9 November armed police fired on a crowd of more than 2000 Nazis who were marching towards the city centre. Sixteen Nazis died in the barrage. With the rising in disarray Hitler fled (Source B). He and Ludendorff were later arrested on the charge of having committed high treason. Hitler appeared to be finished. However, he turned his trial to his advantage, using it to condemn the Weimar government and state and to spread his ideas (Source C). The massive media coverage of his 24-day trial provided Hitler with more publicity than he could ever have dreamt of.

This was not the only stroke of luck he enjoyed; the trial judges were sympathetic to Hitler's views and at the end of the trial he was sentenced to just five years' imprisonment, the minimum possible punishment. Ludendorff was acquitted and freed.

## ACTIVITIES

1 How did Hitler react to the armistice of November 1918? Why was this?
2 How did Hitler get involved with the German Workers' Party?
3 Identify the main points of the 25-Point Programme.
4 For what reasons did Hitler attempt a *putsch* in November 1923?
5 Why did the Munich *putsch* fail?
6 How did Hitler make use of his trial?

## EXTENSION ACTIVITY

'Hitler didn't set up the Nazi Party but he made it what it was.' In what ways did Hitler improve the Nazi Party's chances of success?

## SOURCE C

*Hitler speaking to the judges during his trial, 1924.*

It is not you, gentlemen, who pass judgment on us. That judgment is spoken in the eternal court of history. That court will judge us … as Germans who wanted only the good of their people and fatherland.

## REVISION TIP

The emergence of Adolf Hitler on to the German political scene is an important moment in the history of the Weimar Republic. Examiners will expect you to be able to explain what his ideas were and why he thought November 1923 would be a good time to try and take over the country.

## NAZI REORGANISATION AND GROWTH

### New Tactics

Hitler spent only nine months in prison. He used the time to write down his ideas in a book – *Mein Kampf* (*My Struggle*). He also decided that rather than using force to overthrow the Weimar Republic, the Nazis would use the political system and gain power by standing for election. Once in control they could then destroy the Republic from within (Source A below).

An advertisement for *Mein Kampf*, published in 1925.

Following his release from prison in December 1924 Hitler set about putting his plans into operation. As it had fallen apart during his absence, Hitler re-established the Nazi Party and began to set up branches across Germany, attempting to make it a national rather than regional organisation. The refounded party was based around the 'leadership principle' (*Führerprinzip*), which emphasised absolute obedience to Hitler. As part of this process new Nazi groups were established including the élite *Schutzstaffel* (SS) in 1925 and a Nazi youth movement, the Hitler Youth, in 1926.

At the same time, the use of violence was not completely removed as a tactic. When the occasion demanded the SA was still involved in street fights, particularly against the KPD's equivalent force, the Red Fighting League.

### The 1928 Election

The question of whether these changes would have any impact on the party's electoral fortunes was answered by the results of the 1928 election. The Nazis won only twelve seats in the *Reichstag*. At a time when Germany appeared to be recovering both politically and economically, there seemed to be no real reason to vote for a party whose main policy remained the destruction of the Weimar system.

| Party | Seats | Percentage |
|---|---|---|
| Social Democrats (SPD) | 153 | 29.8 |
| Centre Party (ZP) | 62 | 12.1 |
| Nazis (NSDAP) | 12 | 2.6 |
| Communists (KPD) | 54 | 10.6 |

Table 1.4 Election results, May 1928

### SOURCE A

*Hitler speaking in Landsberg prison on the policy he would follow on release from jail, 1924.*

When I resume active work it will be necessary to pursue a new policy. Instead of working to achieve power by an armed coup we shall have to hold our noses against the Catholic and Marxist deputies. If outvoting them takes longer than out-shooting them, at least the results will be guaranteed by their own constitution! … Sooner or later we shall have a majority – and after that – Germany.

### ACTIVITIES

1 What important change in tactics did Hitler make while he was in prison?
2 How did Hitler reorganise the Nazi Party after 1925?
3 Why was the Nazi Party in a better position to challenge for power by 1928?
4 How did the Nazi Party perform in the 1928 general election? Why was this?

**EXTENSION ACTIVITY**

How successful was Hitler as leader of the Nazi Party during the period 1924–8?

**REVISION TIP**

It is essential that you are able to explain why and how Hitler changed his party's tactics in the aftermath of the Munich *putsch*.

## GERMANY AND THE GREAT DEPRESSION

### Economic Collapse

In October 1929 two disasters befell the Weimar Republic:

1 Gustav Stresemann died, robbing the Republic of its most able supporter.
2 The US economy collapsed with the Wall Street Crash. As a result:
   - all investment from the US stopped
   - those Americans who had invested heavily in Germany insisted that all the money they had provided be repaid as soon as the agreements (most of which were short term) ended.

**SOURCE A**

*Historians John Hite and Chris Hinton assess the impact of the Wall Street Crash on the Weimar Republic.*

The slump had a major effect on the Weimar Republic. It induced a general feeling of gloom and reinforced many Germans' hostility to what they saw as a feeble and failing democratic system … it contributed in March 1930 to the fall of the last Weimar government that had a majority in the Reichstag. In September 1930, it led to a large increase in the number of anti-democratic deputies (especially the Nazis) in the Reichstag. This meant that it became virtually impossible for any government to gain the support of the Reichstag, and parliamentary government declined.

Seeking work this German woman carries a placard that states 'I am a trained shorthand typist, out of work, looking for any kind of work'.

Germany's economy – which, as we have seen, was already weak – collapsed for the second time in six years (Source A on this page). Prices and salaries tumbled, industrial production halved, businesses closed down as demand for their products dried up at home and abroad, unemployment shot up, homelessness increased as people could no longer afford to meet rent payments. As the numbers living on the streets increased, soup kitchens were set up to provide some degree of relief. Agriculture also suffered as thousands of farmers went bankrupt. By September 1930 over three million Germans were unemployed (not counting part-time workers and those who did not register as unemployed) while banks, unable to repay loans, were closing their doors, resulting in a loss of savings for millions. To many it must have seemed as if the world that they lived in was falling apart.

### Political Collapse

Faced with such a range of problems, the Grand Coalition that had been formed after the 1928 general election began to break up and in March 1930 Chancellor Hermann Müller resigned. Heinrich Brüning of the Centre Party took over as Chancellor but still the government remained divided. Several of the coalition's smaller parties wanted to reduce the government's welfare spending as it was struggling to provide payments to so many unemployed; however the Social Democrats refused.

Within months the government finally collapsed and an election was announced for September 1930. The immediate cause was the *Reichstag*'s refusal to support the government's plans to cut spending while increasing taxation. In this election the Nazis and Communists increased their support with the former winning 107 seats and the latter 77. All of the parties committed to supporting Weimar and using democracy lost votes and seats in the *Reichstag*.

| Party | Seats | Percentage |
|---|---|---|
| Social Democrats (SPD) | 143 | 24.5 |
| Centre Party (ZP) | 68 | 11.8 |
| Nazis (NSDAP) | 107 | 18.3 |
| Communists (KPD) | 77 | 14.3 |

Table 1.5 Election results, September 1930

Why did this happen? Put simply, the Weimar government was blamed for the disastrous effects of the Wall Street Crash. People blamed the parties – such as the SPD – who supported the

### SOURCE B

*Historian K. Bracher's assessment of Brüning.*

[Brüning] was not ... the last chancellor before the break-up of the Weimar Republic, but the first chancellor in the process of destroying German democracy.

Weimar Republic and turned to the political extremists such as the Communists and the Nazis. These parties had never been part of the government and so could not be connected with its failures. They alone seemed to offer a way out of the crisis.

Brüning remained as Chancellor despite being incapable of forming a stable government. Unable to get Parliament to agree to his laws, he was forced to ask President Hindenburg to pass laws using Article 48. For the next two years all key laws were passed in this way; as a result democracy was fatally undermined. Germany had become a presidential dictatorship (Source B).

### Brüning's Government

In order to avoid a repeat of the hyperinflation crisis of 1923 Brüning used Article 48 to introduce a range of harsh economic policies.

Hitler campaigning during the 1930 general election.

Heinrich Brüning (1885–1970).

He:

- reduced public spending
- imposed tariffs on imports
- slashed payments to the unemployed
- introduced salary reductions for civil servants.

Brüning's policies were deeply disliked and they earned him the nickname of 'Hunger Chancellor'.

However, by late 1932 there were some signs of recovery even though unemployment stood at over six million. Some historians believe that the Chancellor deliberately allowed the economic mess to continue so as to get reparations stopped. If this was Brüning's intention, he was successful; reparations were suspended in 1931 and then cancelled completely in 1932.

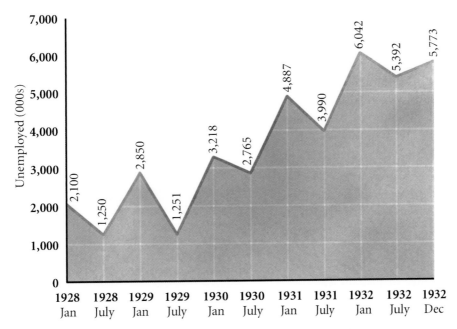

Figure 1.5 Unemployment levels 1928–32.

## ACTIVITIES

1 Why did the collapse of the US stock exchange affect Germany so badly?
2 How did the Wall Street Crash have an impact on Germany:
   - economically?
   - politically?
3 How did the following parts of the Weimar constitution weaken the Weimar Republic at this time:
   - proportional representation?
   - Article 48?
4 What were the successes and failures of Brüning's economic policies?

## EXTENSION ACTIVITY

'Brüning's biggest mistake was calling the 1930 general election.' How true is this statement?

## REVISION TIP

The Wall Street Crash marks the start of a significant turning point in the history of the Weimar Republic. Examiners will expect you to be able to discuss the impact of the crash on Germany's economy and political system. More importantly however, you need to be able to explain how the Weimar constitution worked against the stability of the Republic at this time.

## 1932: THE YEAR OF FOUR ELECTIONS

In March and April 1932 elections were held for the post of President. Hitler decided to stand against Hindenburg and in the first round of the election received over 30 per cent of the votes cast. For victory a candidate had to achieve 50 per cent of the votes and as Hindenburg's total just fell short a second ballot was required. In the second ballot although Hitler increased his vote to nearly 37 per cent (13.4 million votes), Hindenburg was re-elected.

Not long after his re-election Hindenburg forced Brüning to resign as Chancellor by telling him that he would not allow him to use Article 48 any longer. The immediate cause of his dismissal was two actions taken by the Chancellor:

- In April 1932 Brüning banned the SA and SS in response to high levels of violence. This concerned General Kurt von Schleicher, who was an influential adviser of Hindenburg. He believed that the time had come to co-operate with the Nazis.
- Brüning's plan to break up the large estates in Hindenburg's home state of Prussia was too close to socialism for the President's liking.

### Von Papen

On von Schleicher's advice, Hindenburg appointed the Centre Party's Franz von Papen as Chancellor. Papen immediately formed a new government. However, the very make-up of this government was a further indication of how weak democracy had become in Germany. Not one of the new ministers was a member of the *Reichstag*, further undermining its relevance.

Von Papen removed the ban on the SS and SA, deposed the SPD–Centre Party government in the state of Prussia and called a general election for July 1932. As with the results of the 1930 election, only the KPD and NSDAP increased their vote. The Nazis became the largest party with 230 seats.

| Party | Seats | Percentage |
|-------|-------|------------|
| Social Democrats (SPD) | 133 | 21.6 |
| Centre Party (ZP) | 75 | 12.5 |
| Nazis (NSDAP) | 230 | 37.4 |
| Communists (KPD) | 89 | 13.1 |

Table 1.6 Election results, July 1932

Paul von Hindenburg (1847–1934).

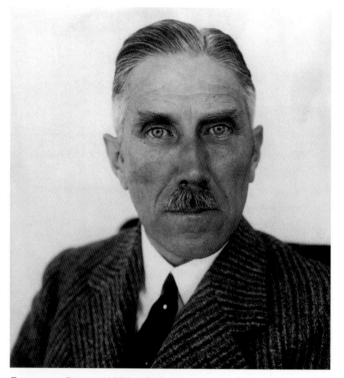

Franz von Papen (1879–1969).

# Why did Support for Nazism Increase?

Apart from the general political and economic situation, there were several specific reasons why Nazi support increased:

- Under the direction of Joseph Goebbels the Nazis used sophisticated propaganda methods such as using an aeroplane to ferry Hitler around the country during the 1932 presidential election campaign and canvassing door to door. Hitler's image and ideas were also plastered across Germany. These strategies were combined with simple messages to win support.
- Nazi groups such as the SA and Hitler Youth won new supporters.
- The SA grew massively in size and launched regular attacks on opposition party meetings (Source A).
- Hitler was a talented orator who portrayed an image of strength. Many other members of the party were also trained as speakers (Source B).

- Nazi policies focused on the groups who had been hardest hit by the depression, such as the middle classes, farmers and young people, and telling them exactly what they wanted to hear:
  - To those who were starving, homeless, unemployed or had lost their businesses, the Nazis promised jobs and the restoration of a vibrant economy. The key phrase used was 'bread and work'.
  - To those angry at Germany's military weakness, Hitler offered the overthrow of Versailles and a return to greatness.
  - To those looking for someone to blame for all of Germany's problems, Hitler pointed to the Jews and the Communists.
- Many Germans, particularly leading industrialists such as Krupp and Thyssen, feared the growth of communism and supported Hitler's rearmament plans. They also sought the restoration of a strong government in Germany. For these reasons they were willing to support the Nazis financially (Source C). For his part Hitler promised to destroy Germany's **trade union** movement following his appointment as Chancellor.
- Hitler also enjoyed the support of Alfred Hugenberg, a very wealthy man and owner of many of the country's newspapers. He used his media empire to help spread the Nazi message.

In addition, it should be noted that none of Germany's other parties came anywhere close to organising as efficient a movement and a propaganda machine as the Nazis.

## SOURCE A

*Moderate Berlin newspaper* Vossische Zeitung *reporting in July 1932 on SA tactics.*

28 July 1932: near Stettin, SA raiders invaded a Social Democrat rally and challenged the speaker to take back a remark he had made about Adolf Hitler … They attacked people in the audience with chairs, injuring 10 of them critically and making the meeting hall a shambles.

## SOURCE B

*Otto Strasser, who left the Nazi Party in 1930, recalls Hitler's speeches.*

Adolf Hitler enters a hall. He sniffs the air. For a minute he gropes, feels his way, senses the atmosphere. Suddenly he bursts forth. His words go like an arrow to their target, he touches each private world on the raw, liberating the mass unconscious, expressing its innermost aspirations, telling it what it most wants to hear … As the spirit moves him, he is promptly transformed into one of the greatest speakers of the century.

## SOURCE C

*Industrialist Fritz Thyssen explaining in his book* I Paid Hitler *(1941) that he gave the Nazis financial support.*

I have personally given altogether one million marks to the Nazi Party … It was during the last years preceding the Nazi seizure of power that the big industrial corporations began to make their contributions … and in all, the amounts given by heavy industry to the Nazis may be estimated at two million marks a year.

However, there were a number of groups unlikely to ever support the Nazis:

- Trade unions disliked them because the Nazis were keen to close them down.
- The movement's lack of discipline resulted in a lack of support from some key industrial figures.
- Church leaders disliked them because they threatened Christian values.
- The anti-feminist nature of Nazi policies lost them the support of some women voters.

## ACTIVITIES

1 Why would Hitler have been pleased with the results of the 1932 presidential election even though he did not win?
2 Why was Brüning forced to resign?
3 What did the make-up of von Papen's cabinet reveal about democracy in Germany by 1932?
4 Create a spider diagram showing the reasons for the growth in support for the Nazi Party by 1932.

## EXTENSION ACTIVITY

Was democracy dead in Germany by 1932?

## REVISION TIP

You need to understand and be able to explain how the Nazis used Weimar's problems to win electoral support by 1932.

## HITLER'S RISE TO POWER

### Two Elections

After the July 1932 election Hitler demanded the Chancellorship. Hindenburg refused and reappointed von Papen (Source A). However von Papen's government lacked support in the *Reichstag* and the Chancellor decided to call yet another election.

The results of the November 1932 general election revealed a fall in support for the Nazis (196 seats) seemingly due to the beginnings of economic recovery and the disappointment among some Nazi voters at Hitler's failure to be appointed Chancellor. The results also showed a further increase in support for the KPD (100 seats).

### SOURCE A

*Hindenburg speaking about Hitler's demands to be appointed Chancellor, 1932*

This Bohemian corporal wants to become *Reich* Chancellor? Never! At most he could be my Postmaster General. Then he can lick me on the stamps.

| Party | Seats | Percentage |
|-------|-------|------------|
| Social Democrats (SPD) | 121 | 20.4 |
| Centre Party (ZP) | 70 | 11.9 |
| Nazis (NSDAP) | 196 | 33.1 |
| Communists (KPD) | 100 | 16.9 |

Table 1.7 Election results, November 1932

'Our last hope – Hitler'. A Nazi propaganda poster produced during the 1932 Presidential election campaign designed to appeal to all of those Germans now experiencing unemployment.

As leader of the largest party, Hitler again requested the position of Chancellor. Again Hindenburg refused. Von Papen wanted to stay on and now planned to replace the *Reichstag* and introduce a constitution that would allow the government to operate as a dictatorship. He also intended to use the army to deal with any opposition. However, von Schleicher advised the President that such plans risked the outbreak of civil war.

## Intrigue

Hindenburg now asked von Schleicher to take on the job himself. He only survived for 57 days, failing in his attempts to strike a coalition deal with some of the more socialist members of the Nazi Party and representatives of the trade unions and incurring Hindenburg's displeasure for requesting the use of Article 48.

Kurt von Schleicher (1882–1934).

A 1933 cartoon from *Punch* magazine showing Hitler being carried to power by Hindenburg and Papen.

Meanwhile, a number of politicians and industrialists were attempting to convince Hindenburg to appoint Hitler as Chancellor. Particularly involved in this was von Papen who had not forgiven von Schleicher for forcing him from office. Von Papen had struck a deal with Hitler whereby he agreed to support Hitler as Chancellor in return for becoming Hitler's deputy. Von Papen then tried to convince Hindenburg to appoint Hitler, assuring the President that with only three Nazi ministers in a cabinet of 12 he would be able to control the Nazi leader (Source B). The President was also being advised by his son, Oskar, to appoint Hitler. At the same time key business leaders and landowners pressed Hindenburg to act to create a stable and effective government. On 30 January 1933, Hindenburg finally asked Hitler to take on the job (Source C).

## ACTIVITIES

1 Why did von Papen become Chancellor rather than Hitler?
2 Why did von Papen call yet another election for November 1932?
3 Would Hitler have been satisfied by the Nazi Party's performance in the November 1932 general election? Explain your answer.
4 What led to von Schleicher replacing von Papen as Chancellor?
5 What developments led to Hitler's appointment as Chancellor on 30 January 1933?

## EXTENSION ACTIVITY

Who was really to blame for the fall of the Weimar Republic?

## REVISION TIP

Examiners will expect you to be aware of the factors that led Hindenburg to appoint Hitler as Chancellor on 30 January 1933. In particular they will expect you to be able to explain the role people like von Papen played in Hitler's appointment.

## SOURCE B

*Otto Meissner, State Secretary in Hindenburg's office, explaining in 1946 how von Papen persuaded the President to appoint Hitler as Chancellor.*

Hindenburg was extremely hesitant, until the end of January, to make Hitler Chancellor ... Papen finally won him over to Hitler with the argument that the representatives of the other right-wing parties which would belong to the government would restrict Hitler's freedom of action.

## SOURCE C

*Historian Ian Kershaw considers if Hitler could have come to power without political intrigue.*

Access to Hindenburg was the key to power ... By January 1933, with other options apparently exhausted, most [élites] ... were prepared to entertain a Hitler government. Had they opposed it, a Hitler Chancellorship would have been inconceivable. Hitler needed the élite to attain power.

## Practice Question (Foundation and Higher)

### Foundation

1 (a)   Below is a list of people linked with the Weimar Republic:

| General Groener | William Cuno | Paul von Hindenburg | Erich von Ludendorff | Franz von Papen |
|---|---|---|---|---|

Match **each** person to the correct description and write your answer in the space provided. The first one has been done for you.

    (i)   Head of the German Army in 1918
        ***General Groener***

    (ii)  Chancellor of Germany in 1932                                       [1]

    (iii) Second president of the Weimar Republic                         [1]

    (iv) Leading WWI general and Nazi supporter                         [1]

    (v)  Chancellor at the time of the 1923 economic crisis              [1]

(b)   Describe **two** actions taken by people living in Germany to protest against Weimar governments between 1919 and 1923.          [4]

(c)   Below are two terms of the Treaty of Versailles signed by Germany in 1919. Choose one term and explain how it affected Germany.

| Loss of Land | Reduction in the Size of Germany's Military |
|---|---|

Term chosen:                                                   [6]

(d)   How did the Great Depression affect the German economy between 1929 and 1932?         [9]

### Higher

1 (a)   Describe **two** terms of the Treaty of Versailles.         [4]

(b)   How did Hitler try to increase support for the Nazi Party following his release from prison?         [6]

(c)   Explain how the Weimar governments dealt with problems between 1929 and 1933. In your answer refer to the bullet points and use other relevant knowledge.

    •   Political problems
    •   Economic problems                                 [15]

# NAZI GERMANY 1933–9

## NAZI CONSOLIDATION OF POWER (I)

### The Reichstag Fire

Hitler might have become Chancellor, but to achieve dictatorship he still had to overcome a number of obstacles. In particular he had to deal with the President, the *Reichstag* and the army, all of which could still prevent his rise to power. In addition, there might be opposition from other parties and Germany's state governments as well as the trade union movement.

Hitler moved almost immediately to gain an overall majority in the *Reichstag*, calling fresh elections for 5 March 1933. If Hitler wanted to achieve a majority of seats he would need to stop people voting for the SPD and KPD. The Nazis attempted to achieve this in the following ways:

- In early February a new law forbade newspapers and public meetings from criticising the new Chancellor and his administration.

- In the state of Prussia, which made up 66 per cent of the whole of Germany, leading Nazi Hermann Göring was Minister of the Interior. He ensured that the SA were enrolled into the police and were used to disrupt the opposition parties' election campaigns.

- The burning of the *Reichstag* building on 27 February gave Hitler his best chance of destroying the KPD's campaign. Because a Dutch Communist, Marinus van der Lubbe, was captured at the scene, the Nazis blamed the Communists for the blaze and raised the spectre of an imminent communist rebellion. However, for many there remained the suspicion that the Nazis were involved in setting the fire (Source A).

Berliners watch the *Reichstag* fire in February 1933.

### SOURCE A

*Sefton Delmer, a British journalist, provides an account of Hitler's reaction to the* Reichstag *fire.*

Twenty to thirty minutes after the fire was discovered Hitler said to von Papen: 'This is a God-given signal. If this fire, as I believe, turns out to be the handiwork of the Communists, then there is nothing that will stop us from crushing out the murderous pest with an iron fist.' ... That evening Hitler said to me, 'God grant that this be the work of the Communists. You are witnessing the beginning of a new age in German history.'

Hitler used the blaze to exploit Hindenburg's fear of a communist takeover and persuaded the President to approve the decree *For the Protection of People and State*. This new law, which remained in place for the duration of Nazi rule, gave the government the power to suspend many of the civil rights that had been guaranteed in the Weimar constitution (Source B). It lost no time in doing so, proceeding to intern opponents, disrupt the election campaigns of opposition parties and intimidate left-wing voters.

## SOURCE B

*Extract from the decree* For the Protection of People and State, *February 1933.*

By the authority of Section 48 (2) of the German constitution the following is decreed as a defensive measure against Communist acts of violence endangering the state:

Sections 114, 115, 117, 118, 123, 124 and 153 of the Constitution ... are suspended until further notice. Thus restrictions on personal liberty, on the right of free expression of opinion, including freedom of the press, on the right of assembly and association, and violations of the privacy of postal, telegraphic and telephonic communications, and warrants for house-searches ... are permissible beyond the legal limits otherwise prescribed.

## Election results

The results of the election revealed that the Nazis had won 288 seats. While this was far more than any other party it was still not an overall majority. The KPD managed to win 81 seats despite the government's underhand tactics, while the SPD won a very respectable 120 seats. However, with the support of the 52 Nationalist Party Deputies, the Nazis could now count on just over 50 per cent of the votes in the *Reichstag*. This left the Nazis in a stronger position within both the cabinet and the government.

| Party | Seats | Percentage |
|---|---|---|
| Social Democrats (SPD) | 120 | 19 |
| Centre Party (ZP) | 74 | 11 |
| Nazis (NSDAP) | 288 | 45 |
| Communists (KPD) | 81 | 13 |

Table 1.8 Election results, March 1933

## Enabling Act

Hitler, however, wanted even more power and moved to amend the constitution to allow the government to introduce laws without the *Reichstag*'s approval for a period of four years. Such a change to the constitution required the support of two-thirds of the *Reichstag* members present. At this point Hitler could count on the support of only 50 per cent of deputies.

To ensure his two-thirds majority, Hitler simply ensured that most opponents were not there to vote against the measure. He used the powers of the decree *For the Protection of People and State* to ban the KPD, thus preventing the Communists from voting against the new law. With the Communist Deputies already in jail, Hitler just needed the support of the Catholic Centre Party to achieve the 66 per cent of votes needed. This was achieved by a promise to cancel the decree *For the Protection of People and State* and an agreement to protect the rights of the Catholic Church. When it came to the vote, it was passed by 441 votes to 94. Only the Social Democrats bravely opposed the measure despite the intimidatory presence of SA men chanting 'We want the Enabling Act' (Source C).

## SOURCE C

*Extract from an account by a member of the SPD, of the* Reichstag *meeting where the Enabling Act was passed, March 1933.*

We tried to dam the flood of Hitler's unjust accusations with interruptions of 'No!', 'An error!', 'False!' but that did us no good. The SA and SS people, who surrounded us in a semicircle along the walls of the hall, hissed loudly and murmured: 'Shut up!', 'Traitors!', 'You'll be strung up today'.

## *Gleichschaltung*

Hitler's government might have been given sweeping power for four years, yet within months he had eliminated most of the remaining political opposition in Germany. This was due to the government's implementation of a process known as *Gleichschaltung* (the co-ordination of all aspects of life to fit in with Nazi ideals).

- In late March all state parliaments were closed down and then re-established with Nazi majorities.
- In April 1933, Jews and other individuals that the Nazis regarded as their political enemies were removed from jobs in the legal profession and civil service. At the same time key positions within Germany's state governments were taken over by Nazis.

The SA move in to occupy trade union buildings in Berlin, 2 May 1933.

- In May 1933 all trade unions were outlawed and replaced by a Nazi union, the DAF (German Labour Front).
- In July 1933, Germany became a one-party state. However, by this stage there were few other parties to get rid of. The Social Democrats had already been outlawed, while the Centre Party had dissolved itself.
- In December 1933 yet more *Reichstag* elections were held. This time the Nazis won 92 per cent of the vote.
- In January 1934 Hitler introduced the *Law for the Reconstruction of the State*. This abolished all of Germany's state governments apart from Prussia's, which was still to be run by Hermann Göring, a key Nazi leader.

## ACTIVITIES

1 What stood in the way of Hitler becoming a dictator in January 1933?
2 How did the *Reichstag* fire help the Nazis?
3 How did Hitler manage to get the Enabling Law passed by the *Reichstag*?
4 How did Hitler use the Enabling Law to help him consolidate his power?
5 Why would Hitler have been so keen to destroy the power of Germany's trade unions?
6 Why did Hitler want to control Germany's state governments?

## EXTENSION ACTIVITY

Were the actions taken by Hitler in the first part of 1933 totally legal?

## REVISION TIP

It was never guaranteed that Hitler would become Dictator of Germany. There were many limitations on his position when he became Chancellor and you should be aware of how he overcame these limitations one by one.

# NAZI CONSOLIDATION OF POWER (II)

## Divisions Within

Hitler's position was still under threat. However, now the danger came from the SA, commanded for the last two years by Ernst Röhm, one of Hitler's longest-serving collaborators. Under Röhm's leadership the Nazi Party's paramilitary wing had expanded to over two million members (some historians say 4.5 million).

Röhm was one of the more left-wing members of the Nazi Party. He believed that Hitler's take-over would be followed by a second revolution in which the authority of Germany's economic old guard and the army would be crushed and the SA would become Germany's new army. Röhm now wanted this second revolution to start. Röhm's plans worried the army, which looked down on the SA as a group of thugs and made clear its displeasure to Hitler. This concerned him because:

- Hitler feared the army. It was the only group that could stop his achievement of dictatorship.
- Hitler needed the army to implement his foreign policy. Many in the army high command supported his foreign policy aims.

Röhm was also opposed by other leading Nazis such as Heinrich Himmler and Hermann Göring (Source A). They believed that the SA leader had become too big for his boots and began trying to convince Hitler that Röhm was disloyal and that aspects of his private life – Röhm was a homosexual – were inappropriate for a leading Nazi.

## The Night of the Long Knives

Hitler finally acted on the night of 30 June 1934, an event that became known as the 'Night of the Long Knives'. Anyone he suspected of preventing his achievement of dictatorship was executed. Key SA leaders, including Röhm, were eliminated. So too were a number of earlier rivals including Gustav von Kahr and General von Schleicher.

Estimates vary widely, but it is believed that somewhere around 100 people were killed on that night and Hitler's achievement of dictatorship took another step forward. The Nazis justified the actions that they had taken by claiming that they had prevented an SA *putsch* from taking place (Source B). On 3 July the *Reichstag* passed a law making the actions taken on the Night of the Long Knives legal. Both the army leadership and President Hindenburg spoke of their appreciation for the actions that Hitler had taken.

### SOURCE A

*Extract from a speech by Hermann Göring, 18 June 1934.*

It does not lie with us to say if a second revolution is necessary. The first revolution was ordered by the Leader and finished by him. If the Leader wishes a second revolution, we stand tomorrow, if he wants us, in the streets. If he wishes no further action we will suppress every one who wants to make a second revolution against the wishes of the Leader.

### SOURCE B

*Extract from the minutes of a meeting of the German cabinet held in the aftermath of the Night of the Long Knives.*

Defence Minister General von Blomberg thanked the *Führer* in the name of the *Reich* Cabinet and the army for his determined and courageous action, by which he had saved the German people from civil war … The *Reich* Cabinet then approved a law on measures for the self-defence of the state. Its single paragraph reads: 'The measures taken on 30 June and 1 and 2 July to suppress the acts of high treason are legal, being necessary for the self-defence of the state.'

Best of enemies: Ernst Röhm (1887–1934) (left) and Heinrich Himmler (1900–45) (right).

A British cartoon from 1934 commenting on the Night of the Long Knives. The caption states 'They salute with both hands now'.

## Führer

With the SA threat gone, Hindenburg was the only person standing in Hitler's way as he moved towards dictatorship. In the event any threat that the elderly President might have posed was very short lived as Hindenburg died on 2 August 1934. A day earlier a new law had been passed which merged together the jobs of President and Chancellor and replaced them with the all-powerful position of *Führer* and *Reich* Chancellor.

The army now demonstrated its gratitude to Hitler for the eradication of the SA threat by swearing an oath of personal loyalty to the *Führer*. Previously, soldiers had promised their loyalty to the constitution. In this new oath each soldier promised to 'render unconditional obedience to Adolf Hitler, the *Führer* of the German nation'. From this point on the army's fate was totally linked to his.

Shortly after, the German people were asked to vote in a plebiscite to indicate their approval for Hitler's new position. Forty-three million – almost 90 per cent of those who voted – agreed with the actions that the *Führer* had taken.

Little more than 18 months after his appointment as a weak Chancellor, Hitler had turned Germany into a **totalitarian** state. What was most remarkable was that most of the

revolutionary changes introduced had been implemented legally, using the powers granted by the March 1933 Enabling Act.

### ACTIVITIES

1 For what reasons did the Night of the Long Knives take place?
2 How did Hitler justify his actions on that night?
3 What events led to Hitler declaring himself Germany's *Führer*?
4 Why did the army not oppose Hitler's actions?

### EXTENSION ACTIVITY

Is it fair to say that Hitler needed the army more than the army needed Hitler?

### REVISION TIP

On the Night of the Long Knives Hitler moved from using the tactics he had employed since the passage of the Enabling Act to employing extreme violence. In doing so he had shown he was prepared to act even against his own movement to ensure total control over Germany.

# NAZI ECONOMIC POLICY (I): UNIONS AND UNEMPLOYMENT

## Destroying the Unions

Hitler was afraid that trade unions could interfere with his plans, so in May 1933 they were outlawed. At the same time taking industrial action was declared illegal. Unions were replaced by the German Labour Front (DAF – *Deutsche Arbeitsfront*) led by Dr Robert Ley (Source A). Within two years all workers – over 20 million people – were members. A branch of the DAF, *Schönheit der Arbeit* (SdA – the Beauty of Labour) was set up to ensure that working conditions were improved through, for example, better lighting or noise reduction.

While the DAF was meant to represent the workers in discussions with their employers, it tended to side with employers and workers found their freedoms restricted (for example, their ability to move jobs) and their working hours increased (Source B). On a positive note, wages improved a little and prices and rents were strictly controlled by the state.

### SOURCE A

*Robert Ley speaking about the DAF, May 1933.*

For we know that without the German worker there is no German nation … Workers, I swear to you we shall not only preserve everything that exists, we shall build up even further the protection of the worker's rights.

### SOURCE B

*Government statement on the role of the DAF, November 1933.*

The high aim of the Labour Front is to educate all Germans who are at work to support the National Socialist State and to indoctrinate them in the National Socialist mentality.

## Free Time

The Nazis were also keen to ensure that their workers were happy outside the workplace. Therefore Strength through Joy (KDF – *Kraft Durch Freude*) was established in November 1933 to improve workers' free time. The KDF provided cheap holidays and organised a broad range of sporting activities. Workers were also given the chance to pay into a savings scheme to own a car, the *Volkswagen* (people's car). However, no cars had been distributed when the war started in 1939.

## Unemployment

Reducing Germany's massive levels of unemployment was one of Hitler's biggest challenges. The Nazis' vote had increased partly as a result of their promises to get Germans back to work. At first glance it would seem that he was largely successful with only 300,000 Germans listed as being without work by 1939.

This was achieved in a number of ways:

1 The scale of existing public work schemes was increased with the establishment of the National Labour Service (RAD – *Reichsarbeitsdienst*). The RAD, which brought

A 1933 poster encouraging workers to join the DAF.

together similar schemes begun by earlier governments, built schools, hospitals and motorways. Its workers were clothed in military-style fatigues and were housed in camps. While no wages were paid, workers did receive their food and some spending money. Six-month membership of the RAD for all men aged 18–25 became compulsory in 1935.

2 Many people – especially professional women and Jews – were forced from the workplace and their jobs were then given to those who were unemployed. Neither of these groups was then counted as unemployed.

3 The introduction of conscription in 1935 had a significant impact on unemployment levels. In 1933 there were 100,000 in the German army. By 1939 there were 1.4 million.

4 As Germany prepared for war, thousands of jobs were created in the armament and associated industries (such as steel and coal). Likewise, the drive for **autarky** resulted in the creation of new industries focused on creating synthetic replacements for raw materials.

## ACTIVITIES

1 Why did the Nazis set up the DAF?
2 What steps did the Nazis take to improve conditions for Germany's workers?
3 What steps did Hitler take to reduce unemployment in Germany?
4 How genuine was the reduction in Germany's unemployment figures?

## EXTENSION ACTIVITY

Did Hitler really care about Germany's workers?

## REVISION TIP

Examiners will expect you to know that while Hitler did reduce unemployment and help Germany's workers, the numbers listed as unemployed were not fully accurate while the Nazis were most anxious about keeping Germany's employers happy.

# NAZI ECONOMIC POLICY (II): STABILITY AND AUTARKY

## New Plan

Hjalmar Schacht (1877–1970).

In May 1933 respected economist Dr Hjalmar Schacht became President of the *Reichsbank*. Within a year he had been appointed Minister of Economics. Schacht's 1934 New Plan – introduced to deal with a **trade deficit** – oversaw the revitalisation of the German economy by:

- Introducing massive cuts to welfare spending.
- Imposing limits on imports.
- Implementing a series of trade agreements with countries to ensure that Germany was supplied with essential natural resources in return for goods manufactured in Germany.
- Introducing targeted government spending on key industries.

Under Schacht's guidance, the German economy recovered; however this was not enough to ensure his survival. By 1936 Hitler was pressurising him to increase spending on military resources. Schacht was unwilling to do this as he feared that it would damage the recovery he had helped create. As a result Schacht was increasingly ignored by Hitler and a year later he resigned from the government.

## Four-Year Plan

Despite his total lack of economic expertise (Source A) Hermann Göring was the man Hitler appointed to create an economy that was ready for war (*Wehrwirtschaft*). In 1936 he introduced the Four-Year Plan (Source B). Its aim was to ensure that Germany had become an autarky in advance of any future conflict.

SOURCE A

*Schacht comments on the Four-Year Plan in his book,* Account Rendered, *written in 1949.*

Göring set out with all the folly and incompetence of the amateur to carry out the programme of economic self-sufficiency, or autarky envisaged in the Four-Year Plan.

SOURCE B

*Hitler setting out his economic aims in the Four-Year Plan Memorandum, August 1936.*

The final solution lies in extending our living space, that is to say, extending the sources of raw materials and foodstuffs of our people ... There is only one interest, the interest of the nation; only one view, the bringing of Germany to the point of political and economic self sufficiency ... I thus set the following tasks:

1 The German armed forces must be operational within four years.
2 The German economy must be fit for war within four years.

Hermann Göring (right) and Adolf Hitler talking in 1938.

The Four-Year Plan introduced a range of strategies to ensure autarky:

- New factories were constructed.
- Industries were placed under strict government control.
- The amount of goods imported by Germany was cut.
- Higher targets were set for the production of essential materials such as oil, rubber and steel.
- Industries were encouraged to develop synthetic substitutes (*ersatz*) for raw materials, particularly rubber and oil.
- Targets were imposed for the production of foodstuffs. The *Reich* Food Estate, which all farmers had to join, provided very strict guidelines on what and how much should be produced.

However, by 1939 Germany was still importing over one-third of the natural resources essential to its economy. It had become clear that the only way to make its economy self-sufficient would be to conquer other countries and so gain complete access to their natural resources.

**ACTIVITIES**

1 What was the New Plan? How successful was it?
2 Why did Schacht leave the government in 1937?
3 Create a spider diagram showing the key elements of the Four-Year Plan.
4 Why was it so important for Hitler that Germany become self-sufficient?

**EXTENSION ACTIVITY**

What was more important to Hitler: economic recovery or preparing the German economy for war?

**REVISION TIP**

It is important that you are able to explain the differences between the New Plan and the Four-Year Plan. In addition, you should also be able to explain whether or not Hitler was successful in making Germany into an autarky.

# HITLER IN CONTROL

To ensure the loyalty of all Germans, the Nazis sought the creation of a *volksgemeinschaft* (people's community). Here, people would know their primary duty was loyalty to the state and to the *Führer*. Achieving this meant that all key institutions would come under Nazi control.

To support the *Führer* a control system was established across the country:

- *Reichsleiter* – leading Nazis
- *Gauleiter* – provincial leaders
- *Kreisleiter* – regional leaders
- *Ortsgruppeführer* – local group leaders
- *Zellenleiter* – cell leaders
- *Blockleiter* – local leaders.

While this system helped ensure that the party was aware of the mood, thoughts and behaviour of the population, establishing total control would require even greater interference. There would be no group or institution within Germany that the Nazi government would not try to control.

## Women

For the Nazis, the role of women was neatly encapsulated by the Three Ks: *Kinder, Kirche und Küche* – Children, Church and Cooking (Source A, page 37). A number of strategies were implemented to achieve this:

- Some women, particularly those married or in the professions (such as medicine or law), were forced from the workplace.
- By giving every newly married couple a loan of 1000 marks, 25 per cent of which was written off for every child born, the *Law for the Encouragement of Marriage* of June 1933 encouraged women to marry and have large families.
- Awards were created to encourage women to have as many children as possible. There were different levels of the Mother's Cross, depending on how many children the recipient had had. These women were also able to benefit from lower taxation levels and increased state benefits.
- Contraception and abortion became much harder to get hold of.
- Divorces to end childless marriages were made easier to obtain.
- Unmarried mothers were encouraged to live in homes (*Lebensborn* – Spring of Life) where Aryan SS men could impregnate them.

At the same time, the Nazis were only looking for the birth rate to improve if it resulted in a greater number of healthy Aryan offspring (Source B, page 37). The 1935 Marriage Law demanded evidence of racial purity and health before marriages could go ahead. Women deemed to be unfit mothers or likely to produce unhealthy children faced sterilisation. By 1939 an estimated 350,000 women had been dealt with in this way.

These policies had mixed results. Although the birth rate had increased by 1939, it remained lower than it was during the 'Golden Twenties'. The numbers getting married also increased, but

*The Aryan Family*, a painting by Wolfgang Willrich (1897–1948).

only for a few years; by 1935 the numbers were levelling off. A large number of women kept their jobs because of a lack of replacement workers, although the numbers of professional women did go down. The numbers of women in jobs actually went up in the later 1930s as the drive for rearmament and autarky took off.

---

**SOURCE A**

*Joseph Goebbels commenting on the role of women under National Socialism, 1929.*

The mission of women is to be beautiful and bring children into the world.

---

**SOURCE B**

*A viewpoint on the Nazis' policies towards women, published in 1939.*

Young girls from the age of 10 onwards were taken into organisations where they were taught only two things: to take care of their bodies so they could bear as many children as the state needed and to be loyal to National Socialism.

---

**ACTIVITIES**

1 Explain what the Nazis meant by the Three Ks.
2 What steps did the Nazis take to implement their policies for women?
3 How successful were the Nazis' policies towards women?

---

**EXTENSION ACTIVITY**

What evidence is there that the Nazis were ignoring their own policies towards women by the late 1930s?

---

**REVISION TIP**

The Nazis had very particular ideas as far as women were concerned. Examiners will expect you to be able to explain what their ideas were, how they tried to put them into practice and how successful they finally were.

---

## YOUTH

### Inside School

The Nazis saw **indoctrination** of youth with National Socialist ideas as the key to their future control of the country. To this end they set about influencing children inside and outside school (Source A, below).

Inside school, the Nazis sought to train students to accept that 'individuals must be willing and ready to sacrifice themselves for nation and *Führer*' (extract from 'Education and Instruction', the official teaching instruction booklet). Therefore the government:

- Dismissed Jewish teachers and those regarded as unreliable.
- Encouraged teachers to join the NSLB (National Socialist Teachers' League). Within six years all but three per cent of teachers had joined up.
- Nazified the curriculum to reflect the importance of subjects such as history, biology, geography and PE (which was allowed to take up 15 per cent of the timetable) (Source B, below).
- Prepared boys for life in the military and girls for their role as mothers.
- Established special schools (*Napolas* and Adolf Hitler Schools) to teach Germany's future leaders. Boys identified as high fliers went to *Ordensburgen* (Castles of Order).

---

**SOURCE A**

*The Nazi Minister of Education explains the role of education under National Socialism.*

The whole purpose of education is to create Nazis.

---

**SOURCE B**

*Explanation of the role of different subjects for Nazi education. Contained in* Der Angriff, *October 1939.*

All subjects, German language, history, geography, chemistry and mathematics must concentrate on military subjects, the glorification of military service and of German heroes and leaders.

## Free Time

The Hitler Youth Movement was established to control the activities of young people outside the classroom. Led by Baldur von Schirach, membership became compulsory for certain ages in 1936 and for most others in 1939. By that stage there were more than seven million members in the Hitler Youth Movement.

As Table 1.9 shows, there were a number of different sections to the movement, which again stressed the particular role of boys (military) and girls (motherhood) in the future of Germany.

The Nazis' youth policies had mixed results. Most young people did not oppose and would have been influenced by the Nazi policies both inside and outside the classroom. On the other hand evidence suggests that the quality and breadth of education suffered badly with traditional subjects losing out under the regime.

| Age | Boys' organisations | Girls' organisations |
|---|---|---|
| 6–10 | Pimpfen (Cubs) | |
| 10–14 | Deutsches Jungvolk (Young German Folk) | Jung Mädel (Young Girls) |
| 14–18 | Hitler Jugend (Hitler Youth) | Bund Deutscher Mädel (League of German Girls) |
| 18–21 | | Glaube und Schönheit (Faith and Beauty) |

Table 1.9 The main Nazi youth movements

Nor were all young people in love with the Hitler Youth. A significant minority (perhaps as many as one million) avoided joining the Nazi youth movements. Some of these even established rival youth groups. The two most notable were the Edelweiss Pirates and the Swing Youth.

A recruitment poster for the Hitler Youth.

## ACTIVITIES

1 Why did the Nazis see Germany's young people as so important for the future of the **Third Reich**?
2 What steps did the Nazis take to ensure that children were taught Nazi ideas in school?
3 How did the Nazis try to control young people's free time?
4 How successful were the Nazis' youth policies?

## EXTENSION ACTIVITY

'The Nazis' youth policies did more harm than good.' Discuss.

## REVISION TIP

It is essential that you can explain the Nazis' policies both inside and outside of school. The examiners will also want you to be able to tell them whether these policies were successful or not.

# RELIGION

Given the country's long tradition of Christianity, Hitler knew that it would be almost impossible to destroy Germany's different Churches; however he was determined to limit their influence as much as possible (Source A).

## Catholicism

In July 1933 a special agreement (concordat) was signed with the Catholic Church. The Church agreed not to involve itself in German politics; in return it was permitted to continue to run its own schools and activities for young people. Initially, this arrangement worked well, but by 1936 some of the terms – particularly those guaranteeing the rights of Catholic organisations such at youth groups – were being ignored. In 1937 Pope Pius XI responded by condemning the Nazi regime while later some German Church leaders spoke out strongly and successfully against Nazi policies in areas such as euthanasia of the mentally ill (a programme known as Operation T4) (Source B, page 40).

## Lutheranism

The **Lutheran** Church was split over its attitude to Nazism. Pro-Nazi Lutherans were known as the German Christians. Their symbol was a cross with the swastika at its centre, and their version of the Bible was altered to omit many references to the Jews. They were led by Ludwig Müller who became the first *Reich* Bishop in July 1933. In 1934 those Lutherans who disagreed with Nazism set up the Confessional Church. One of their leaders was Pastor Martin Niemöller who was arrested by the Nazis in 1937 and sent to Dachau **concentration camp**.

> ### SOURCE A
>
> *Joseph Goebbels writing about Hitler's views of religion, December 1939.*
>
> The *Führer* is deeply religious although completely anti-Christian. He views Christianity as a symptom of decay.

Pope Pius XI (1857–1939).

Bishop Ludwig Müller (1883–1945).

*Bishop von Galen condemning Nazi policies, August 1941.*

If you establish the principle that you can kill unproductive fellow human beings then woe betide us all when we become old and frail ... Woe to mankind, woe to our German nation if God's holy commandment 'Thou shalt not kill' ... is not only broken, but ... tolerated and permitted to go unpunished.

The Nazis also created their own Church, the German Faith Movement. Its beliefs owed much more to pagan values (such as worship of the sun) than to the ideas of Christianity and attracted few members.

Overall the Nazis were somewhat successful in their aim of undermining the influence of Germany's Churches. Although a number of individual clerics spoke out against aspects of the regime, by and large the Churches remained more concerned about ensuring their survival.

### ACTIVITIES

1 Why did the Nazis want to limit the power of the different Churches in Germany?
2 What steps did the Nazis take to control the Catholic and Lutheran Churches?
3 How successful were Hitler's religious policies?

### EXTENSION ACTIVITY

'Religion did not oppose Nazism enough in Germany.' Discuss.

### REVISION TIP

It is easy to get confused about the different parts of Hitler's religious policies. Make sure you can explain the steps he took to control the different Churches and can tell the examiners which policies were or were not successful.

## THE POLICE STATE

### 'Protective Custody'

Just in case anyone remained unpersuaded by Nazism, the security and justice systems also came under state control. The decree *For the Protection of People and State* allowed for opponents to be arrested and placed in 'protective custody' in newly constructed concentration camps, the first of which was established at Dachau in Bavaria in March 1933. By mid-1934 these camps were being run by part of the SS known as Death's Head Units.

While most early inmates tended to be political prisoners, before long other groups suffered **internment** including:

- criminals
- gypsies
- tramps
- the 'work shy'
- the 'anti-social'
- homosexuals
- Jews.

All of these prisoners had to endure extremely harsh conditions in the concentration camps.

### Security Forces

Following the Night of the Long Knives (see page 31) Heinrich Himmler's SS took over responsibility for party security from the SA. Along with the *Gestapo* and SD (both branches of the SS), the SS removed any real or potential opponents of the state. Historians argue that the SS became so powerful that it became a 'state within a state'.

The *Gestapo* (GEheime STAats POlizei – the secret state police and a branch of the SS) arrested opponents who became known as 'enemies of the state'. Also led by Himmler, much of the information it worked on came from ordinary Germans denouncing their fellow countrymen (Source A). The SD (*Sicherheitdienst*) was the intelligence arm of the SS; headed by Himmler's protégé Reinhard Heydrich, it monitored the security of the *Reich*.

### Judiciary

The judicial system also came under state control. The aim was to ensure that the legal system did not protect those that the state wanted to punish. Special People's Courts were established in 1934 to judge those accused of crimes against the state. It is estimated that in the period up to 1939 the judicial system sentenced nearly a quarter of a million Germans found guilty of political crimes to more than 600,000 years in prison.

Overall, the police state was very successful. Although individuals might have grumbled about aspects of the Nazi state, in general there was no organised opposition to the regime until the Second World War. Undoubtedly the fact that several hundred thousand Germans ended up being imprisoned for political crimes would have had a significant impact on the willingness of people to speak out against the regime.

## ACTIVITIES

1 What is a police state?
2 Identify and explain the different parts of the Nazi police state.
3 Was the police state successful in eliminating opposition to the Nazi government?

## EXTENSION ACTIVITY

What does the use of the police state suggest about the attitude of ordinary Germans to the Nazi system?

## SOURCE A

*Historian Jacques Delarue assesses the role of the Gestapo in Nazi Germany.*

Never before, in no other land and at no other time, had an organisation … possessed such power and reached such a degree of 'completeness' in its ability to arouse terror and horror, as well as its actual effectiveness.

## REVISION TIP

The use of terror was central to the success of the Nazi regime. Make sure that you can explain to the examiners what the police state was, what methods it used and how successful it was in achieving its aims.

Heinrich Himmler (left) and Reinhard Heydrich (1904–42) (right).

# PROPAGANDA

One of the easiest ways of ensuring conformity was by getting people to support the new government. This was the job of Dr Joseph Goebbels, Minister for Popular Enlightenment and Propaganda (Source A). To help him in this task, Goebbels established the *Reich* Chamber of Culture. This was subdivided into six sections, one for each major propaganda method.

One of the most impressive propaganda methods the Nazis employed was the annual Nuremberg rallies. Light, sound and costume were used to create a mesmeric atmosphere among crowds of up to half a million people. Other smaller-scale rallies and festivals were held throughout the year. Nazi propaganda efforts probably reached their height with the spectacle of the 1936 Olympic Games which were held in Berlin.

Joseph Goebbels (1897–1945) (left).

**SOURCE A**

*Extract from* Mein Kampf *on the importance of propaganda for the Nazis.*

The capacity of the masses for perception is extremely limited and weak. Bearing this in mind, any effective propaganda must be reduced to the minimum of essential concepts ... Only constant repetition can finally bring success in the matter of instilling ideas into the memory of the crowd ... The most important thing ... is to paint your contrasts in black and white.

## Controlling the Media

Control of the media was also a key aim. This was achieved in a variety of ways:

- Most newspapers were bought up by *Eher Verlag*, the Nazi publishers. By 1939 the Nazis owned 69 per cent of the newspaper titles in circulation.
- The *Editors' Law* held editors responsible for the content of their newspapers.
- Only journalists that were approved by the government could work in the media.
- Newspapers that printed stories the regime disapproved of were shut down.
- Editors went to a daily Propaganda Ministry briefing to be told what to print.
- The Nazis took control of all radio stations.
- Strong efforts were made to persuade Germans to buy cheap radios made by the *Reich* Radio Company. These could only pick up Nazi broadcasts. By 1939 70 per cent of households owned one, the highest percentage of radio ownership for any country in the world (Source B).
- Loudspeakers were erected in public places and in workplaces.

## Censorship

The Propaganda Ministry also controlled **censorship**. It censored cinema, theatre, music and literature, to ensure that they reflected Nazi thinking. In May 1933, 20,000 books were symbolically burned in Berlin. The 1934 law against malicious gossip outlawed anti-Nazi stories and jokes. Exhibitions of 'degenerate' art were organised showing people the 'distorted' work of modern artists such as George Grosz and Otto Dix.

The Nuremberg Rally of 1936.

Unacceptable music such as jazz was condemned. The writings of over 2500 authors were banned. Propaganda films such as *The Eternal Jew* were produced to portray the Jewish race in a derogatory way. Listening to foreign radio broadcasts was also made illegal.

It is difficult to decide the extent to which ordinary Germans believed Nazi ideas. It is probably safe to say that Nazi propaganda helped reinforce existing beliefs but was less successful in trying to get people to accept new ideas. Censorship ensured that the quality of much of Germany's culture was damaged. Only in the area of cinema was high-quality work produced, particularly by Leni Riefenstahl. Her most famous works were the documentaries *Olympia* (about the 1936 Olympics) and *Triumph of the Will* (about the 1934 Nuremberg Rally).

## ACTIVITIES

1 Who was in charge of propaganda in the Nazi government?
2 Why was propaganda so important to the Nazi state?
3 What were the main methods of propaganda used by the Nazis?
4 What steps did the Nazis take to censor alternative viewpoints?
5 How successful were Nazis' propaganda and censorship policies?

## EXTENSION ACTIVITY

'Propaganda and censorship were the Nazis' greatest areas of achievement.' Discuss.

## SOURCE B

*Nazi Minister Albert Speer comments on the importance of radio for Nazi propaganda.*

Through technical devices like the radio and the loudspeaker, 80 million people were deprived of independent thought. It was thereby possible to subject them to the will of one man.

## REVISION TIP

The use of propaganda and censorship were absolutely central to the success of the Nazi regime. Examiners will expect you to be able to identify the different methods used and explain how and why they were so successful.

## ANTI-SEMITISM AND THE PERSECUTION OF MINORITIES

Jewish people had experienced anti-Semitism in many European countries for several centuries. In Germany, however, there was a perception that Jews were more influential than their numbers merited. Hitler and the Nazis used propaganda to tell Germans that Jews were to blame for many of the problems that they had faced since the end of the First World War.

Allied to this were the Nazis' belief in the existence of a *Herrenvolk* or Aryan race, a master race of human beings who were superior to and would eventually overcome all other races (the *Untermenschen*), including the Jews (Source A). The Nazis also viewed groups such as those listed on page 40, as well as the disabled, prostitutes, alcoholics, Jehovah's Witnesses, and other minorities as *Untermenschen*. They enacted policies designed to prevent them from reproducing, to remove them from society or to eliminate them altogether.

However, the Nazis reserved their greatest hatred for Germany's Jews and so once in power, Hitler wasted no time in putting his anti-Semitism into operation:

### SOURCE A

*Hitler outlining his aims for the Jews, 1922.*

As soon as I have power, I shall have gallows after gallows erected ... Then the Jews will be hanged one after another, and they will stay hanging until they stink.

| | | | |
|---|---|---|---|
| April 1933 | Boycott of Jewish shops introduced (Source B). Jews banned from government jobs. | October 1938 | Jews to have their passports stamped with a J-shaped symbol. Jews forced to use new names: Israel for men, Sarah for women. |
| September 1933 | Jews banned from owning land. | November 1938 | The murder of a Nazi diplomat by a Jew in Paris on 7 November was the catalyst for a massive outbreak of anti-Jewish persecution. It became known as *Kristallnacht* (Source D, page 46). More than 400 synagogues and 7500 shops were destroyed. Ninety-one Jews were killed and over the following months 20,000 were sent to concentration camps. The Nazis fined the Jews one billion marks for the damage caused on *Kristallnacht*. They also had to clean up the streets in the aftermath of the attacks. Remaining Jewish businesses confiscated or closed down. Jews not allowed to attend German schools. |
| October 1933 | Jews banned from key media jobs. | | |
| September 1935 | Nuremberg Laws (Source C). There were two main elements: <br>• Jews deprived of many political and economic rights (*Reich* Citizenship Law). <br>• Illegal for Jews and Aryans to marry or engage in sexual relations outside marriage (Law for the Protection of German Blood and German Honour). | | |
| May 1935 | Jews banned from joining the army. | | |
| August 1936 | Persecution of the Jews eased off during the 1936 Olympic Games, which were held in Berlin. | | |
| January 1937 | Jews banned from the key professions including teaching, accountancy and dentistry. | | |
| April 1938 | Jews ordered to register all wealth and property. | January 1939 | Jews encouraged to emigrate from Germany. Hitler spoke of future annihilation of Jews. |
| June 1938 | Jews to register all businesses. | | |
| July/August 1938 | Jews had to carry identity cards. | | |
| September 1938 | Jews banned from all legal practices. | July 1939 | Jews forbidden from holding government jobs. |

*The Nazi newspaper,* Völkischer Beobachter, *calling for a boycott of Jewish businesses, 30 March 1933.*

On 1 April 1933, at the stroke of 10, the boycott of all Jewish businesses, doctors, lawyers begins – 10,000 mass gatherings. The Jews have declared war on 65 million, now they are to be hit where it hurts them most.

*Extract from the Nuremberg Laws, September 1935.*

Reich Citizenship Law: Article IV: (1) A Jew cannot be a citizen of the Reich.

The Law for the Protection of German Blood and Honour: Article I: (1) Any marriages between Jews and citizens of German or kindred blood are herewith forbidden.

A combination of support (especially resulting from propaganda), education, ignorance or fear ensured that persecution of the Jews was able to go ahead.

An anti-Semitic illustration from a 1936 children's textbook.

SA men posting instructions in 1933 for Germans to boycott a Jewish shop.

The aftermath of *Kristallnacht* in 1938.

## SOURCE D

*Instructions issued by the* Reich *Security Bureau about the events of 9–10 November 1938.*

Only such measures may be employed as will not endanger German lives or property, for example, synagogues may only be burnt when there is no risk that fire will spread to neighbouring structures. Jewish stores and dwellings may be destroyed ... The police must not interfere with the demonstrations that will occur.

## ACTIVITIES

1 Explain Hitler's ideas about race.
2 Which social groups did the Nazis regard as *Untermenschen*?
3 Why was there so much anti-Semitism in Germany in the early twentieth century?
4 What impact did the Nuremberg Laws have on the position of Jews in Germany?
5 Explain *Kristallnacht* under the following headings:
  * Reasons.
  * Events.
  * Results.

## EXTENSION ACTIVITY

Why do you think there was not more opposition within Germany to the Nazis' racial policies?

## REVISION TIP

This is a very important topic. Examiners will expect you to be aware of the different ways in which the Nazis discriminated against Germany's Jews and other minority groups.

# Practice Question (Foundation and Higher)

## Foundation

1  (a)  Below is a list of words linked to the Nazi consolidation of power between 1933 and 1934:

| Hindenburg | Socialist Party (SPD) | Communist Party (KPD) | Van Der Lubbe | Röhm |
|---|---|---|---|---|

Match **each** word to the correct description. The first one has been done for you.

Man who set fire to the *Reichstag* building in 1933.
***Van Der Lubbe***

SA leader killed on the Night of the Long Knives.                          [1]

President who appointed Hitler as Chancellor in January 1933.              [1]

Political party blamed by the Nazis for the *Reichstag* fire.             [1]

The only political party to vote against the Enabling Act.                [1]

(b)  Describe **two** actions which show how the Nazis tried to control young people in Germany between 1933 and 1939.                          [4]

(c)  Below are two actions taken by the Nazis to ensure control of the media.

| Editors' Law | Daily briefing at the Propaganda Ministry |
|---|---|

Choose **one** action and explain how it allowed the Nazis to control the media.   [6]

(d)  Why did the Nazis want to control the lives of women in Germany between 1933 and 1939?                          [9]

## Higher

1  (a)  Describe **two** actions taken by Hitler to consolidate his power in 1934.   [4]

(b)  In what ways did the Nazis change the lives of young people in Germany between 1933 and 1939?                          [6]

(c)  Explain how and why the Nazis implemented their anti-Semitic policies in Germany between 1933 and 1939. In your answer refer to the bullet points and use other relevant knowledge.

- Aryan beliefs
- 1935 Nuremberg Laws                          [15]

# NAZI POLICIES AND ACTIONS IN EUROPE 1933–41

## NAZI FOREIGN POLICY

### Aims

Hitler had three main foreign policy aims (Source A) which he had elaborated in a number of writings including *Mein Kampf* (Sources B and C) and his less famous *Secret Book* (written in 1928 and published in 1958) (Source D):

1 To restore the strength of Germany's armed forces by removing the military restrictions imposed by the 1919 Treaty of Versailles. Achieving this would be the first step to undertaking his other foreign policy aims.

2 To unite all those claiming German nationality into the Third *Reich* (*Grossdeutschland*). This would require the alterations of Germany's borders as they had existed since 1919.

3 To create *lebensraum* (living space) by acquiring new territory from 'racially inferior' central and eastern Europe states (especially the USSR) to support the needs of the growing population.

At first Hitler moved cautiously in his foreign policy, but within a few years, as his dictatorship strengthened and as Germany's military strength began to return, he was moving rapidly to achieve his foreign policy aims.

**Figure 1.6** Locations of Germans living outside the Third *Reich*.

### SOURCE A

*Extract from the 25-Point Programme.*

1 We demand the union of all Germans in a Greater Germany on the basis of the right of national self-determination.

2 We demand equality of rights for the German people in its dealings with other nations, and the revocation of the peace treaties of Versailles and St Germain.

3 We demand land and territory [colonies] to feed our people and to settle our surplus population.

### SOURCE B

*Hitler writing in* Mein Kampf *about the impact of the Treaty of Versailles on Germany.*

The treaty … is engraved on the minds and hearts of the German people and burned into them. Sixty million people will find their souls aflame with a feeling of rage and shame. Then the people will join in a common cry: 'We will have arms again.'

### SOURCE C

*Extract from* Mein Kampf *about the need for living space.*

Only a sufficiently large space on this earth can ensure the independent existence of a nation … The acquisition of land and soil [must be] the objective of our foreign policy … We are … turning our eyes towards the land in the east.

### SOURCE D

*Extract from Hitler's* Secret Book, *written in 1928 and published 30 years later.*

Every healthy, vigorous people sees nothing sinful in territorial acquisition, but something quite in keeping with nature … Hence … a vigorous nation will always find ways of adapting its territory to its population size.

## DISARMAMENT

At the 1919 Paris Peace Conference it had been agreed that all countries would disarm. However, Germany was the only country that had done so. It was decided in the 1920s that an international conference would be held to sort out this problem once and for all. The conference first met in Geneva in 1932.

At the conference Germany demanded that the other major powers disarm as it had been forced to do at the end of the First World War. The French government refused to agree to this demand and in response Hitler ordered the German representatives to walk out of the conference and withdrew Germany from the League of Nations. At the same time he balanced what might have been seen as a warlike act by signing a **non-aggression pact** with Poland in January 1934 (Source A, page 50).

The signing of the non-aggression pact with Poland, January 1934. Pictured are Polish leader Jozef Pilsudski (1867–1935) (second left) and Joseph Goebbels (second right).

## SOURCE A

*An historian's view of the non-aggression pact signed between Germany and Poland in January 1934.*

*Much to everyone's surprise ... Hitler concluded a non-aggression pact with Poland ... Hitler said privately at the time, 'I have no intention of maintaining a serious friendship with Poland.'*

## REARMAMENT

Throughout the Weimar years Germany had been using its friendship with Moscow to secretly rearm within the USSR, despite the restrictions imposed by the Treaty of Versailles. At first Hitler continued with this cautious policy, but once he felt secure in power, military expenditure tripled to nine billion marks and rearmament was speeded up with the opening of new factories:

- The navy began to construct new vessels including submarines.
- The air force (*Luftwaffe*) was officially set up in 1935 and soon expanded rapidly to over 2500 aircraft.
- Conscription was publicly announced in March 1935 although the army had already quadrupled in size from the official 100,000 set at Versailles.

All of these actions broke the terms of the Treaty of Versailles. In response, the leaders of Britain, Italy and France met at Stresa in northern Italy in April 1935 to condemn German breaches of the treaty. However, within weeks this partnership had collapsed. This was because Germany and Britain signed a naval agreement in June 1935 which permitted Germany to increase its fleet until it was 35 per cent of the size of the Royal Navy. Britain's aim in signing this agreement was to ensure that it remained the strongest naval power in Europe.

This agreement was a massive diplomatic victory for Hitler:

- The anti-German coalition was broken up.
- The German navy was only one-tenth of the size of the British fleet; now it could increase massively.
- The naval agreement was yet another breach of the Treaty of Versailles. The difference this time, however, was that one of the countries that had signed the treaty was involved in the breaking of its terms.

There were also other notable successes for Hitler at this time. The Versailles settlement had provided for a future plebiscite to decide who would control the Saar region. This vote finally took place in January 1935. Nearly 91 per cent voted for a return to German rule.

Evidence of Germany's growing military might. Newly constructed tanks on parade at a Nazi Party gathering.

## ACTIVITIES

1 Hitler's early foreign policy actions were quite cautious: why was this?
2 Why would the other European powers have been worried about Germany by 1935? What evidence do we have that they were concerned?
3 Explain why the Anglo-German naval agreement was such an achievement for Hitler.
4 Construct a timeline showing Hitler's main foreign policy actions for 1933–5.

## EXTENSION ACTIVITY

Had Hitler any reason to be satisfied by his foreign policy achievements 1933–5?

## REVISION TIP

You need to be able to show the examiners that you understand how and why Hitler acted with caution in his foreign policy in the years up to 1935.

## SOURCE A

*An account written in 1949 by Hitler's interpreter on his feelings over the remilitarisation of the Rhineland.*

More than once, even during the war, I heard Hitler say: 'The 48 hours after the march into the Rhineland were the most nerve-wracking in my life.' He always added, 'If the French had then marched into the Rhineland we would have had to withdraw with our tails between our legs, for the military resources at our disposal would have been completely inadequate for even moderate resistance.'

## SOURCE B

*Lord Lothian commenting on the remilitarisation of the Rhineland, March 1936.*

The Germans ... are only going into their own back garden.

## 1936–8: BECOMING BOLDER

### The Rhineland

Hitler detested how the Treaty of Versailles had left Germany's border with France undefended. Therefore, in March 1936, thousands of German troops reoccupied the hitherto demilitarised Rhineland, which violated the terms of both the Versailles and Locarno Treaties (see pages 6 and 13). Hitler was clearly testing the waters to see how the Allies would react. He knew that German forces were still comparatively weak (Source A on this page).

However, France and Britain took no action. Their leaders preferred to achieve a peaceful solution to the problem (Source B). This strategy became known as **appeasement** and until 1939 it allowed Germany to expand. Neville Chamberlain (British Prime Minister 1937–40) strongly supported this policy. His willingness to concede to Hitler's demands only increased the latter's belief in the Allies' weakness.

Hitler's success in the Rhineland massively boosted his popularity at home. A plebiscite was held in late March for Germans to give their opinions on the remilitarisation; all but one per cent of those that voted supported Hitler's actions.

### Alliances

Hitler also moved to ensure that Germany would not be alone if a war was ever to break out. By the end of 1936 military agreements had been made with:

- Italy (the Rome–Berlin Axis).
- Japan (the Anti-**Comintern** Pact).

Like the Italian leader, Benito Mussolini, Hitler also got involved in the Spanish Civil War (1936–9). Over 10,000 military personnel were dispatched to support the Nationalists under the command of General Francisco Franco. Not only was this an attempt to help establish a like-minded system and perhaps secure another ally; it also allowed the *Luftwaffe*, flying as the Condor Legion, to perfect bombing techniques that would later be used in the Second World War.

By 1936 it was clear that Hitler was intending to go to war. In that year he gave Göring the task of overseeing the creation of a war economy through the Four-Year Plan (see pages 34–5). A year later, as recorded in the Hossbach Memorandum, Hitler secretly told his generals that he envisaged Germany being involved in a major war by the mid-1940s.

## Anschluss

### Failure

In July 1934, Nazis in Austria made an attempt to seize power in Vienna. Hitler, however, failed to support them. There were two main reasons for this:

1 Germany was still militarily weak.
2 Italy's leader, Benito Mussolini, at that stage was not a supporter of Hitler's foreign policy and had threatened to intervene militarily to prevent his neighbour from becoming a Nazi-controlled state.

Austrian crowds show their support for the *Anschluss* in 1938.

By 1938 things were very different:

- Italy was now Germany's closest ally.
- Secret contacts with France and Britain had suggested that these countries would not oppose Germany gaining control of Austria.
- Austria was economically weak and more likely to be open to increased links with an increasingly prosperous Germany.
- Hitler felt that Germany was strong enough militarily to attempt an *Anschluss*.

### Success

In early 1938 Hitler forced Austrian Chancellor Schuschnigg into appointing Nazis to his government. Schuschnigg was so concerned about the impact of Hitler's increased influence in his country that he announced there would be a plebiscite over Austria's future. He hoped that Austrians would use the opportunity to vote against an *Anschluss*.

Hitler was outraged and demanded the cancellation of plans for a plebiscite. He also demanded that Schuschnigg resign the chancellorship. Schuschnigg agreed and was replaced by Artur Seyss-Inquart, an Austrian National Socialist. Once in power, Seyss-Inquart asked Hitler to send the German army into Austria. With no one to oppose them, the troops began to move in on 12 March 1938. On the next day Hitler announced that the *Anschluss* had taken place and Austria had become part of Germany (Source C). A subsequent referendum on the *Anschluss* resulted in 99 per cent approval for the action.

Versailles had again been broken. By acquiring unheld territory, Hitler was moving forward with his plans for a *Grossdeutschland*. Germany had also gained access to the Austrian Army's resources. Again the Allies protested but did nothing else, thus encouraging further expansion.

### SOURCE C

*Hitler's justification of the* Anschluss *with Austria, March 1938.*

What injustice have we done to any country, whose interests have we violated, when we concur with the desire of the overwhelming majority of the Austrian population to be Germans?

## Czechoslovakia

### The Sudeten Crisis

Hitler's next target was the neighbouring state of Czechoslovakia, which included within its borders a sizeable German minority. His first tactic was to launch a misinformation campaign against the Czech government, arguing that it was allowing the mistreatment of the three million Germans living in the industrially developed Sudetenland region. He also encouraged the pro-Nazi Sudeten German Party, led by Konrad Henlein, to make impossible demands of the Czech government and to engage in civil unrest when these demands were not granted (Source D).

British Prime Minister Neville Chamberlain was so concerned about the prospect of war that he flew to meet Hitler at Berchtesgaden in September 1938. At this meeting Hitler demanded that Germany be given all parts of the Sudetenland that were over 50 per cent German.

---

**SOURCE D**

*German Foreign Office record of Hitler's meeting with the Hungarian Prime Minister, September 1938.*

He, the *Führer*, was determined to settle the Czech question even at risk of a world war.

---

Adolf Hitler taking the salute from German soldiers on the streets of Prague, October 1938.

Britain and France persuaded Czechoslovakia to accept these demands.

Hitler, however, wanted more and now upped the pressure by demanding that all of the Sudetenland be handed over to him by 1 October. This time, however, the Czechs refused and negotiations broke down. With war seemingly inevitable another meeting was organised to be held in the Bavarian capital Munich. Before this meeting took place Hitler declared that once he had gained the Sudetenland he would demand territory off no other European country.

### Munich

The Munich conference marked the lowest point of the policy of appeasement. Apart from Chamberlain and Hitler, the conference was attended by the leaders of France (Édouard Daladier) and Italy (Mussolini). Amazingly however, Czechoslovakia's leader, (Edvard Beneš), was excluded while Czechoslovakia's ally, the Soviet Union, was not invited. There were three main terms:

1 Germany would gain the Sudetenland.
2 Hitler agreed to the holding of plebiscites in mixed areas of Czechoslovakia (to work out the wishes of the other minority groups in the country).
3 Germany promised to respect the independence of what remained of Czechoslovakia.

---

**ACTIVITIES**

1 Explain what is meant by appeasement.
2 Why did Britain and France support the policy of appeasement?
3 Why was the successful remilitarisation of the Rhineland such an important turning point in Nazi foreign policy?
4 Explain why an *Anschluss* was possible in 1938 when it was not four years earlier.
5 Why did Hitler want control of the Sudetenland?
6 Would the following have regarded the Munich conference as a success or a failure:
   • Germany?
   • Britain and France?
   • Czechoslovakia and the USSR?
   Explain your answer.
7 Construct a timeline showing Hitler's main foreign policy actions for 1934–8.

---

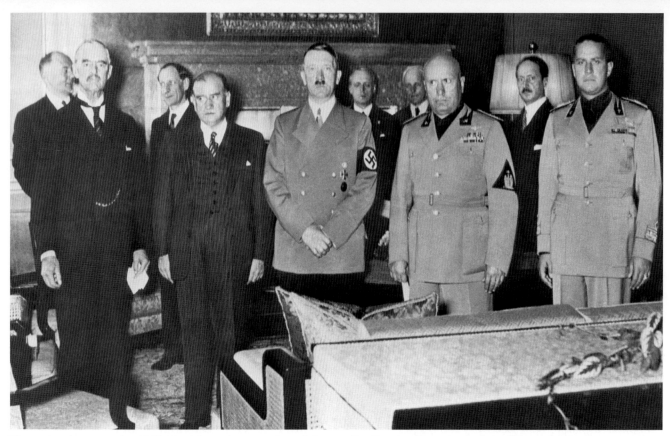

The main players at the 1938 Munich conference. From left, Neville Chamberlain (1869–1940), Édouard Deladier (1884–1970), Adolf Hitler and Benito Mussolini (1883–1945).

## EXTENSION ACTIVITY

Was appeasement a success or a failure?

## REVISION TIP

It is important that you understand how appeasement allowed Hitler to grow in strength while also convincing him that Britain and France would never stand up to him.

## THE ROAD TO WAR

### Broken Promises

However, despite all that he had gained and all that he had promised, Hitler still was not satisfied. In March 1939, he forced the Czech government to hand over the provinces of Bohemia and Moravia (which had German minorities). For the first time Hitler had taken over non-German territory. Days later the remaining parts of Czechoslovakia were also dealt with. Slovakia came under German protection while the province of Ruthenia was handed over to Hungary, which had shown support for German foreign policy.

Britain and France's immediate response was to issue yet another protest against Germany's actions (Source A). Not surprisingly Hitler paid no heed to their condemnations and continued in the same vein by successfully demanding the former German port of Memel from Lithuania. The latter had seized the port in 1923.

## SOURCE A

*Historian William Carr comments on the reaction of the Western powers to the destruction of Czechoslovakia in March 1939.*

What [Hitler] did not anticipate was the deep impression the events of March 1939 made upon public opinion in Britain. Overnight, appeasement was discredited.

## Nazi–Soviet Pact

In March 1939 Hitler turned his attention to Poland. His main interest lay in the return of the Polish corridor (see Figure 1.3 on page 7) and the former German port of Danzig. Hitler's initial demands were for the return of Danzig and the provision of a road and rail link across the Polish corridor to connect East Prussia with the rest of Germany.

Finally, realising that Hitler could not be trusted, Britain and France offered Poland a security guarantee on 30 March 1939. Hitler believed that Britain and France would find it hard to protect Poland and chose to ignore their actions. Germany stated it no longer supported the 1934 non-aggression pact and preparations for an invasion were stepped up. Perhaps to guarantee that he had some allies, a full military alliance, the Pact of Steel, was signed with Italy in May.

Tied in with *lebensraum* was Hitler's desire for the destruction of Communist Russia allied with access to its immense natural resources, including oil. Other powers were astonished, therefore, when Nazi Germany and the Soviet Union, two countries whose political ideas were completely opposed, signed the Nazi–Soviet Pact on 23 August 1939.

As well as agreeing not to attack each other for 10 years, the pact contained a secret clause that divided Poland up between the two countries. This left Germany free to attack Poland without taking the risk of having to face opposition from Soviet troops.

As far as Hitler was concerned the Nazi–Soviet Pact cancelled out any threat of Britain and

A cartoon from *Punch* commenting on what the 1939 Nazi–Soviet Pact meant for Poland.

France defending Poland. On 1 September 1939 therefore, Germany launched an invasion of Poland. Two days later Britain and France responded by declaring war on Germany.

The signing of the Nazi–Soviet Pact, August 1939 by the USSR's Foreign Minister Vyacheslav Molotov (1890–1986). Joseph Stalin (1878–1953) looks on approvingly in the background (standing, second from left).

### ACTIVITIES

1. Why did Hitler continue to seize land despite the promises he made at Munich?
2. How did Britain and France respond to the fall of Bohemia and Moravia? Why did this not worry Hitler?
3. Why was the signing of the Nazi–Soviet Pact in August 1939 so significant?

### EXTENSION ACTIVITY

Should Britain and France not have declared war on Germany long before September 1939?

### REVISION TIP

Things happened very quickly in German foreign policy in 1939. Make sure that you understand and can explain what happened in these crucial months.

## Practice Question (Foundation and Higher)

### Foundation

1 (a) The following are words linked to the aims and early actions of the Nazis in foreign policy:

| Lebensraum | Britain | Versailles | Austria | Luftwaffe |
|---|---|---|---|---|

Match **each** word to the correct description. The first one has been done for you.

Aim of Germany to expand into central and eastern Europe.
**Lebensraum**

Country that Germany failed to take over in 1934. [1]

Airforce set up in 1935. [1]

Country with which Germany signed a naval agreement in 1935. [1]

Treaty that Hitler wanted to destroy. [1]

(b) Describe **two** reasons why Hitler wanted to take over the Sudetenland in 1938. [6]

(c) Below are two actions taken by Hitler to break the terms of the Treaty of Versailles.

Choose **one** action and explain how Hitler broke the Treaty.

| Conscription | Rhineland |
|---|---|

Action chosen: _____ [6]

(d) How was Hitler able to take over the Sudetenland and the rest of Czechoslovakia by 1939? [9]

### Higher

1 (a) Give **two** reasons why Germany invaded Poland in 1939. [4]

(b) How did Hitler restore Germany's military power between 1933 and 1935? [6]

(c) Explain how and why Hitler broke the terms of the Treaty of Versailles between 1936 and 1938. In your answer refer to the bullet points and use other relevant knowledge.

- Austria
- The Sudetenland [15]

# Peace, War and Neutrality: Britain, Northern Ireland and Ireland 1932–49

## ANGLO-IRISH RELATIONS BEFORE THE SECOND WORLD WAR

### IRELAND BEFORE 1932

#### Partition

Between 1801 and 1920 Ireland was ruled by Britain from Westminster. For much of that time Ireland's **Nationalist** politicians sought the establishment of a **home rule** Parliament in Dublin. This demand was strongly opposed by Ireland's **Unionist** population, many of whom lived in the north-eastern part of the island.

In 1912 Britain's Liberal government agreed to introduce home rule to Ireland by 1914. In the aftermath of this decision both sides set up their own private armies. Their intention was to ensure that they got their way in terms of either getting or stopping home rule. The Nationalists set up the Irish Volunteers; the Unionists established the Ulster Volunteer Force (UVF). Both armies imported weapons from Germany.

By mid-1914 it seemed as if **civil war** was about to break out between the two sides; however, with the start of the First World War in August 1914 it was agreed to postpone the introduction of home rule until the conflict had ended. Both sides agreed to send their private armies to fight for the **Allies** in the war although a section of the Irish Volunteers refused to fight for Britain and remained at home.

#### The Easter Rising and its Aftermath

Not everyone was prepared to wait for the end of the war. In April 1916 a group of **republicans** staged a rebellion against British rule and declared Ireland a **republic**. While the rebellion failed, the harsh way in which the British government reacted to it meant that many Nationalists now demanded that Ireland be given full independence.

Nationalist leader John Redmond is portrayed in this *Punch* cartoon herding a group of pigs (representing the four provinces of Ireland) through a gate (representing Home Rule). One pig (representing the Unionist part of the province of Ulster) is trying to get away.

In the December 1918 **general election** Sinn Féin, led by Éamon de Valera, replaced the more moderate Irish Parliamentary Party as Ireland's largest political party. Rather than send its MPs to Westminster, Sinn Féin decided to set up its own parliament in Dublin. This was known as Dáil Éireann and with its calls for the creation of an independent Irish Republic, the scene was set for some sort of clash with the British government.

The conflict was not long in coming. In January 1919 the Irish Republican Army (IRA) began what became known as the Anglo-Irish War against the British forces in Ireland. The IRA had been formed from those members of the Irish Volunteers who had refused to go off and fight in the First World War.

While the Anglo-Irish War was being fought in the south, **sectarian** violence – involving the revived UVF and the IRA – erupted in the

## POBLACHT NA H EIREANN.

## THE PROVISIONAL GOVERNMENT
### OF THE
## IRISH REPUBLIC
### TO THE PEOPLE OF IRELAND.

IRISHMEN AND IRISHWOMEN: In the name of God and of the dead generations from which she receives her old tradition of nationhood, Ireland, through us, summons her children to her flag and strikes for her freedom.

Having organised and trained her manhood through her secret revolutionary organisation, the Irish Republican Brotherhood, and through her open military organisations, the Irish Volunteers and the Irish Citizen Army, having patiently perfected her discipline, having resolutely waited for the right moment to reveal itself, she now seizes that moment, and, supported by her exiled children in America and by gallant allies in Europe, but relying in the first on her own strength, she strikes in full confidence of victory.

We declare the right of the people of Ireland to the ownership of Ireland, and to the unfettered control of Irish destinies, to be sovereign and indefeasible. The long usurpation of that right by a foreign people and government has not extinguished the right, nor can it ever be extinguished except by the destruction of the Irish people. In every generation the Irish people have asserted their right to national freedom and sovereignty; six times during the past three hundred years they have asserted it in arms. Standing on that fundamental right and again asserting it in arms in the face of the world, we hereby proclaim the Irish Republic as a Sovereign Independent State, and we pledge our lives and the lives of our comrades-in-arms to the cause of its freedom, of its welfare, and of its exaltation among the nations.

The Irish Republic is entitled to, and hereby claims, the allegiance of every Irishman and Irishwoman. The Republic guarantees religious and civil liberty, equal rights and equal opportunities to all its citizens, and declares its resolve to pursue the happiness and prosperity of the whole nation and of all its parts, cherishing all the children of the nation equally, and oblivious of the differences carefully fostered by an alien government, which have divided a minority from the majority in the past.

Until our arms have brought the opportune moment for the establishment of a permanent National Government, representative of the whole people of Ireland and elected by the suffrages of all her men and women, the Provisional Government, hereby constituted, will administer the civil and military affairs of the Republic in trust for the people.

We place the cause of the Irish Republic under the protection of the Most High God, Whose blessing we invoke upon our arms, and we pray that no one who serves that cause will dishonour it by cowardice, inhumanity, or rapine. In this supreme hour the Irish nation must, by its valour and discipline and by the readiness of its children to sacrifice themselves for the common good, prove itself worthy of the august destiny to which it is called.

Signed on behalf of the Provisional Government.

THOMAS J. CLARKE.
SEAN MacDIARMADA. THOMAS MacDONAGH.
P. H. PEARSE. EAMONN CEANNT.
JAMES CONNOLLY. JOSEPH PLUNKETT.

The proclamation of the Irish Republic as published in 1916.

A painting by Irish artist Sean Keating (1889–1977) showing IRA men during the Anglo-Irish War.

northern counties. The violence was particularly fierce in the cities of Belfast and Derry/Londonderry. Westminster's response was the establishment of the mainly Protestant Ulster Special Constabulary. It had a part-time section called the B Specials who were particularly feared by Catholics.

## The Government of Ireland Act 1920

While fighting this war, the British government began the search for a political solution that it hoped would be acceptable to all sides. The result was the 1920 Government of Ireland Act which partitioned the island. Two new states were set up, Northern Ireland (looking after the six north-eastern counties) and Southern Ireland (governing the remaining 26 counties). These states would have control over areas such as education, health and transport. Proportional representation would be used to ensure that the minorities in both areas would be properly represented. Westminster would keep responsibility for defence, foreign policy and taxation.

## Irish Free State

The terms of the Government of Ireland Act were unacceptable to Irish Republicans. They wanted much more power than the new law gave them and so the Anglo-Irish War went on. It was not until July 1921 that both sides agreed a ceasefire and began to talk about a political solution. The outcome of these negotiations was the signing, in December 1921, of the Anglo-Irish Treaty. This established the Irish Free State as a dominion of the British Commonwealth.

Although it was still not full independence, it gave Dublin more power than the Government of Ireland Act had done. In the words of Michael Collins, one of the Irish leaders who signed the treaty, it gave Irish politicians 'freedom, not the ultimate freedom that all nations desire and develop to, but the freedom to achieve it' (Source A on page 59).

Not all of Collins' colleagues agreed however, and the Anglo-Irish Treaty divided Irish Republicans. There were two parts of the treaty in particular which caused problems:

1 The continuation of strong links with the British Commonwealth.

By signing the treaty the Irish accepted that the Irish Free State would retain links with the UK. This relationship would be symbolised by:
- An oath of allegiance to the British monarch, to be sworn by members of the Irish Parliament (Source B on page 59).

- The appointment of an official by the London government who would represent the monarch in the Irish Free State. This official would be given the title of **Governor General**.
- The right of citizens of the Irish Free State to appeal judgements of Irish courts to the British **Privy Council**.

In addition, the British also held on to three military/naval bases in the Irish Free State. These 'treaty ports' were located in Berehaven, Cobh and Lough Swilly.

2 The confirmation of the partitioning of Ireland as introduced by the 1920 Government of Ireland Act.

During the negotiations leading to the treaty, the Sinn Féin delegation reluctantly accepted the partition of Ireland as a temporary price to pay for political independence. They were helped here by the British promise to set up a Boundary Commission to examine the location of the border at a future date. The Irish delegation was told that this commission would take land off of Northern Ireland and leave it too small to survive. In this way, they believed, Ireland would be united again.

This promise did not convince all Republicans. The anti-treaty members of Sinn Féin, led by Éamon de Valera, attacked the treaty for its acceptance of partition (as well as for its offer of less than an independent republic). They argued that it meant the abandonment of half a million Nationalists living inside the new state of Northern Ireland (Source C).

The divisions were so serious that a civil war was fought between 1922 and 1923. The pro-treaty side was victorious and, under the leadership of Cumann na nGaedheal (the pro-treaty party), the Free State set about increasing its independence from Britain. This process ended with the passage of the 1931 Statute of Westminster, which stated that dominions were independent countries that could leave the Commonwealth without Britain's permission.

During this period Éamon de Valera continued to lead the anti-treaty side. In 1926 he established a new party, Fianna Fáil. It entered the Dáil in 1927 and within a year had become the official opposition party.

---

### SOURCE A

*Seán MacEoin gives a supporter's view of the treaty, December 1921.*

To me this treaty gives me what I and my colleagues fought for; it gives us for the first time in 700 years, the evacuation of Britain's armed forces out of Ireland.

---

### SOURCE B

*Extract from the oath of allegiance (Article 4, Anglo-Irish Treaty, 1921).*

I — do solemnly swear true faith and allegiance to the Constitution of the Irish Free State as by law established and that I will be faithful to His Majesty King George V, his heirs and successors by law, in virtue of the common citizenship of Ireland with Great Britain and her adherence to and membership of the group of nations forming the British Commonwealth of Nations.

A cartoon from *Dublin Opinion* suggesting that the 1921 treaty may not be good for Ireland.

**ACTIVITIES**

1 Explain the background to the 1921 treaty.
2 How did members of Sinn Féin react to the 1921 treaty?
3 Explain the reasons for opposition to the treaty under the following headings:
   • Partition.
   • Links with Britain.
4 Which two political parties were set up in the Irish Free State after the civil war?

**EXTENSION ACTIVITY**

Did the treaty give the Free State 'freedom, not the ultimate freedom that all nations desire and develop to, but the freedom to achieve it'?

**REVISION TIP**

Although this information is background to the period that you will be examined on it is still important information for you to understand. In particular you need to be aware of why there were divisions in the Free State over the 1921 treaty.

## NORTHERN IRELAND

The Government of Ireland Act delighted Unionists, ensuring as it did that they would have control over their own affairs (Source A). They lost no time in holding elections for their new Parliament, winning 40 of the available 52 seats. As a result Sir James Craig (Lord Craigavon from 1927), the Unionist leader, became Northern Ireland's first Prime Minister.

The creation of Northern Ireland was bitterly opposed by the majority of Nationalists (Source B). Many of them were convinced that the provision of the Boundary Commission in the 1921 Anglo-Irish Treaty meant that partition would not last and so they refused to give any recognition to the new state. As a result, Unionists were convinced that Nationalists wanted to destroy Northern Ireland. The doubts and suspicions that were being experienced by both sides were increased by the high levels of sectarian violence in the early months of Northern Ireland's existence.

Sir James Craig/Lord Craigavon (1871–1940).

**SOURCE A**

*Protestant attitude to the setting up of the Northern Ireland Parliament as stated by historian Patrick Buckland in* A History of Northern Ireland.

[Unionists] fully realised that there was little sympathy and affection for them in Britain and feared that Westminster might try and force them into the South. Therefore they saw safety in 'Having a parliament of our own, for we believe that once a parliament is ... working well ... we should fear no one, and we feel that we would then be in a position of absolute security.'

## SOURCE B

*The Catholic attitude to the new Northern Ireland state as expressed by Mgr George Crolly, Parish Priest of St Matthew's, Belfast, April 1921.*

This so-called northern parliament is a danger to our liberties and a barrier to the permanent solution of the Irish problem, we [Nationalists] can neither give it recognition nor lend it support.

In the end the Nationalists were to be disappointed. Although the Boundary Commission finally met in 1925 it did not lead to any change in the border. The commission's report actually recommended handing some of the Irish Free State's land to Northern Ireland, something that Dublin had never considered. For that reason all sides agreed to leave the border as it was and the Irish Free State was let off making the contributions to the UK's national debt that it had agreed to pay in the 1921 treaty.

From that point it became clear that partition would be permanent and Nationalist MPs finally took up their seats in the Northern Ireland Parliament.

## ACTIVITIES

1 Who won the elections held for the first Northern Ireland Parliament?
2 How much power did the new Northern Ireland Parliament have?
3 How did Northern Nationalists react to the establishment of Northern Ireland?
4 Why was the failure of the Boundary Commission so important for the future of Northern Ireland?

## EXTENSION ACTIVITY

Was Northern Ireland 'a Protestant state' (as later stated by Craigavon)?

## REVISION TIP

As with the previous chapter, this information is background to the period that you will be examined on. However, you still need to understand the reasons why Northern Ireland was such a divided state.

King George V (1865–1936) arriving to open Northern Ireland's first Parliament in June 1921.

# THE FREE STATE UNDER DE VALERA

## The 1932 General Election

Following a general election in March 1932 Fianna Fáil, with the support of the Irish Labour Party, became the Free State's government. The IRA, declared illegal by the previous government, was legalised and began to organise openly again, even attacking Cumann na nGaedheal members. It responded by setting up the Army Comrades Association (ACA) which became known as the Blueshirts. In 1933 Cumann na nGaedheal and the Blueshirts joined together to become Fine Gael. In 1936 de Valera responded to continuing illegal activities by IRA members by declaring it illegal.

Éamon de Valera (1882–1975).

## Cementing Independence

Now in power de Valera (also serving as the Free State's Minister for External Affairs) began to change parts of the Anglo-Irish Treaty he was most unhappy about (Source A). Bit by bit, and making use of the legal means available, de Valera began to remove the Free State's remaining links with Britain (Source B), as established by the 1921 treaty.

### SOURCE A

*De Valera outlining his policy aims at a rally commemorating the 1916 Easter Rising, April 1933.*

Let it be clear that we yield no willing assent to any form or symbol that is out of keeping with Ireland's right as a sovereign nation. Let us remove these forms one by one, so that this state we control may become a republic in fact.

Éamon de Valera destroying the 'Commonwealth Bridge'.

## SOURCE B

*Historian M.E. Collins reflects on the methods used by de Valera to undermine the Anglo-Irish Treaty.*

[De Valera] adopted a step-by-step approach and kept carefully within the law. This made it difficult for the British to retaliate.

In November 1932 the London government recalled Governor General James MacNeill because Fianna Fáil ministers were engaged in a policy of snubbing him as he was the King's official representative. MacNeill was replaced by Fianna Fáil politician Domhnall O'Buachalla who, instead of being called Governor General, was titled *an seanasca* (Chief Steward). De Valera acted in other ways to undermine the position that O'Buachalla now held, and thus play down the Free State's link with the British crown. O'Buachalla's powers were limited, he never lived in the Governor General's official residence in Dublin's Phoenix Park and he undertook no official duties.

In May 1933, the Dublin government passed the Removal of the Oath Act, which removed the oath of allegiance that all Dáil members had to swear to the King. This action followed on from de Valera's victory in a snap election in January 1933. That election had been called to prove that the government had public support for the policies that it was following.

In May 1933 the Free State constitution was changed to prevent citizens appealing Irish court verdicts to the British Privy Council. In 1935 London challenged these actions before the Privy Council itself, but it ruled that the 1931 Statute of Westminster (see page 59) gave de Valera the power to introduce the changes he was making.

De Valera used the December 1936 abdication crisis to pass the External Relations Act. Under this new law, the King's official role within the Free State came to an end even though in legal terms Ireland remained a member of the Commonwealth. As a result, the position of Governor General also ceased to exist.

## EXTENSION ACTIVITY

Did the changes introduced by de Valera during 1932–6 make any real difference to life in the Irish Free State?

## REVISION TIP

Some very important changes to the constitutional position of the Irish Free State took place between 1932 and 1936. You need to be able to explain to the examiner why de Valera wanted to make these changes and how the 1931 Statute of Westminster had made it possible for him to do so.

## ACTIVITIES

1 Why was de Valera so opposed to the oath of allegiance?
2 Make a copy of the following table and fill it in showing the steps de Valera took to weaken the terms of the 1921 Treaty:

| Area | Date | Action taken | Result |
|------|------|--------------|--------|
| Oath of allegiance<br>Governor General<br>Privy Council<br>Position of monarch | | | |

3 How did de Valera ensure that it would be difficult for the British government to oppose the actions that he took?

# THE ECONOMIC WAR

## Land Annuities

Land reform was one of the biggest issues in Irish history in the nineteenth century. The 1870 Land Act had tried to resolve it by giving tenants the chance to buy the land they were farming from the landowners. To make this happen, the British government had loaned tenants the funds. Each year the farmers had paid back part of these loans, in payments known as land annuities, worth an estimated £5m per year to the British government. Between 1922 and 1932 the Irish government collected the money and sent it to London.

Irish farmers, believing that they owned the land, disliked paying annuities and so de Valera stopped them. He argued that:

- The Irish economy was suffering from the consequences of a global economic depression and could not spare the money.
- The British government had abolished land annuities for Northern Ireland's farmers. It was only fair that the same concession should be extended to farmers in the Free State.

## The War Begins

Britain, angry that de Valera's government refused to pay monies that the previous government had paid, responded to Dublin's actions by imposing duties of 20 per cent on Free State imports. The Irish government reacted in two ways:

1 In January 1933 de Valera called the snap general election, as mentioned above (page 63), which gave him enough seats to rule without the Labour Party. Thus there would be no other party threatening to leave the government during the crisis, strengthening de Valera's position.
2 The Dublin government imposed similar duties on imports all over the UK, including Northern Ireland. Maybe de Valera hoped that making British goods more expensive would encourage Irish people to set up their own business and produce similar goods more cheaply. If there were any complaints about the harshness of the economic situation, de Valera could simply blame the British for starting it (Source A).

## SOURCE A

*De Valera commenting on the importance of the Economic War, November 1932.*

If the British government should succeed in beating us in this fight then we could have no freedom, but at every step they could threaten you … and force you again to obey the British. What is involved is whether the Irish nation is going to be free or not.

This standoff (known as the Economic War) continued for six years, although in 1935 both sides seemed to want to improve relations by agreeing a Coal–Cattle Pact that made trade in these two essential commodities much easier.

Given that 90 per cent of Irish exports went to Britain, the Economic War had a significant impact.

## SOURCE B

*Historian M.E. Collins writing about the Economic War in Ireland, 1868–1966.*

The attempt to get self-sufficiency had failed. Agricultural exports to Britain were still the mainstay of the economy.

## The Irish economy

While the Dublin government benefited from keeping the £5m worth of annuities, Irish farmers probably suffered most with a 35 per cent reduction in cattle exports (from 1929 levels), resulting in massive overproduction of beef and many Irish farmers going bankrupt. Much of this reduction came from a decrease in trade with Britain, the Free State's biggest export market; however it partly also resulted from the loss of cross-border trade with Northern Ireland. Alternative markets were unavailable due to the impact of the ongoing world economic depression. Subsistence farmers in Éire probably suffered less as they benefited from the reduction in their annuities.

The Dublin government attempted to encourage farmers to explore new markets by offering subsidies to increase production of crops such as sugar beet and wheat. However, this was unsuccessful as these crops were grown instead of other more traditional crops such as barley, and only the bigger farmers switched. Small-scale farmers kept on growing traditional crops and so did not benefit from the subsidies. As a result, living standards fell even though taxes were raised to compensate farmers. At the same time, small-scale farmers did benefit from the reduction of the land annuities, now made to the Dublin government.

While the industrial sector was not quite as badly hit as agriculture, it was not a massive success either. De Valera hoped that increasing the price of British goods in the Irish Free State would stop people buying those products and encourage new Irish industry. Despite the appointment of Sean Lemass as Minister for Industry and Commerce, this did not happen, mainly from a lack of investment. To make matters worse, the new Irish industries could not sell their products abroad, as they were not prepared for the export marked. The economy experienced a **trade deficit** as well as cutbacks in electricity generation and rail transport. The lack of coal imports from the UK did result in coal shortages, which particularly impacted upon the poor, but also saw the local peat industry grow (Source B, page 64). Additionally, cement factories were established in Drogheda and Limerick, while the Dublin government spent £1 million on improving bridges and rural cottages.

'On the other hand, it's quite possible his story of taking a wrong turning could be perfectly true'. A cartoon published during the Anglo-Irish Economic War comments humorously on the increase in cross-border smuggling.

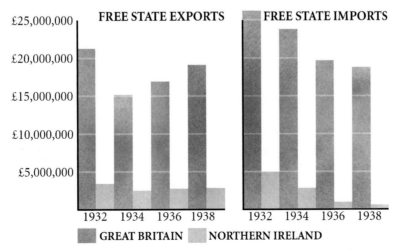

**Figure 2.1** Trade between the Irish Free State, Britain and Northern Ireland, 1932–8.

## The British and Northern Irish Economies

The Economic War led to a deterioration in Dublin's relations with both London and Belfast (Source C). Economically it had a much greater impact on the Northern Irish economy than the more diverse British economy. However, some evidence suggests that unemployment in Britain did increase somewhat because of the Economic War, not least in the ports that had handled Free State trade. Welsh coalmine owners were also scared of losing the Irish market to other coal importers. That said, while Britain had many other markets, much of Northern Ireland's economic prosperity was due to strong cross-border trade with the Free State. This prosperity was hit by the import duties de Valera imposed. All such trade stopped during the Economic War, although smuggling increased. On the other hand, Northern Ireland's farmers were helped by being able to provide Britain with produce no longer supplied by the Irish Free State due to the impact of import duties.

### SOURCE C

*Historian D. Kennedy describes Northern Ireland's reaction to the Economic War.*

De Valera's confrontation policy ... was seen in the north as a strategy to destroy the treaty settlement and reopen the question of unity.

### ACTIVITIES

1 What were the land annuities?
2 Why did de Valera decide to stop paying this money to the British government?
3 What economic steps were taken by each side to begin the Economic War?
4 In what ways did de Valera hope the Economic War would benefit the Free State's economy? Was he correct?
5 Explain the impact of the Economic War under the following headings:
   • The Irish economy.
   • The British economy.
   • The Northern Irish economy.

### EXTENSION ACTIVITY

Did de Valera make a mistake in starting the Economic War?

### REVISION TIP

Examiners will expect you to be able to explain the reasons why the Economic War started and the impact that it had on the economies of both islands.

## THE 1937 CONSTITUTION

### Bunreacht na hÉireann

In 1937 de Valera made an important break with the Irish Free State by introducing a new constitution, *Bunreacht na hÉireann* (Source A). It included three significant changes from the Irish Free State's Constitution of 1922:

1 The Irish Free State would henceforth be known as Éire.
2 The title of the head of government would be *Taoiseach*.
3 The head of state, whose duties would be mainly ceremonial, would have the title of President. The position would be decided by an election, held every seven years. In 1938 Douglas Hyde, a well-known Gaelic scholar, was elected as the first President of Éire.

### SOURCE A

*Extracts from* Bunreacht na hÉireann *(the Irish constitution), 1937.*

| | |
|---|---|
| Article II | The national territory consists of the whole island of Ireland, its islands and territorial seas. |
| Article III | While maintaining the right to rule all 32 counties in Ireland, the laws passed by the Dublin Parliament will apply only to the 26 counties until Ireland is reunified. |
| Article XLIV | The state recognises the special position of the Holy Catholic Apostolic and Roman Church as the guardian of the faith professed by the great majority of the citizens. |

The Constitution recognised Irish as the official language of the state. It also said that the Catholic Church would have a 'special position … as the guardian of the faith professed by the great majority of the citizens' although 'freedom of conscience and the free profession and practice of religion' was granted to other faiths. Article II claimed that Dublin had the right to rule over the whole island. However, Article III added that until the end of partition Éire's laws would only apply to the 26 counties that were currently controlled by the Dublin government.

Nowhere in the new constitution could any reference to the King be found. Éire had become a republic in all but name, yet despite this, de Valera did not declare Éire a republic and the country still remained part of the Commonwealth. Speaking in the Dáil on the passage of the new constitution, de Valera suggested that breaking the link completely would make partition even harder to end.

## Reactions

Unsure whether Éire remained in the Commonwealth or not, London decided that the changes introduced by the new constitution were relatively unimportant and did not change their existing relationship with Dublin (Source B on page 68). Unionists were not so calm. *Bunreacht na hÉireann* reinforced their fears and suspicions of their neighbours and strengthened their determination to remain within the UK.

The Unionist government – located at Stormont since 1932 – strongly criticised *Bunreacht na hÉireann* (Source C on page 68). In particular, it condemned Éire's territorial claim over Northern Ireland (contained in Article II) and denounced the new constitution's particular mention of the position of the Catholic Church and the Irish language. Lord Craigavon used the opportunity to call a snap general election in 1938, resulting in an increased Unionist majority at Stormont.

Éire's first President, Douglas Hyde (1860–1949), on the way to his inauguration in 1938.

## SOURCE B

*London's response to* Bunreacht na hÉireann.

His Majesty's government ... [is] prepared to treat the new constitution as not effecting a great change in the position of the Irish Free State.

## SOURCE C

*Stormont's attitude towards the new Irish constitution.*

The effect of ... this new constitution ... will be to strengthen ... the determination of Ulster to resist attacks from there [Éire] and make the links between Britain and ourselves stronger.

Some historians believe that northern Nationalists also had a lot to be dissatisfied with following the introduction of *Bunreacht na hÉireann*. In many ways, despite the inclusion of Articles II and III, it could be argued that by removing almost all links with Britain and the Commonwealth, *Bunreacht na hÉireann* had actually strengthened partition and so had made eventual reunification even more unlikely. The realisation of this fact made Northern Nationalists feel even more cut off.

## ACTIVITIES

1 Why was *Bunreacht na hÉireann* introduced?
2 List the key points of the 1937 constitution.
3 What impact did *Bunreacht na hÉireann* have on the Free State's relationship with Britain?
4 Why did de Valera not declare that the Free State was now a republic?
5 Identify and explain the different reactions to the new constitution.

## EXTENSION ACTIVITY

Do you agree that the 1937 constitution made the reunification of Ireland even less likely than before?

## REVISION TIP

The 1937 constitution makes an important stage in the development of Ireland as a republic. Examiners will want you to be able to explain the reasons why de Valera made the changes that he did.

## BRITAIN AND THE THREAT OF WAR

### Tensions in Europe

By the mid-1930s, the risk of war in Europe seemed to be growing. Leaders such as Hitler in Germany and Mussolini in Italy seemed determined to increase their countries' influence, even to the extent of taking over other nations. Mussolini had already begun a war in Abyssinia in 1935, while Hitler had begun to undo the military restrictions placed on Germany by the Treaty of Versailles. On top of this, Stalin's programme of economic development in the USSR led some to fear that the Soviet Union might also try to spread the influence of **communism**.

As the risk of war grew, the British government had to choose between the following alternative policy options: neutrality, rearmament or **appeasement**.

Neville Chamberlain (1869–1940), Britain's Prime Minister from 1937 to 1940.

## Neutrality

A neutral Britain would not get involved in any war. While there were many who supported such a policy for reasons such as fear of the devastation of another war, belief in the League of Nations and concerns about the cost of rearmament, Britain also had to consider that the security of its empire might not be well served by such a policy.

## Rearmament

While rearmament would be costly and unpopular at a time of economic crisis, a 1935 report on Britain's military readiness made depressing reading. It revealed that Britain's army, navy and air force were all very far from being able to defend Britain and the empire. Faced with Germany's military expansion Britain was forced to increase defence spending.

## Appeasement

Appeasement was the policy whereby Britain (and France) made concessions to their opponents to buy them off. Britain adopted appeasement as its main policy for the following reasons:

- Britain's economy was still recovering from the impact of the First World War and the Great Depression and was not in a position to bear the expenditure that rapid rearmament would demand.
- People still remembered the brutality of the 1914–18 war and were keen that the government did not commit itself to another conflict.
- Many leaders – particularly British Prime Minister Neville Chamberlain – viewed Hitler as a realistic man with sensible demands who could be dealt with by reasonable policies (Source A).

## Impact

Apart from avoiding an immediate conflict, appeasement allowed Britain to begin to rebuild its military albeit at a slower rate. Improvements were made to the size of the Royal Navy and the Royal Air Force (RAF). The RAF also benefited from reorganisation, the development of modern fighter and bomber aircraft and a chain of radar stations along the south coast of England, which allowed detection of enemy aircraft from 30 miles away. The government also ordered the building of anti-aircraft weapons, searchlights and barrage balloons while large orders were placed for air raid shelters. Britain also passed the Air Raid Precaution Act, created Air Raid Protection wardens, provided gas masks, and made evacuation plans from London and other cities to prepare its population for war.

Hitler, however, used appeasement to his advantage. While there was no great public opposition to the 1936 German remilitarisation of the Rhineland, the 1938 *Anschluss* with Austria and particularly Hitler's treatment of Czechoslovakia in 1938 and 1939 led to appeasement being discredited. (See pages 51–4.)

At that late stage Britain and France realised that appeasement would have to be abandoned and, in April 1939, they offered military guarantees to Poland to try to prevent an expected German attack. It was too little too late. Confident that the August 1939 Nazi–Soviet Pact neutralised the USSR as an opponent, Hitler ignored the Anglo-French guarantees and invaded Poland in September 1939. When Britain's ultimatum to withdraw was ignored, war was declared on 3 September 1939 (Source B on page 70).

### SOURCE A

*Report of Chamberlain's address to the British cabinet, 8 December 1937 (adapted).*

The Chiefs of Staff ... said they could not foresee the time when our defence forces would be strong enough to safeguard Britain's territory, trade and vital interests against Germany, Italy and Japan at the same time. They had urged that Britain's foreign policy must be governed by this consideration. Chamberlain argued that Germany was the real key to the question. In the light of the recent consideration given by the cabinet to the question of improving relations with Germany, it was necessary to develop that theme further.

## ACTIVITIES

1 Explain briefly why there was increasing unrest in Europe in the mid-1930s.
2 Make a copy of the following table and fill it in:

| Option | Arguments for | Arguments against |
|---|---|---|
| Neutrality Rearmament Appeasement | | |

3 Why did Britain finally give up the policy of appeasement?

## THE ANGLO-IRISH AGREEMENTS

The British Prime Minister Neville Chamberlain decided that relations between London and Dublin would have to improve. This would mean:

- ending the Economic War
- resolving the issue of the treaty ports.

He recognised the strategic value of the ports, but also knew they were out of date as they had not had any investment since the time of the treaty. He therefore decided that returning them would help end the Economic War and would, through de Valera's gratitude, result in Éire's assistance if war broke out (Source A).

Keen to get the ports back, de Valera believed that Britain's continued control would weaken Éire's claims to neutrality and leave it open to attack.

Representatives of the two governments began to talk in January 1938. On 25 April 1938, the British and Irish delegations signed three separate agreements on defence, finance and trade. As a result the Economic War was ended, improving

trade links, and the three treaty ports were returned to Éire. As a result, another symbolic link between the two countries was broken, the terms of the 1921 Anglo-Irish Treaty were further undermined and Éire's independence was further reinforced. Éire agreed to pay Britain £10 million to resolve the annuities question (see page 64), an estimated £78m, while all duties imposed by both countries during the Economic War were removed.

The end to the trade war between Éire and Britain did not apply to cross-border trade with Northern Ireland, which was subject to a long-running boycott. Both sides also approved a three-year trade agreement. Overall, de Valera was delighted with the outcome of the agreements (Source B) which, historians agree, were much more favourable to Éire. However, during the negotiations resulting from the signing of the Agreements, Éire refused to end partition in return for a defence agreement between Britain and Éire.

While the agreements received a favourable response from most people, the return of the treaty ports was criticised sharply by British politicians such as Winston Churchill who had described the returned ports as the 'sentinel towers of the western approaches'. He did not share Chamberlain's belief that Éire would allow Britain to use the ports during a future war. Unionists were also concerned by the agreements, fearing that the obvious improvement in Anglo-Irish relations might lead to the reunification of Ireland. Craigavon also agreed with Churchill's view that the return of the treaty ports would weaken the security of both the UK and Éire (Source C on page 72).

> ## SOURCE B
>
> *De Valera's reaction to the return of the ports, April 1938.*
>
> Handing over the treaty ports recognises and finally establishes Irish sovereignty over the 26 counties.

British forces preparing to leave the military facility at Cobh in 1938.

## SOURCE C

*Craig recalls his concern over the danger of returning the treaty ports to Éire, November 1940.*

I gave the most solemn warnings to British ministers on the dangers of such unnecessary action as surrendering these valuable bases for British use as protection not only for Great Britain and Ulster, but for southern Ireland also.

## ACTIVITIES

1 Why did Chamberlain want to improve Britain's relationship with Éire?
2 What benefits did Chamberlain see in returning the treaty ports to Éire?
3 Why would de Valera have been so pleased at the return of the treaty ports?
4 Which side gained most economically from the 1938 agreements?
5 Explain the different reactions to the agreements.

## EXTENSION ACTIVITY

Who were the winners and losers in the 1938 Anglo-Irish agreements?

## REVISION TIP

While examiners will expect you to be able to write about the economic terms of the 1938 Anglo-Irish agreements, they will be more interested in whether or not you are aware of the agreements' implications for both British and Irish foreign policy.

# DEVELOPMENTS IN NORTHERN IRELAND 1939

## Conscription

In April 1939 the British government announced the introduction of **conscription** in Great Britain. However, the fear of a negative Nationalist reaction, and the desire not to worsen relations with Dublin, meant that conscription was not extended to Northern Ireland. An irate Craigavon demanded that this decision be reversed as a demonstration of Northern Ireland's unity with Britain.

Craigavon's demand annoyed Nationalists and the North's Catholic bishops issued a statement opposing his appeal. Cardinal Joseph MacRory, the Archbishop of Armagh and the head of the Irish Catholic Church stated that resisting the introduction of conscription would be morally justified. De Valera also voiced his concerns as did a range of other groups and individuals (Source A).

In May 1939 Chamberlain met Craigavon to explain that the reason for the decision not to introduce conscription was Northern Ireland's 'special difficulties'. Craigavon was unhappy but accepted the decision (Source B, page 73).

To compensate for the refusal to extend conscription, Northern Ireland was awarded over £6 million in defence contracts. Particularly involved were the Short & Harland aircraft factory and the Harland & Wolff shipyard. While this investment resulted in a fall of over 30,000 in the number of unemployed during 1939, it also meant that Belfast could be a target for enemy bombers if war broke out.

In May 1940, a series of rallies was held across the North; however the response was not as positive as Craigavon might have hoped. The memories of the carnage of the Battle of the Somme may have contributed to this, as well as that the Minister of Agriculture, Sir Basil Brooke, was chosen to lead it. Many still remembered his 1933 speech when he had urged unionist employers to 'employ good Protestant lads and lassies'.

The aftermath of an IRA bomb in Coventry in 1939.

## SOURCE A

*Historian Brian Barton illustrates just how far news of the controversy about introducing conscription to Northern Ireland spread.*

This hostile response [to the suggested introduction of conscription] was even referred to in a speech by Hitler.

## SOURCE B

*Lady Craigavon writing about how Chamberlain persuaded Craig not to push for the extension of conscription to Northern Ireland, May 1939.*

J. [James] was asked flat out by Chamberlain, 'is Ulster out to help Britain in her war effort?' To which, of course, he answered, 'you know we are. I have offered personally all the resources at our disposal to help you, and we have passed resolutions in our Parliament to the same effect.' Chamberlain said, 'if you really want to help us, don't press for conscription, it will only be an embarrassment', What else could J. do than say, 'Very well then, I won't!'

## ACTIVITIES

1 Why did Unionists want conscription and Nationalists oppose it?
2 Why did Britain not extend conscription to Northern Ireland in 1939?
3 How successful was the Northern Ireland Government's May 1940 recruitment drive? Why was this?

## EXTENSION ACTIVITY

What did the conscription issue reveal about attitudes of the two communities in Northern Ireland to Britain?

## REVISION TIP

Examiners will expect you to be able to explain the reasons for the refusal of the British government to extend conscription to Northern Ireland in 1939.

## DECLARATION OF WAR

On 1 September 1939 German forces invaded Poland. The Second World War began two days later on 3 September 1939 when Germany refused to abide by Britain and France's ultimatum to withdraw from Poland. The onset of war resulted in different reactions in Belfast and Dublin.

### Northern Ireland

The Northern Ireland Parliament met on 4 September to discuss the declaration of war. The war provided the Stormont government with the opportunity to declare and demonstrate its loyalty to Great Britain (Source A). In this way the union with Great Britain could be strengthened. Speaking during the debate, Craigavon reassured the London government of Northern Ireland's readiness to play its part in the forthcoming war effort. Just how ready Northern Ireland was remained to be seen (Source B).

### Éire and Neutrality

The reaction to the start of the war was somewhat different south of the border. The day after Britain declared war on Germany de Valera announced Éire's neutrality (Source C). There were several reasons for the Éire government's decision to introduce this policy:

- De Valera correctly assumed that people would support neutrality to reinforce Éire's independence from Britain (Source D).
- The continued existence of partition ruled out Éire's involvement in the war.
- Éire was divided over whether or not to support the British war effort; some may even have sympathised with Germany.
- Many in Éire believed Germany posed no threat to Éire – and if there was a threat, Britain would protect Éire, as a member of the Commonwealth.
- Éire was not equipped to fight a war, economically or militarily.
- The Dublin government wanted to unite its people against invasion and protect them against the hardships of war.

By and large neutrality was a popular policy, though people remained largely sympathetic to the Allied cause. Indeed, de Valera agreed to appoint a British representative to Dublin to avoid any misunderstandings with London.

The government also introduced the Emergency Powers Act, increasing its control over the country. This gave the government extensive powers to ensure that the policy of neutrality was maintained. For example, **censorship** was introduced and strictly enforced.

### Britain's Attitude

Great Britain accepted Éire's declaration of neutrality only grudgingly. Some viewed it as potentially damaging to the war effort while fears were expressed that Germany might use Éire as a

---

### SOURCE A

*Lord Craigavon speaking in the Northern Ireland Parliament on 4 September 1939.*

[There will be] no slackening in [Ulster's] loyalty. There is no falling off in our determination to place the whole of our resources at the command of the [Westminster] government … anything we can do to facilitate them … they have only just got to let us know.

---

### SOURCE B

*Historian Jonathan Bardon comments on Northern Ireland's readiness for war.*

During the first year of the war … Craigavon proclaimed the unyielding support of the people of Northern Ireland without having the slightest idea of what that might involve.

---

### SOURCE C

*Historian F.S.L. Lyons on the meaning of Éire's neutrality (adapted).*

Neutrality … was the outward and visible sign of absolute sovereignty. To be free to choose between peace and war was the mark of independence, to be free to choose between peace and a *British* war demonstrated to all of the world just how complete that independence really was.

War is declared, September 1939.

base from which to invade Great Britain. Particular opposition came from Winston Churchill, soon to be appointed Prime Minister. Reactions in Northern Ireland were even less positive. There was strong resentment in the north at Éire's declaration of neutrality, which was viewed as an act of betrayal and a threat to the security of Britain.

## SOURCE D

*Sir John Maffey, the British government's representative in Dublin, commenting on Irish attitudes to neutrality.*

The policy of neutrality commands widespread approval among all classes and interests in Éire.

## ACTIVITIES

1 How did Belfast react to the start of the Second World War?
2 Why was Lord Craigavon so keen to offer Northern Ireland's support and assistance during the war?
3 Why did de Valera decide to declare Éire neutral at the start of the Second World War?
4 How did Britain react to these two different responses?

## EXTENSION ACTIVITY

'The declaration of war was good news for de Valera.' Discuss.

## REVISION TIP

It is essential that you can identify and explain the reasons for the different reactions to war in Northern Ireland and Éire.

## Practice Question (Foundation)

### Foundation

Answer all questions

1  (a)  Below is a list of questions on relations between Britain, Northern Ireland and Ireland during the years 1932–1949. Write your answer to **each** question.

(i)  The Minister of Agriculture who became Prime Minister of Northern Ireland in 1943?  [1]

(ii)  The law passed by de Valera which ended the King's role within the Irish Free State?  [1]

(iii)  Payments collected by Dublin from Irish farmers for loans given?  [1]

(iv)  The name of the Irish Prime Minister after 1937?  [1]

(v)  The first President of Éire?  [1]

(vi)  The name of one of the Treaty Ports?  [1]

(b)  This question is about relations between the Free State and Britain in the years 1932 to 1937.

Study Sources A (the cartoon on page 62) and B (Source B on page 63) and answer the questions which follow.

(i)  Study Source A.

Using Source A, give two ways de Valera wanted to change the relationship between the Free State and Britain.  [4]

(ii)  Study Sources A and B.

Using Sources A and B, and your own knowledge, describe how de Valera tried to destroy the Anglo-Irish Treaty in the years 1932–1937.  [10]

(c)  This question is about the Economic War.

In what ways did the Economic War change life in Britain and Éire?  [12]

(d)  In this question up to 5 additional marks are available for your use of spelling, punctuation and grammar.

This question is about Northern Ireland during the Second World War.

Explain the important role played by Northern Ireland in helping Britain during the Second World War.

Use the following three paragraph headings to help you with your answer:

Military Support
Economic Support
Strategic Support  [18] and [SPaG 5]

# THE EFFECTS OF THE SECOND WORLD WAR ON NORTHERN IRELAND

## READY FOR WAR?

### Complacency?

Northern Ireland was not ready for war when it started on 3 September 1939. While the Stormont government was quick to promise its support to London, there is less evidence that it had really thought through what being at war might mean for the people of Northern Ireland. For example, the administration continued to believe that the province was beyond the range of enemy aircraft and so appropriate defence measures (both aerial and ground based) were not put in place (Source A).

### SOURCE A

*The view of Edmond Warnock (Parliamentary Secretary at the Ministry of Home Affairs), on the possibility of a Luftwaffe attack on Belfast, June 1939.*

An attack on Northern Ireland would involve a flight of over 1000 miles. For aeroplanes of the bombing type, loaded, this is a very big undertaking … the enemy aeroplanes must twice pass through the active gun, searchlight and aeroplane defences of Great Britain … it is possible that we might escape attack.

An anti-aircraft battery outside Belfast.

Even with the war underway the government still remained slow to act. It was not until well into 1941 that the majority of Northern Ireland was covered by radar and steps had been taken to establish a number of anti-aircraft batteries. Even then some feared that enemy planes could still approach Northern Ireland without being picked up while others suggested that far too few anti-aircraft defences (including anti-aircraft guns, night-fighters and searchlights) were in place.

### RAF Reorganisation

By June 1940 German forces had defeated France and reached the Channel and the possibility of air attacks increased. This led to a significant reorganisation of the RAF within Northern Ireland which included:

- An increase in the number of RAF squadrons within Northern Ireland.
- The provision of up-to-date Hurricane fighter aircraft.
- The construction of airfields in location such as Aldergrove and Ballykelly.

While these developments did improve the RAF's ability to protect Northern Ireland from *Luftwaffe* attack, it is probably fair to say that on the whole the RAF remained too poorly resourced to be able to defend Northern Ireland as completely as it would have wanted.

### Prepared for Enemy Attack?

Nor did Northern Ireland compare well to the wide-ranging evacuation and air raid protection schemes that had been implemented across Britain prior to the outbreak of war.

- The Stormont government introduced an Air Raid Precautions Act in 1938; however, unlike the rest of the UK it did not make local council provision of civil defence measures compulsory. As a result Northern Ireland's population was not as well prepared for enemy attacks.
- Public responses to the dangers of air attack were almost as inept as those of the government. **ARP** (Air Raid Protection) wardens, who had the job of enforcing blackouts, were not taken seriously as they went about their duties and blackouts were routinely ignored. By early 1941, recorded

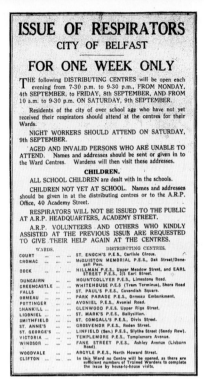

ISSUE OF RESPIRATORS
CITY OF BELFAST

FOR ONE WEEK ONLY

An official evacuation notice from 1940.

blackout offences in Belfast alone had reached nearly 1,000 per month. That said, the blackout of the headlights of cars, buses and bicycles was adhered to by the public, even though it made travel at nighttime very difficult!

- When people were offered the chance to be evacuated from Belfast in case of air raids, few availed of the opportunity.
- When Belfast was bombed in 1941 (see page 84), there were insufficient recruits for the various civil defence services.
- In spite of constant government advice and warnings, the majority of people did not carry gas masks (issued at the start of the war) until after the Belfast blitz (see pages 84–5).
- It was not until July 1940 that a local evacuation plan was launched and even this only resulted in 7000 out of a possible 70,000 children being evacuated from Belfast.
- Nearly a year after the declaration of war only 15 per cent of the Belfast households entitled to an **Anderson air raid shelter** had taken delivery of one.

## MacDermott's Reforms

Thereafter things began to improve a little. In June 1940 John MacDermott was appointed to the new post of Minister of Public Security. MacDermott organised:

- the rapid erection of public air-raid shelters
- the reinforcement of the emergency services
- efforts to evacuate children from Belfast.

At the same time, blackout curtains were used to stop lights alerting *Luftwaffe* pilots of the locations of towns and cities across Northern Ireland.

However, it was too little too late and when, in April and May 1941, the *Luftwaffe* bombed Belfast, the city still only had 22 anti-aircraft guns, insufficient air cover from fighter aircraft and public shelters capable of housing no more than a quarter of the city's population (Source B).

John MacDermott (1896–1979) was appointed Northern Ireland's Minister of Public Security in June 1940.

### SOURCE B

*Historian Jonathan Bardon commenting on MacDermott's work.*

Again and again his efforts were frustrated by public apathy and lack of support from his colleagues.

### ACTIVITIES

1 Why had the Stormont government not prepared Northern Ireland effectively for war?
2 How well were Northern Ireland's people prepared for enemy attack?
3 Explain the steps taken to prepare Northern Ireland for war under the following headings:
   - Air defence.
   - Precaution against air raids.

**EXTENSION ACTIVITY**

What does the state of Northern Ireland's readiness for war tell us about the quality of the Stormont government?

**REVISION TIP**

Northern Ireland's preparations for war compared very poorly with those taken across the Irish Sea. Examiners will expect you to be able to explain these differences and the reasons for them. They will also expect you to be able to identify the improvements introduced by John MacDermott.

# THE BATTLE OF BRITAIN

## Preparing for War

By the end of June 1940 all of Western Europe had been conquered by Hitler's armies; Britain now stood alone against Germany. However, its army was low in numbers and did not have the equipment needed. To deal with this:

- Factories worked multiple shifts to produce aircraft, tanks and heavy weapons and a government campaign began for scrap metal from Britain's households.
- Over 500,000 rifles were ordered from the USA.
- The Local Defence Volunteers (later renamed the Home Guard) was established in May 1940. In just over a year it had over a million members.

Although the Royal Navy had begun a blockade of the North Sea and was patrolling the Channel to defend against German warships and U-boats, the RAF was in a stronger position than other branches of the military due to its ongoing improvements since 1935. The provision of radar, as well as providing early warning of the approach of enemy aircraft, also enabled RAF fighters to be directed accurately to intercept enemy planes. The RAF was reorganised into three sections:

- Fighter Command
- Bomber Command
- Coastal Command.

Britain's preparations for war also included the development of a civil defence plan. This comprised:

- Mass evacuation plans for women and children.
- The distribution of gas masks.
- The provision of 400,000 Anderson air raid shelters.
- The establishment of the ARP force. Its job was to enforce strict blackout rules, particularly in urban areas.

## Battle for the Skies

In July 1940, Great Britain – now led by Winston Churchill – rejected Hitler's attempts to negotiate a peaceful conclusion to the war. The German leader responded by ordering the implementation of Operation Sealion, the invasion of Britain. Before this could take place, however, the RAF would have to be destroyed. This was because its control of the skies over the English Channel would prevent a successful sea invasion from France (Source A, page 80).

Winston Churchill (1874–1965), Britain's wartime Prime Minister from 1940 to 1945.

**SOURCE A**

*Churchill's speech to the House of Commons, 18 June 1940.*

The battle of France is over. I expect that the Battle of Britain is about to begin … Hitler knows that he will have to break us in this island or lose the war … Let us therefore brace ourselves to our duty and so bear ourselves that if the British Commonwealth and Empire lasts for a thousand years, men will still say, 'This was their finest hour.'

On 12 August 1940 the *Luftwaffe* launched Operation Eagle, its attack on the RAF. Although initial *Luftwaffe* losses were greater (225 aircraft losses against the RAF's 117), it had significantly more aircraft and so it is likely that if these attacks had continued the RAF would eventually have been worn down. However on 7 September the *Luftwaffe* switched tactics; instead of attacking RAF bases it started to bomb London. This was in response to recent RAF raids on Berlin. The bombing raids continued for months and were quickly extended to include other British cities (such as Coventry, Liverpool and Glasgow).

While the nightly blitz caused massive devastation to cities and Britain's civilian population, the change of tactics allowed the RAF to reorganise and obtain newly manufactured aircraft. This meant that the RAF continued to control the skies over Britain and for this reason Operation Sealion was finally called off in October 1940 (Source B).

**SOURCE B**

*Historian Jack Watson explains the reasons for the RAF's victory in the Battle of Britain.*

The pre-war development of the RAF proved to have been just adequate. Under the command of Air Chief Marshal Dowding, with Beaverbrook in charge of aircraft production, with the valuable help of radar and, above all, with the heroism of the 'few' fighter pilots who flew the Hurricanes and Spitfires, the RAF defied the might of Göring's *Luftwaffe*.

**ACTIVITIES**

1. Why was Britain in such a vulnerable position after June 1940?
2. What steps were taken to prepare Britain for war?
3. Why did Germany need to gain control of the skies over Britain and the Channel?
4. Explain the different stages of the Battle of Britain.
5. Why was the RAF's victory in the Battle of Britain so important?

**EXTENSION ACTIVITY**

'Britain did not win the Battle of Britain – Germany lost it.' Discuss.

**REVISION TIP**

Examiners will expect you to be able to write about the important part that the RAF played during the Battle of Britain. They will also want you to be able to explain why Germany lost this battle when it had such superiority in numbers.

## NORTHERN IRELAND'S WAR EFFORT (I): STRATEGIC

### Conscription Again

In the aftermath of the Belfast blitz, the British Labour Minister, Ernest Bevin, again raised the possibility of conscription being introduced in Northern Ireland. Again most Nationalists opposed the move, seeing this as Britain's war, not theirs. Aside from de Valera condemning the proposal, thousands of Nationalists took to the streets of Belfast in protest, supported by local Catholic bishops and Nationalist politicians.

The strength of Nationalist opposition meant that the Unionist leadership, after initially welcoming the prospect of conscription, now decided that introducing it would create more problems than it would solve. Moreover, the Royal Ulster Constabulary (RUC) Inspector-General informed the government of his fear that any attempt to introduce conscription could lead to serious public disorder. Once more London announced that conscription would not be extended to Northern Ireland.

## Military Service

Many Irish people still fought in the war though.

- It is estimated that close to 40,000 people from Northern Ireland joined one of the services. Just over 10 per cent of this number died. It is probable that more of Northern Ireland's Unionist population would have joined up were it not for the fact that they were employed in **reserved occupations**. Many of those who joined up served with considerable distinction. One such individual was James Magennis, a Royal Navy sailor who was awarded the **Victoria Cross** for the part he played in sinking a Japanese cruiser off the coast of Borneo.
- In excess of 43,000 Irish citizens fought for the Allies. Their reasons ranged from support of the Allied cause to desperation to escape from poverty. However, the recent history of poor Anglo-Irish relations meant that their contribution was not recognised at home.

## The Home Guard

Northern Ireland's experience of the Home Guard differed noticeably from Britain's. Craigavon's fear of Republican infiltration if the force was created through open enrolment meant that the B Specials

Members of the Northern Ireland Home Guard on parade.

**SOURCE A**

*Historian Brian Barton comments on the sectarian nature of the Home Guard in Northern Ireland (adapted).*

There was obvious justification in the view that the government had succeeded in transforming the Home Guard into a sectarian body. MacDermott (Minister of Public Security) recalled that a few Catholics did enlist but that 'virtually all left because they hated the B Specials'.

formed the core of the Northern Ireland Home Guard. Unlike Britain, the RUC rather than the army controlled them.

As a result Catholic membership was limited and the Home Guard was seen as little more than a sectarian force (Source A above). Although some of the British government expressed unease at this, in the end nothing was done to change the situation.

Much of the focus of the Home Guard was on counteracting the IRA threat. Pro-German sentiments were evident in some Republican circles and in September 1939 the government had responded to the declaration of war by introducing **internment** to deal with IRA activists. After several additional moves against Republican suspects – including the arrest of IRA Chief of Staff Hugh McAteer in 1942 – IRA activity dropped off.

## Strategic Significance

Northern Ireland's geographical location ensured that it played a key role in the war, particularly after the return of the treaty ports to Éire (1938) and Eire's declaration of neutrality in September 1939. Once France fell to the Germans in 1940 Allied shipping went north of Ireland and thus Northern Ireland's strategic significance increased.

- Naval bases, such as Lisahally outside Derry/ Londonderry, provided vital support and services for those vessels involved in the **Battle of the Atlantic** and acted as bases for ships and submarines keeping sea lanes open (Source B, page 82). The port at Londonderry/ Derry was the biggest base in Britain for warships protecting merchant ships, and 43 German U-boats surrendered here at the end of the war.

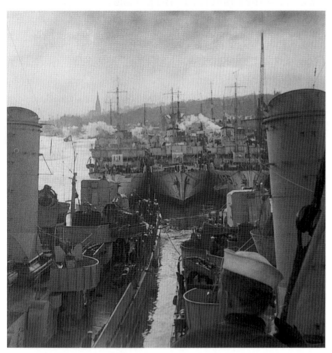

Allied shipping moored in Derry/Londonderry during the Battle of the Atlantic.

- Derry/Londonderry itself became an important base for service personnel, including large numbers from the USA and other Allied countries. By mid-1943 there were nearly 150 ships based at the port while by the end of the same year there were an estimated 40,000 military personnel in and around the city.
- Natural inlets such as Lough Foyle provided refuge from U-boat attack for **merchant shipping** on their trans-Atlantic journeys.
- Air bases at locations such as Aldergrove, Ballykelly, Eglinton, Limavady, Nutts Corner, Long Kesh and Castle Archdale (for Coastal Command) provided much needed cover for **convoys**. Aircraft from Castle Archdale sank 18 U-boats in 1943.

- A variety of US forces used Northern Ireland between 1942 and 1944. Apart from training troops, bases to service aircraft and shipping were established. Most notable among these service bases was Langford Lodge on the shores of Lough Neagh. Magee College in Derry/Londonderry served as the main communication base for US forces across Europe.
- Northern Ireland was also used as a base for preparations for operations in north Africa and southern Italy and for **D-Day**. By 1943 there were close to 300,000 military personnel stationed in various locations throughout the province. One unforeseen consequence of such huge numbers was that there where was sometimes friction with the local male population, unhappy at the 'challenge' of those in uniform!

## ACTIVITIES

1 Why did the issue of conscription re-emerge in 1941?
2 Why did the British government decide not to introduce conscription in 1941?
3 What part did Irish people play in the fighting of the war?
4 Why did the Northern Irish Home Guard become an issue of controversy?
5 Create a spider diagram showing the different ways in which Northern Ireland contributed to the war effort strategically.
6 How significant was Northern Ireland's strategic role in the Second World War?

## EXTENSION ACTIVITY

'Northern Ireland played a crucial part in the Allies' victory in the Second World War.' Discuss.

## REVISION TIP

While there may not have been conscription in Northern Ireland during the Second World War, there is no doubt that the region played an important part in the Allies' eventual victory. Make sure that you can identify and explain all of the reasons why this was the case.

# NORTHERN IRELAND'S WAR EFFORT (II): ECONOMIC

## Agriculture

The best-performing section of the Northern Ireland wartime economy was agriculture.

- With increasing demand from Britain for food, the amount of land used for growing crops increased by 60 per cent as farmers switched from livestock to arable farming.
- Particularly significant were the increases in the production of flax, wheat and potatoes.
- The number of allotments increased fourfold in the war years. Careful planning by the government ensured that sufficient artificial fertilizers were made available to support this increase which became known as the 'Dig for victory'.
- The numbers of cattle and poultry increased significantly. Northern Ireland's chickens were responsible for providing Britain with 20 per cent of its egg consumption.
- Along with eggs Britain received sheep, cattle and dairy produce from Northern Ireland (£3 million-worth per year); Scotland received 100,000 litres of Northern Ireland milk each day.

As a result of this Ulster's farmers grew wealthy. There were two main reasons for this impressive performance:

- the continued availability of fertilisers
- the more than 100-fold increase in tractor numbers.

Much of the credit for the agricultural sector's success belongs to the Minister for Agriculture, Basil Brooke. He took to the countryside to persuade Northern Ireland's farmers to increase production. His success contributed to his appointment as Prime Minister in 1943.

## Rationing

The war resulted in the introduction of rationing to discourage waste and encourage self-reliance. Although shortages did not bite as quickly as they did in Britain, by 1941 goods such as fresh meat and dairy produce became much more difficult to source, particularly in towns. Fuel shortages had a massive impact on the use of cars and as a result the use of public transport increased. For some, particularly those close to the border, smuggling eased the shortages; for others the solution was to buy goods on the black market.

## Industry

The fortunes of Northern Ireland's industrial economy were not quite as impressive as those of the agricultural sector. For the first two years of the war output was hit by:

- Bad management.
- A lack of planning. A year and a half into the war, no new factories had been built.
- A shortage of skilled workers coupled with questionable working practices.
- A series of strikes (even though strikes were supposed to be illegal).

| Year | Number of unemployed people |
|------|------------------------------|
| 1941 | 70,000 |
| 1942 | 50,000 |
| 1943 | 19,000 |
| 1944 | 10,000 |

Table 2.1 Unemployment levels 1941–4

Although things began to improve in late 1941, it was 1943 before any real improvement could be seen in Northern Ireland's industrial output. By the time the war ended much of the industrial unrest had disappeared. After initially increasing,

Aircraft being manufactured at Short & Harland.

unemployment had dropped from a high of 70,000 (late 1941) to just 10,000, production figures had begun an upward climb and wages and the standard of living had improved. A variety of Northern Ireland firms produced a significant number of tanks, ships, aircraft and munitions. This is best illustrated by examining the performance of two of Northern Ireland's largest companies during the war years:

- Harland & Wolff:
  - 140 warships (incl. 3 destroyers and 6 carriers)
  - 123 merchant ships (10% of Britain's total wartime production)
  - 3000 ships repaired or converted to other uses
  - 500 tanks
  - over 13 million aircraft components.
- Short & Harland:
  - 1500 Stirling bombers
  - 125 Sunderland flying boats
  - 150 Hereford bombers
  - over 3000 aircraft repairs.

Between 1939 and 1945 other local companies (especially James Mackie and Sons) produced other wartime essentials including weapons and ammunition, nets and ropes as well as uniforms and parachutes. In total, local factories produced close to 75 million shells, 180 million bullets 50,000 bayonets, 50,000 camouflage/cargo nets, 30,000 shirts, 200,000 yards of cloth (for uniforms), two million flax cloth parachutes and 250,000 tons of rope (one third of the total used by the British army). While these figures are impressive, historical research would suggest that Northern Ireland's economic performance might still have been better (Sources A and B on this page).

## ACTIVITIES

1 How did Northern Ireland's agricultural sector perform during the Second World War?
2 What impact did rationing have on Northern Ireland?
3 How did Northern Ireland's industrial sector perform during the Second World War?
4 Create a spider diagram showing the different ways in which Northern Ireland contributed to the war effort economically.
5 How significant was Northern Ireland's economic role in the Second World War?

## EXTENSION ACTIVITY

'Northern Ireland's economy did not contribute as much to the war effort as it could have done.' Discuss.

## REVISION TIP

There were both positive and negative aspects of Northern Ireland's contribution to the war effort. Make sure that you know what they were and the reasons for them.

## SOURCE A

*Historian Brian Barton comments on the performance of Northern Ireland's wartime economy.*

Despite Northern Ireland's impressive wartime output, production levels were consistently lower in the region than in any other part of the UK.

## SOURCE B

*Historian M.E. Collins reflects on the less impressive aspects of Northern Ireland's economic performance during the war.*

The Northern economy boomed during the war [but] wartime expansion was marred by bad management, poor productivity rates and bad work practices. Industrial unrest flared up from time to time with several strikes, in spite of the fact that they were illegal.

## THE BELFAST BLITZ

### Targeting Belfast

In 1941 Belfast was targeted by over 150 *Luftwaffe* bombers. This was because:

- Germany was aware of the key role that a number of the city's industries were playing in the war effort.
- Northern Ireland was playing an important strategic role in the war.

The *Luftwaffe* visited Belfast four times in 1941 (7–8 April, 15–16 April, 4–5 May and 5–6 May) (Source A, page 85). As a result:

Luftwaffe map from 1940 showing key targets in Belfast.

## SOURCE A

*Historian Jonathan Bardon writing about the first air raid of 7–8 April 1941.*

After returning to their bases in northern France, *Luftwaffe* bomber crews reported that Belfast's defences were 'inferior in quality, scanty and insufficient'. Sirens had sounded only after the first bombs had fallen.

- The city's most densely populated areas were targeted. As a consequence 955 civilians were killed and 2436 were injured.
- Almost 57,000 homes were damaged or destroyed, leaving in excess of 100,000 people temporarily homeless and 15,000 permanently affected.
- In the short term many thousands fled Belfast to the rest of Northern Ireland and even to Éire, enduring harsh conditions in the process.
- Belfast's industrial infrastructure, the bombers' main target, suffered extensive damage. As a result it took six months for industrial production to recover.

## SOURCE B

*Ernst von Kuhren, a German journalist reporting his impressions of the blitz of 4–5 May 1941 (adapted).*

I can really say that I could not believe my eyes. When we approached the target … we stared silently into a sea of flames such as none of us had seen before … In Belfast there was not a large number of fires, but just one enormous fire which spread over the entire harbour and industrial area.

All told, Belfast suffered more, relatively speaking, from *Luftwaffe* attacks than other British cities had, at least up to that point (Source B). The 745 deaths that resulted from the raid of 15–16 April was greater than the number of deaths resulting from a single raid elsewhere in the UK. Many of the reasons for this have already been highlighted and include:

- the Stormont government's failure to prepare properly for possible air raids
- the poor level of anti-aircraft defences in and around Belfast.

Other parts of Northern Ireland also suffered, although not on the same scale. Derry/Londonderry was also raided in April 1941 and although it is probable that the intended target was military, the bombs fell on civilian housing killing 15 people. Also attacked were Bangor (where five civilians lost their lives) and Newtownards Airport (where 10 guards died).

### Leadership Changes

The blitz highlighted the dreadful conditions that many of Belfast's citizens were living in as well as the poor effort that the Stormont government was making of the Northern Ireland war effort. On his death in 1940, Craigavon had been replaced as Prime Minister by his Finance Minister, J.M. Andrews. Unfortunately Andrews was not up to the demands of the job, yet he obstinately refused to make up for his own shortcomings by promoting younger, more able ministers.

Despite its loyalty to the Unionist Party, Northern Ireland's voting public was not beyond letting it know that they were not happy. In 1942 two safe seats were lost in by-elections. By 1943 the situation had deteriorated further with more and more complaints from within the government about the quality of leadership on offer. Faced with the threatened resignation of his two most able ministers, Basil Brooke and John MacDermott (along with up to four others), Andrews finally resigned in April 1943 (Source C). The new Prime Minister was Basil Brooke.

## SOURCE C

*Brian Barton explains why Andrews had to resign.*

The Andrews government collapsed under the accumulated weight of its own incompetence. It had proved incapable of responding adequately to the demands of war.

## ACTIVITIES

1 Why did German bombers see Northern Ireland as a target?
2 What impact did the 1941 air raids have on Belfast?
3 What evidence can you find of divisions within the Ulster Unionist Party at this time?

## EXTENSION ACTIVITY

'The impact of the Belfast Blitz was made worse by the performance of the Stormont government.' Discuss.

## REVISION TIP

You must be able to explain the impact that the blitz had on Belfast and Derry/Londonderry. Examiners will also expect you to be able to identify how the Unionist voters reacted to the way in which the Stormont government was running the war effort.

# WAR AND THE FREE STATE (I): MILITARY PREPARATIONS

## Military Preparations

Despite de Valera's declaration of neutrality, there remained the possibility that Ireland might be invaded by Germany as the first stage of an invasion of Britain. This possibility was discussed by representatives of both governments. The outcome of their talks was the agreement that members of the British army based in Northern Ireland could move back into Éire to secure its vulnerable western flanks.

Well aware of the limitations in its armed forces (Source A), the government increased Éire's military capacity by:

- Increasing the size of the army to over 40,000.
- Creating a reserve force in the shape of the Local Defence Force. However, this force was poorly equipped.
- Extending the size of the navy.
- Establishing an air force.

## SOURCE A

*Historian M.E. Collins comments on the Éire army's ability to defend the country from invasion.*

These men had no decent equipment. Little had been spent on defence during the 1930s and there was no native arms industry.

## The IRA

De Valera moved against the IRA as a result of that organisation's rather clumsy efforts to conspire with the Third *Reich* against the British and because its members had stolen a million rounds of ammunition from a Dublin magazine. Using the Offences Against the State Act, the government introduced internment without trial against suspected IRA members. At least 1000 individuals were targeted in this way. Six IRA members were hanged and when a further three went on hunger strike nothing was done to prevent their deaths. De Valera's stance was supported by the vast majority of the population. In the event the government's onslaught left the IRA broken (Source B, page 87).

## SOURCE B

*Historian M.E. Collins reflects on de Valera's attitude to the IRA during the emergency.*

Once war broke out IRA activity became a threat to neutrality ... De Valera struck ruthlessly against this threat [and] by 1943 the IRA had almost ceased to exist.

## ACTIVITIES

1  What changes did the Dublin government make to Éire's military forces at the start of the war?
2  What steps did the Dublin government take against the IRA during the war? How effective were these measures?

## EXTENSION ACTIVITY

'Éire was ready to repel any invading force.' Discuss.

## REVISION TIP

You must be able to explain to the examiners the steps that Dublin took to prepare itself against invasion. You should also be able to comment on how effective these preparations were.

## WAR AND THE FREE STATE (II): ASSESSING NEUTRALITY

### Joining the War?

After Winston Churchill became Prime Minister in May 1940, Britain made two main attempts to encourage Ireland on to its side:

- In June 1940 London proposed the reunification of Ireland if Éire joined the Allies (Source A on this page). In return the Dublin government would allow British forces to be stationed in Éire and make use of naval

## SOURCE A

*Extract from Britain's proposal of a united Ireland if Éire helped Britain in the Second World War, June 1940.*

There should be a declaration of a United Ireland in principle ... Ulster to remain involved in the war, Éire to remain neutral ... for the time being ... A joint defence council to be set up at once ... British naval ships to be allowed into Éire's ports, British troops and aeroplanes to be stationed at certain agreed points in the territory, the British government to provide additional equipment for Éire's forces.

facilities. However, de Valera rejected the offer on the strength of Éire's 'unpreparedness', the negative impact it would have on Éire's independence and the fact that there was no guarantee that Northern Ireland would agree since its government had not even been consulted (Source B below). When he became aware of the British offer, Lord Craigavon informed the British government 'to such treachery to loyal Ulster I will never be party'.

- Early in the morning following the Japanese attack on Pearl Harbor (7 December 1941), Churchill telegrammed de Valera. His offer of 'Now is your chance. Now or never "A nation once again" ', was understood by de Valera to refer to the possibility of Irish unity if he joined the Allies, but again he declined.

In 1942 Churchill attempted to regain the use of the treaty ports. Once again his efforts were rejected by de Valera.

## SOURCE B

*De Valera's response to the British offer.*

[This] plan would commit us definitely to an immediate abandonment of our neutrality. [However] it gives no guarantee that in the end we would have a united Ireland.

A 1940 cartoon from Britain's *Daily Mail* commenting on the dangers for Éire if it continued with its policy of neutrality.

## Totally Neutral?

Éire asserted its neutrality during the war in several ways:

- It refused military assistance to both sides.
- The Allies were denied use of Éire's ports and airfields.
- News bulletins gave purely factual reports about the war.
- Weather forecasts ceased to be broadcast in case they helped either side.
- De Valera resisted US pressure to end neutrality when the US entered the war in late 1941.

On occasion, though, de Valera went to quite extraordinary lengths in his efforts to display even-handedness. He irritated the US government by protesting at the arrival of US troops in Northern Ireland in 1942. He further annoyed Allied opinion when, in April 1945, he visited the German ambassador to express sympathy over Hitler's death. Earlier the same month, however, he had carried out a similar visit to the US embassy as a mark of respect to the late US President, Franklin Delano Roosevelt.

Frequently, however, Dublin's actions made it appear that their neutrality was biased in favour of the Allies:

### MR. DE VALERA'S SYMPATHY
#### Wholehearted Help for Belfast

MR. DE VALERA, speaking at Castle-bar on Saturday, expressed sympathy with the victims of the air attack on Belfast, and promised " any help we can give them."

" This is the first time I have spoken in public since the disaster in Belfast," he said, " and I know you will wish me to express, on your behalf and on behalf of the Government, our sympathy with the people who are suffering there.

" In the past, and probably in the present, too, a number of them did not see eye to eye with us politically," Mr. de Valera continued, " but they are all our people, they are one and the same people, and their sorrows in the present instance are also our sorrows

" I want to say that any help we can give them in the present time we will give to them wholeheartedly—(applause)—believing that were the circumstances reversed they would also give us their help wholeheartedly."

Newspaper report on de Valera's reaction to the Belfast blitz.

- The German ambassador's radio transmitter was confiscated.
- German pilots who bailed out over Éire were imprisoned while Allied airmen were

surreptitiously allowed to cross the border into Northern Ireland.

- During the Belfast blitz, de Valera sent 13 fire engines (with 71 crew) to help. In its aftermath, relief centres were set up close to the border, relief funds were started and officials from both governments met to discuss how best the refugee problem could be handled.
- Allied airmen patrolling the **Western approaches** or refuelling on trans-Atlantic missions were permitted to fly over Irish territory through the 'Donegal air corridor' (from Beleek to the coast). Later in the war US airmen were also permitted to use this route.
- In the final months of the war, de Valera allowed the RAF to establish a number of secret radar bases on Irish territory.

## Whose Credit?

It is important to consider the real reasons for Éire's ability to remain neutral:

- Éire benefited from the sympathetic attitude of the representatives of the British and German governments in Dublin, and their recommendations to their respective governments not to do anything that would compromise that neutrality.
- If the Allies had found it strategically necessary to invade the South there is little doubt that they would have done so. That they did not was due mainly to the significant strategic role that Northern Ireland played during the conflict.

The possibility of an Allied invasion was revealed in a speech delivered by Churchill on the war's conclusion when he condemned de Valera's role in the conflict (Source C). At the same time Churchill praised the part played by Northern Ireland that prevented Great Britain from having 'to come to close quarters with Mr de Valera, or perish forever from the earth'.

De Valera used his response to score a few points of his own (Source D). He asked Churchill if he could not 'find in his heart the generosity to acknowledge that there is a small nation that stood alone, not for one year or two, but for several hundred years against aggression?'

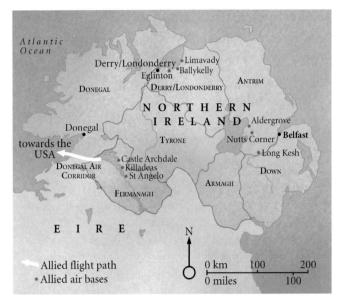

**Figure 2.2** The location of the Donegal air corridor.

### SOURCE C

*Excerpt from Churchill's end of war broadcast in which he praised Northern Ireland's wartime contribution while condemning Éire's neutrality, May 1945.*

Owing to the action of Mr de Valera ... the approaches which the southern Irish ports and airfields could so easily have guarded were closed by hostile aircraft and U-boats. This was indeed a deadly moment in our life, and had it not been for the loyalty and friendship of Northern Ireland, we should have been forced to come to close quarters with Mr de Valera, or perish forever from the earth.

### SOURCE D

*De Valera's response to Churchill's rebuke, May 1945.*

Mr Churchill is proud of Britain's stand alone ... Could he not find in his heart the generosity to acknowledge that there is a small nation [Ireland] that stood alone, not for one year or two, but for several hundred years against aggression; a small nation that could never be got to accept defeat and has never surrendered her soul?

## The Impact of the 'Emergency'

The war – or 'Emergency' as it was called – had an impact on Ireland in a number of ways:

- Poor *Luftwaffe* navigation resulted in Dublin being bombed several times. In one attack in May 1941, 28 people died (some historians put the fatalities at 34 while a recent account puts the death-toll at over 40), at least 90 were injured (again, estimates vary) and several hundred houses were damaged or destroyed.
- The Ministry of Supplies was set up under Sean Lemass to ensure that Ireland was not left totally without essential materials. Lemass established the Irish Shipping Company to carry supplies previously brought by British ships. However, factories still had to close because they could not get hold of sufficient natural resources or manufacturing equipment. Particularly in short supply were petrol and coal. As a result of the lack of the former, usage of public transport increased. As a result of the lack of the latter, the use of turf increased many times over.
- Ireland benefited from a food surplus. However, the lack of available artificial fertilisers damaged productivity even though over one and a half times more land was being used to grow crops. In addition, other imports such as tea and sugar had to be rationed due to the lack of imports. Attempts were made to increase wheat production to support the production of bread. Unfortunately the Irish climate was not best suited to this crop and so rationing had to be introduced.
- The lack of maize meant that home-grown grain had to be used to feed livestock.
- Other goods that were rationed included butter while fruit and chocolate became unavailable. As a result cross-border smuggling increased. However, the availability of most meat and dairy produce in addition to the potato meant that most people were able to survive without having to tighten their belts too much.
- The closure of factories had an impact on employment levels and many Irish people began to seek their fortunes in Britain. It is estimated that between 1939 and 1945 about 200,000 (estimates vary) Irish people crossed the Irish Sea. Many of these emigrants worked in British munitions factories.

At the same time there were no wartime blackouts in Éire and the state's cinemas and theatres remained open for business. As a consequence large numbers of servicemen and better-off northerners crossed the border for entertainment and nights out.

Despite the general support for neutrality among the Éire population, the harsh economic situation meant that Fianna Fáil still lost 10 seats in the 1943 general election. Within a year all but one of these seats had been regained in another election. This snap election was called by de Valera to take advantage of the increased popularity of his government as a result of the Allies' decision to isolate Ireland in advance of D-Day. The reason for the Allies' action was de Valera's refusal of an American request to shut down the German and Japanese embassies in Dublin to prevent leaks of the Allied invasion plans.

### ACTIVITIES

1 What evidence is there that Britain was keen to get Éire involved in the war?
2 What evidence is there to indicate that Éire was not totally neutral during the Second World War?
3 What problems did Éire's neutrality pose for the British?
4 Assess the impact of the War on Éire using the following headings:
   - emigration
   - shipping
   - rationing.

### EXTENSION ACTIVITY

How and why was Éire's neutrality biased towards the Allies during the Second World War?

### REVISION TIP

You should be able to explain the impact that 'the Emergency' had on the people of Éire. You will also be expected to be able to explain just how neutral Éire was during the war.

## Practice Question (Higher)

### Higher

Answer all questions

1 (a) (i) Study Source A (the cartoon on page 62).

Using Source A, and your own knowledge, describe how de Valera planned to change the relationship between the Free State and Britain.                                    [6]

(ii) Study Source B (Source A on page 66).

Using Source B, and your own knowledge, explain the importance of the 1937 Constitution on relations between Britain and Éire.                                        [9]

(iii) Study Source C (Source B on page 73).

Source C suggests that Chamberlain did not want conscription to be introduced in Northern Ireland.

How far do you agree with Chamberlain's view that introducing conscription in Northern Ireland would have been 'an embarrassment'?

Explain your answer using Source C and your own knowledge.                            [12]

(b) In what ways did the standard of living differ between Northern Ireland and Éire in the period 1945 to 1949?                                                            [6]

(c) In this question 5 additional marks are available for your use of spelling, punctuation and grammar.

'The preparations made between 1938 and 1941 for the defence of Northern Ireland and its people were inadequate'. Do you agree? Explain your answer.          [17] and [SPaG 5]

# POST-WAR SOCIAL AND POLITICAL CHANGES

## THE WELFARE STATE (I): GREAT BRITAIN

### Labour in Power

In May 1945 the Second World War ended in Europe; two months later the Labour Party led by Clement Attlee won the British general election. Although Churchill and the Conservatives had led Great Britain to victory, voters were more attracted by Labour's promises of jobs for all, government ownership of Britain's industries and, most importantly of all, the introduction of a free health care, education and benefits system available to all British citizens (Source A). This system was based on ideas first developed by Lord Beveridge in 1942 and would become known as the **Welfare State**.

Taking up office just after six years of total war, the new government faced a very difficult situation:

- The country was almost broke.
- Poverty was widespread.
- Most of the goods being made in Britain were being sold abroad so that food could be bought in from other countries.
- Coal, bread and potato supplies had almost run out. In 1946 rationing of bread was introduced. A year later potatoes were also rationed.

> ### SOURCE A
>
> *Extract from the Labour Party's manifesto for the 1945 general election. The manifesto was entitled* Let us Face the Future.
>
> The nation wants food, work and homes. It wants more than that – it wants good food in plenty, useful work for all, and comfortable, labour-saving homes … It wants a high and rising standard of living, security for all against a rainy day, an educational system that will give every boy and every girl a chance to develop the best that is in them.

As a result the immediate post-war period in Britain was known as the 'age of austerity'.

### Reforms

The Labour Party believed that the government should control Britain's key industries and service providers. This policy of **nationalisation** was implemented as follows:

- 1947: coal mines and electricity
- 1948: railways
- 1949: iron and steel.

A Labour election poster of 1945.

The Labour government began to construct large numbers of houses in order to eliminate Britain's slums and as a response to the damage caused by German bombs. A massive 680,000 houses were erected between 1947 and 1950.

The National Health Service (NHS) came into operation in July 1948. At first it faced opposition from those in the middle and upper classes concerned about the costs in terms of increased taxation and from doctors fearing that it would limit their freedoms, restrict their ability to earn money and turn them in to glorified civil servants. In the end, however, the NHS was joined by 90% of doctors and was hugely successful even if it was massively expensive, and it greatly benefited public health in Britain.

## THE WELFARE STATE (II): NORTHERN IRELAND

### Reforms in Northern Ireland

Despite the need for massive reforms in healthcare and housing following years of poverty and deprivation, many in Northern Ireland were worried about what Labour's reforming policies might mean for them. The middle classes and doctors voiced the same objections as their equivalents had done across the Irish Sea. Unionist business leaders feared the implications of nationalisation. Meanwhile, apart from its suspicions of what it saw as the Labour government's socialism, the Stormont administration feared the loss of power to a centralising government and wondered how it was to finance the introduction of similar reforms (Source A below). Not surprisingly, the less well-off welcomed the Welfare State as it promised improvements in their quality of life while Nationalists welcomed the initiative as they viewed a Labour government as potentially more sympathetic to their situation.

### SOURCE A

Historian J.J. Lee explains Stormont's attitude to the prospect of a Welfare State.

The Unionist cabinet contemplated with distaste the election of a Labour government in Britain … [however] it decided it had no option but to adhere to the existing constitutional arrangement and do its best to modify the more repellent features of Labour's welfare legislation.

Labour's socialist medicine: a bitter medicine for the Stormont government?

## SOURCE B

*Historian M.E. Collins explains how the Welfare State was financed in Northern Ireland.*

Since the North could not afford [the Welfare State reforms] out of its own resources, the Unionist government made an agreement with London that Britain would subsidise them ... This subsidy allowed the Northern government to give its citizens a far higher level of health care, social service and education than they could otherwise have afforded.

It need not have worried; the Labour government demonstrated its gratitude for Northern Ireland's contribution to the war effort by helping to cover the costs of the introduction of the Welfare State through the provision of generous subsidies (Source B). As a result improvements were effected in a range of areas.

### Health and Welfare

The biggest development was the introduction of the health service, similar to the programme initiated in Britain. The new system came online in 1948 and took root quickly. It was soon waging highly successful campaigns against diseases such as polio and tuberculosis. By 1962 Northern Ireland's death rate was the lowest in the UK; in 1939 it had had the highest. Northern Ireland's population was also assisted through the introduction of a range of other welfare initiatives including **family allowance, national assistance** and **non-contributing pensions.**

### Housing

An already serious housing shortage in Northern Ireland was made worse by the impact of the war. A report commissioned by Brooke soon after he became Prime Minister was published in 1944. It estimated that 37 per cent of homes (43,000) in Belfast were unsuitable for living in and more than 100,000 new homes were required for the whole of Northern Ireland. In 1945 the Northern Ireland Housing Trust was established to oversee their construction. This was a massive undertaking that took two decades to complete. Local councils were also encouraged to construct dwellings through the provision of generous subsidies, however they were not as successful. Also, discrepancies in how those council houses were allocated meant that not all benefited equally.

### Education

Radical changes were also introduced to the education sector by the 1947 Education Act when the school-leaving age was raised to 15 (with transfer to post-primary education at the age of 11). For the first time, children could stay at school free of charge until they were fifteen, and children who passed the 11+ examination could attend grammar schools, again without payment. As a result the numbers of students in post-primary education doubled over the following eight years. In addition, local education authorities were required to provide free services to all schools including transport, milk, meals, books, stationery and healthcare.

New secondary schools were constructed to cope with the massively increased numbers in education, while funding for the voluntary sector increased from 50 to 65 per cent (much higher than equivalent grants in England). Scholarships were also provided to allow more people to access third level education. Teacher training provision was also improved in both Catholic and Protestant sectors.

Despite lower levels of financial support, the Catholic population gained considerably from these reforms. In spite of the poverty from which they came, more Catholic children were able to access secondary and university-level education. As a result of the 1947 Education Act the educational system in Northern Ireland was modernised, even if the old religious divisions remained and were, in many senses, deepened.

### Economy

The Stormont government also made efforts to improve the North's economy, particularly given the long-term decline in some of Northern Ireland's traditional industries such as linen and shipbuilding. The 1945 Industrial Development Act provided the land and incentives for the building of new factories.

At the same time, while living standards undoubtedly improved, the reforms did mean that Stormont came to rely more and more on the British government for money. This fact was resented by some unionist politicians.

**ACTIVITIES**

1 How did the Stormont government react to Labour's plans? How did Labour overcome this opposition?
2 What steps did the Northern Ireland government take in the following areas:
   - health and welfare?    - education?
   - housing?               - economy?

**EXTENSION ACTIVITY**

To what extent did Northern Ireland's contribution to the war effort benefit it after 1945?

**REVISION TIP**

The introduction of the Welfare State in Northern Ireland was a development of great significance. Make sure that you can identify and explain its different elements, the variety of reactions to it and its overall impact.

## ÉIRE: POST-WAR PROBLEMS

### Depression

After 1945 Éire found itself isolated economically, particularly by its nearest neighbour, Britain, and its allies. The reason was London's dissatisfaction with Éire's decision to remain neutral during the Second World War. The result was a severe economic depression, which was made worse by poor weather in 1946 and 1947 (Source A):

- Unemployment numbers shot up.
- Building materials, particularly timber, became almost unobtainable.
- The lack of fertilisers during the war meant that the land was short of essential nutrients, thus limiting productivity. Poor weather in summer 1946 further had an impact on crop production.
- Britain withheld coal imports.
- Éire experienced severe fuel shortages in 1947 as a result of increased demand during the harsh winter weather.

- Wartime rationing remained in force and was extended to include bread from the start of 1947.
- Inflation began to rise and as workers failed to achieve sufficient wage increases, a wave of strikes broke out.
- Emigration rates remained high with as many as 24,000 leaving Éire each year. This in itself had a significant economic impact.

By 1947 the situation had deteriorated to the point where de Valera declared that Éire remained in a State of Emergency.

Unlike Northern Ireland, which was now beginning to benefit from Labour's modernising policies, state benefits (unemployment, family allowance) in Éire were almost non-existent and there was no welfare state to look after people. Instead people had to pay for their own medical care.

The end result was increased unpopularity for the Fianna Fáil government; as a result it lost the 1948 general election.

**SOURCE A**

An assessment of Éire's economic situation after 1945 by Dermot Keogh in his book Twentieth Century Ireland.

It was a case of wartime conditions without a war.

ILL-PAID EIRE WORKER: "WOULDN'T I JUST LIKE TO LIVE IN THAT SAME 'BLACK' NORTH!"

The grass is greener on the other side of the fence!

## The Inter-party Government

As a result of Fianna Fáil's defeat a **coalition** government took power in Éire. This was made up of a range of political parties:

- Fine Gael was the largest of the parties. It was set up in 1933 as a union of a number of parties/ groups including Cumann na nGaedheal. It was led by General Richard Mulcahy.
- Two different and antagonistic Labour parties.
- Farmers were represented by Clann na Talmhan.
- Clann na Poblachta was a Republican and socialist party. It was led by Seán MacBride, former Chief of Staff of the IRA, 1936–1938.
- The government also had the support of 12 independent TDs (*Teachta Dála* – Deputy to the Dáil, Member of Dáil Éireann).

As leader of the largest party, Mulcahy should have become *Taoiseach*. However, he was unacceptable to MacBride because of his involvement in the Irish civil war. For this reason senior Fine Gael politician John A. Costello was appointed as *Taoiseach* (Source B).

John A. Costello (1891–1976).

## Reforms

The new government introduced a range of policies that were designed to modernise the Irish economy. These measures included:

- The establishment in 1949 of the Industrial Development Authority (IDA). Its purpose was to revitalise Éire's economy.
- The creation of Córas Tráchtála, a government body set up to increase the country's trade with North America.
- A house-building programme which resulted in the erection of close to 12,000 new houses annually by 1950.
- The initiation of huge land reclamation projects and the extension of electrification schemes.
- The signing of a trade agreement with Britain in 1948. This improved profit margins for Irish agricultural exports.

As a result of these measures, the Irish economy entered into a slow, if steady, period of improvement; however the government's failure to engage in longer-term economic planning meant that the economy did not develop as

### ACTIVITIES

1. How well did the Éire economy perform in the post-war period? Why was this?
2. How did this situation differ from the North, both economically and socially?
3. Why did de Valera lose power in 1948?
4. What type of government took over from Fianna Fáil in 1948?
5. What economic policies did the inter-party government introduce during its term of office?

### SOURCE B

*Historian M.E. Collins assesses the reasons for the inter-party government's survival.*

The new government looked weak and unlikely to last. It contained an uneasy blend of old and young, of Republicans and Free Staters, of conservatives and socialists. In practice, however, it worked well. Costello was an excellent *Taoiseach*. He gave each minister a good deal of freedom to pursue his own policies.

### EXTENSION ACTIVITY

Was de Valera right to keep Éire out of the war given the conditions it found itself in after 1945?

### REVISION TIP

North–South differences were made worse by the impact of the Second World War. Make sure that you give all of the reasons why this was the case.

The Republic is declared. Crowds gather outside Dublin's General Post Office, 1949.

quickly as it might. At the same time, the problem of emigration continued to bleed away the potential of the Irish population.

## ÉIRE BECOMES A REPUBLIC

### Reasons

The members of the inter-party government – particularly Clann na Poblachta – felt that the 1937 constitution had made Éire a republic in all but name and had left the country's relationship with Britain in a confused state, neither fully in nor fully out of the Commonwealth. Therefore, in November 1948 the Republic of Ireland Bill was introduced into the Dáil. It came into effect on Easter Monday 1949 (Source A).

### Reactions

As Éire was the first country to leave the Commonwealth there was concern about how Britain would react. If London responded negatively it could have a major impact on the Irish economy and on the position of Irish people living and working in Great Britain (Source B). However, Australia and Canada supported Éire, stating that there was no reason why an Irish

### SOURCE A

*Historian M.E. Collins assesses the significance of the Declaration of a Republic in 1949.*

Ireland at last cut the few tenuous links which had bound her to the British Commonwealth. This changed nothing of the reality of independence which had existed since 1937–8. But it did mark a final end to the old quarrel over the treaty. The question of Irish independence was finally laid to rest. As evidence of its new-asserted independence, the Dublin government declined the invitation to join NATO in 1949, arguing that membership would compromise its neutrality and recognise the partition of Ireland.

### SOURCE B

*Attlee's view of Éire's decision to leave the British Commonwealth, 1948.*

The government of Éire considered the cutting of the last tie which united Éire to the British Commonwealth as a more important objective than ending partition.

Republic could not continue to work closely with the members of the Commonwealth.

London agreed and decided that it would not treat Éire as a foreign country but as a near neighbour with whom it enjoyed a special relationship.

As a result:

- Passports were not needed for travel between the two countries.
- Working permits were not required for Irish workers in the UK or British workers in the Republic of Ireland.
- Citizens of both nations had voting rights in each other's elections if they were living in the other country.
- Éire would continue to enjoy preferential treatment compared to non-Commonwealth countries when it came to trade.

Reactions to developments in Dublin were mixed north of the border:

- Northern Nationalists unsuccessfully demanded seats in the Dáil so that their views could be heard. Many of them felt abandoned by Dublin and objected to the inter-party government's claim that it represented the whole island. Some continued to call the Republic the Irish

Basil Brooke (1888–1973) (left) and Clement Attlee (1883–1967) (right) discussing the implications of the declaration of the Republic of Ireland.

Free State, believing that the former term should be reserved for a 32-county Irish Republic.
- Unionists felt threatened by the declaration of the Republic. Fearing – correctly – that the Republic would now make a determined effort to reunite Ireland, Unionists rejected Dublin's offer of any reasonable guarantees to respect their rights if they were to agree to end partition.

Leinster House, Dublin, seat of the Irish Parliament and government.

Instead the Stormont government pledged its defiance to the declaration of the Republic and used the border issue as the justification for calling a general election for February 1949. Brooke urged Unionists to vote in support of Northern Ireland's continued membership of the UK (Source C).

Nationalists – represented by the Anti-Partition League – were urged to vote in favour of a united Ireland. The election became known as the 'chapel gate election' as much of the money used to fund the Nationalists' campaign was raised mainly through collections outside churches in the South. This fact alone caused great resentment within the Unionist community.

The outcome – after a bitter campaign marred by sectarian violence – was an increased share of votes and seats for both Unionists and Nationalists although it was the former who still controlled Stormont. Brooke used his increased support as justification for demanding a British guarantee of Northern Ireland's future within the UK.

### The Ireland Act

Westminster's response was the Ireland Act of June 1949. It stated that 'In no event will Northern Ireland … cease to be part of … the

> **SOURCE C**
>
> *Extract from an election speech delivered by Brooke, 1949.*
>
> Our country is in danger … we fight to defend our very existence and the heritage of our Ulster children … Loyalists must stand united, pledging themselves … that, come what may, we shall maintain our province as part and parcel of the United Kingdom.

United Kingdom without the consent of the Parliament of Northern Ireland'. Put simply, the Northern Ireland Parliament had been given the final word in any future debate about the ending of partition. Not surprisingly Unionists felt reassured by these guarantees. A royal visit to Northern Ireland in 1949 further cemented their sense of union with the other parts of the UK.

Dublin and the North's Nationalists, on the other hand, were outraged and strongly expressed their displeasure with the Act. However, nothing was changed; Attlee felt that as Dublin had not consulted him about the declaration of the Republic, he was free to give whatever guarantees he wanted to the North.

Parliament Buildings, Stormont, location of the Northern Ireland Parliament and government 1932–72.

## ACTIVITIES

1 For what reasons did the inter-party government declare Ireland a republic?
2 How did the following react to this declaration:
   - Commonwealth countries?
   - Britain?
   - the different groups in Northern Ireland?
3 What was the purpose of the Ireland Act?
4 Explain how the following groups responded to the Ireland Act:
   - Unionists
   - Dublin government
   - Northern Nationalists.

## EXTENSION ACTIVITY

Attlee claimed that 'The government of Éire considered the cutting of the last tie which united Éire to the British Commonwealth as a more important objective than ending partition.' Do you agree?

## REVISION TIP

The passage of the 1949 Ireland Act was of huge importance to Northern Ireland's Unionist population. Make sure you are able to explain what the Act stated and why Westminster was prepared to pass it in the first place.

## NORTHERN IRELAND IN THE 1960S AND ITS RELATIONS WITH THE REPUBLIC OF IRELAND

### INTRODUCTION: THE EMERGENCE AND DEVELOPMENT OF NORTHERN IRELAND 1920–63

Northern Ireland was established by the 1920 Government of Ireland Act. This Act **partitioned** Ireland into two parts:

1 A 26-county Southern Ireland (which after the 1921 treaty became the Irish Free State).
2 A six-county Northern Ireland.

The first elections for the new Northern Ireland Parliament were held in May 1921 and it met for the first time the following month.

### Reactions to the New State

The population of the North reacted to the new arrangements rather differently:

- **Unionists** – who were mostly Protestants – were delighted. The new state had a substantial Protestant majority and so their control of the government was more or less guaranteed. Indeed, in the May 1921 elections Unionists won 40 out of the 52 seats available.
- **Nationalists** – most of whom were Catholics – were deeply upset; they wanted to be part of the rest of Ireland and governed by a parliament in Dublin.

### Violence and Discrimination

As a result of this desire, most Unionists felt that Nationalists could not be trusted and in this atmosphere of distrust the number of **sectarian** murders rocketed. The London government had already responded to increasing tensions by establishing the Ulster Special Constabulary (populated mainly by former members of the UVF). The new Northern Ireland government

added to its powers by passing the Special Powers Act (1922), which allowed them to arrest and detain suspects without holding a trial.

Other political responses to the seeming threat of Nationalism included:

- The abolition of **proportional representation** for local elections. This meant that fewer Nationalists would be elected to councils.
- The redrawing of the boundaries of local council areas to ensure Unionist control even where there was a Nationalist majority. This was known as **gerrymandering**.
- Allowing only those who paid **rates** to vote in local elections. For every £10 paid in rates one vote was given, up to a maximum of seven. This usually resulted in extra votes for the wealthy – who tended to be Protestant – and no votes for the poor – who were mostly, but not wholly, Catholic.

Discrimination was also practised against Catholics in other ways:

- Catholics were given fewer houses than Protestants by the Unionist-controlled councils as ownership of a house gave a vote in local elections.
- The quality of much Catholic housing was inferior.
- Catholics were less likely to have a job than Protestants.

### Developments up to 1963

The situation created in the early 1920s remained unchanged until the 1960s. Northern Ireland played a valuable part in the Allied war effort 1939–45, and in the late 1940s the **Welfare State** was introduced to improve living conditions.

However, relations with the South (the **Republic** of Ireland since 1949) remained tense, particularly as Articles II and III of the South's 1937 **constitution** laid claim to all of the island. Furthermore, an IRA campaign between 1956 and 1962 opposing the border reinforced the government's view that Nationalists were untrustworthy, though the campaign failed due to a lack of Nationalist support.

## O'NEILL'S POLICIES (I): ECONOMIC

### A New Premier

In March 1963 the hard-line Lord Brookeborough resigned as Prime Minister of Northern Ireland. His replacement was the Minister of Finance, Captain Terence O'Neill. Right from the start O'Neill's leadership was weak, as most of the Official Unionist Party's (OUP) MPs had wanted another minister, Brian Faulkner, to get the job. However, at that time the party's leader was decided by a group of senior party members, not by election. This lack of widespread support within his party would undermine O'Neill throughout his premiership.

### Improving the Economy

O'Neill's early statements suggested the prospect of change and progress in Northern Ireland. He believed that 'the face of Ulster' had to be transformed if it was to prosper (Source A). To achieve this goal O'Neill promised to introduce 'bold and imaginative measures'.

O'Neill's main concern lay with improving the economy (Source B). To this end a number of key economic measures were either proposed or introduced during his time as Prime Minister:

- £900 million of investment and the creation of five economic zones to update existing industries and attract new ones.
- Modernisation of the road and railway network (including closing seemingly unprofitable railway lines).
- Co-operation with the Dublin-based Irish Trades Union Congress, whose support was important for economic development.
- The establishment of an economic council under Brian Faulkner to drive forward the modernisation of the economy.

Terence O'Neill (1914–90), Northern Ireland's Prime Minister from 1963 to 1969.

### SOURCE A

*Historian Sabine Wichert writing in her book* Northern Ireland Since 1945 *(1991) (adapted).*

O'Neill wanted greater economic and social equality within Northern Ireland. He believed that a modern, industrialised system could not work properly without the involvement of all its citizens.

### SOURCE B

*Terence O'Neill sketching out his economic vision in 1963 (adapted).*

It is a new motorway driving deeper into the province. It is a new airport worthy of our position as the busiest air centre in Britain outside London. It is a new hospital in Londonderry – the most modern in the British Isles. It is new laboratories and research facilities at Queen's to carry us to the frontiers of existing knowledge and beyond. It is replacement of derelict slums by modern housing estates.

- The creation of a Ministry of Development to drive economic revival.
- The establishment of a new city based on the existing towns of Lurgan and Portadown. The new city was to be called Craigavon.
- The development of a new university in the market town of Coleraine to help develop a skilled workforce.

## Success and Failure

It was soon clear that these policies were having a positive impact:

- A number of multinational firms such as Michelin, DuPont, Goodyear, ICI and Grundig took advantage of generous investment grants and tax allowances to open factories in Northern Ireland.
- The construction of a motorway system was started.
- An oil refinery was opened in Belfast.
- A new airport was under development.
- Links with the Republic of Ireland resulted in the signing of an agreement on the supply of electricity from the south.

In total over 35,000 new jobs were created during the 1960s, but at the same time over 20,000 were lost in the ailing traditional industries such as linen manufacture.

This was not the only bad economic news:

- Between 1963 and 1969 the government had to give money to shipbuilders Harland & Wolff to keep it afloat.
- Unemployment averaged between 7 and 8 per cent.
- Several companies refused government grants to open factories west of the River Bann, seeing the area as too remote from their export markets.

This last fact alone had significant implications, not only for unemployment in the west (over 12.5 per cent) but also for feeding allegations of bias in government policy. This was because the majority of the population in the west was Nationalist.

### REVISION TIP

Make sure that you are able to explain the successes and failures of O'Neill's economic policies.

### ACTIVITIES

1 Give one reason why O'Neill wanted to improve the Northern Ireland economy.
2 Describe two measures taken by O'Neill to improve the economy of Northern Ireland.
3 What weakness did O'Neill face in his position right from the time of his appointment as Prime Minister of Northern Ireland?
4 Construct a spider diagram showing the economic policies introduced by O'Neill.
5 Explain what O'Neill hoped to achieve with his economic policies.
6 Make a copy of the following table:

| Economic successes | Economic failures |
| --- | --- |
|  |  |

Using the information on the left, fill in the table as appropriate. Now look at your results; would you say that O'Neill's economic policies were a success or a failure? Provide evidence to support your answer.

### EXTENSION ACTIVITY

Discuss how O'Neill's method of appointment would always make the achievement of his aims difficult.

## O'NEILL'S POLICIES (II): POLITICAL

### Political Changes

O'Neill realised that his economic policies would not change Northern Ireland on their own. There would also have to be social and political modernisation within Northern Ireland – to end discrimination and help nationalists to identify more strongly with the state – and improvements in relations with the Republic of Ireland – to benefit the economy. As someone with both Gaelic and **planter** ancestry, O'Neill believed that he was the right man for the job. However introducing such changes would increase the chances of division within unionism.

### The Hand of Friendship: Dublin

On 14 January 1965 the first face-to-face meeting of Ireland's main leaders since 1925 took place at **Stormont** when O'Neill met with the *Taoiseach* Sean Lemass. That this was the first such meeting in 40 years was an indication of the tensions that had existed between the two parts of the island (Source A below). Speaking later on television, O'Neill defended the meeting by arguing that both systems shared 'the same rivers, the same mountains and some of the same problems'.

O'Neill made a return visit to Dublin four weeks later. Both meetings focused on areas of economic co-operation and did not consider political issues. Discussions also took place between northern and southern ministers on issues such as tourism and electrical link-ups.

### The Hand of Friendship: Northern Nationalists

Within Northern Ireland O'Neill tried to improve relations with the Nationalist community by:

- Visiting Cardinal William Conway, Archbishop of Armagh, and spiritual leader of Ireland's Catholics.
- Offering official condolences to the Catholic Church on Pope John XXIII's death (June 1963).
- Visiting schools and hospitals run by the Catholic Church.
- Increasing the financial support provided for Catholic schools and hospitals (such as Belfast's Mater Infirmorum Hospital) and schools.

These steps were courageous and were well received by the Nationalist community. However, whether in the end they would go far enough for one community or be seen as too much for another remained to be seen (Source B).

---

**SOURCE A**

*Terence O'Neill reflecting on the likely fallout of the visit of Sean Lemass in* Ulster at the Crossroads.

[Lemass] suddenly said, 'I shall get into terrible trouble for this.' 'No, Mr Lemass,' I replied, 'it is I who will get into trouble for this.'

Terence O'Neill meeting Sean Lemass (1899–1971) at Stormont on 14 January 1965.

---

**SOURCE B**

*Historian Sabine Wichert writing in her book* Northern Ireland Since 1945 *(1991), (adapted).*

O'Neill's policies were clearly meant to make Catholics feel more a part of the state. However in the face of opposition from within the OUP it was difficult to make real changes. Therefore, his attempts at anti-sectarianism remained little more than words.

---

**ACTIVITIES**

1 Name the two Irish leaders who met at Stormont in 1965.
2 Name two actions taken by O'Neill that aimed to improve relations between the communities in Northern Ireland.
3 Construct a spider diagram showing all of the political policies introduced by O'Neill.
4 What do you think could have been the benefits and dangers for O'Neill in holding out the hand of friendship both within Northern Ireland and towards the South?

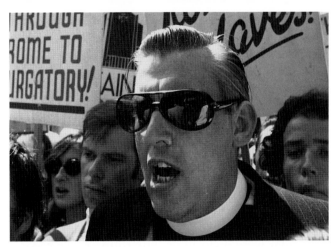

Ian Paisley (1926–2014) leading a protest march against **ecumenism**.

## REACTIONS TO O'NEILL'S POLICIES 1963–7

O'Neill's economic and political policies raised a mixture of fear and expectation within Northern Ireland's two communities.

### Unionist Reactions

There was both support and opposition within the Unionist community for O'Neill's attempts to change Northern Ireland. The mixed reaction was due to the desire of many moderate Unionists for reform and the fear among others of the changes that such reform might bring to their own position.

O'Neill's support among ordinary members of the OUP had never been total. Indeed, O'Neill did not even inform his own cabinet colleagues of Sean Lemass' January 1965 visit in advance (Source A below). This indicated his concerns about their possible reaction and also suggests that the idea for the visit was his alone.

Evidence of the divisions within the OUP over the visit was clear when Brian Faulkner condemned O'Neill's failure to consult his cabinet. That said, when Lemass' successor as *Taoiseach*, Jack Lynch, visited Northern Ireland in

December 1967, the visit was agreed in cabinet, implying that by then such a visit had become more acceptable to its members.

### The Emergence of Reverend Ian Paisley

While there was no widespread hostile public reaction to the Lemass visit, there was strong objection from the **Moderator** of the Free Presbyterian Church, Reverend Ian Paisley. Apart from longstanding Protestant concerns about the influence of the Catholic Church in the Republic, Paisley objected to any links with the South, especially as Articles II and III of its constitution laid claim to the whole island of Ireland. When Lynch visited in 1967 Paisley illustrated his continuing opposition by snowballing the Taoiseach's car. On the same day, Paisley and his supporters also carried placards describing O'Neill as a '**Lundy**'.

Throughout the rest of the decade Paisley's support grew as many Unionists came to fear the implications of O'Neill's new policies and to resent the failure of such policies to improve their own lives. In the short term, however, O'Neill was delighted with the success the OUP enjoyed in the November 1965 **general election** when it won 38 out of 52 seats. This result seemed to suggest that many people were satisfied with his policies.

### Violence and Division

Before long, however, the situation in Northern Ireland deteriorated. Tensions increased in 1966 with the commemorations for the fiftieth anniversaries of the Easter Rising and the Battle of the Somme and rioting broke out. Yet this was not the worst of the violence: two Catholics died in May and June 1966, the result of a series of gun attacks by the re-emerging UVF. O'Neill responded by banning the organisation.

As the situation worsened, O'Neill found that support within his own party was weakening. In September 1966 he revealed a plot by OUP **backbenchers** to get rid of him as leader. There were also growing rumours of opposition within his own cabinet from Deputy Prime Minister Brian Faulkner and Agriculture Minister Harry West.

By late 1967 the levels of O'Neill's support within unionism in general and the OUP in particular were dwindling. The ruling party was divided over strategy while opinion polls indicated increasing support within the Unionist population for Paisley's policies.

## Nationalist Reactions: Satisfaction and Disappointment

O'Neill's policies received similarly mixed reactions from the Nationalist community. Initial support for his policies soon gave way to frustration as the better future that seemed to have been promised failed to materialise. This annoyance was particularly felt among a new generation of Catholics (Source B).

At first Catholic leaders, political and religious, reacted warmly to O'Neill's attempts to hold out the

**SOURCE B**

*Irish historian Professor J.J. Lee, writing in* Ireland 1912–1985: Politics and Society *(1989), (adapted).*

A generation of Catholics brought up on the Welfare State, educated to a higher standard than ever before, began to emerge from the late 1950s … relatively well-educated Catholics felt increasingly bitter at what they believed to be discrimination.

hand of friendship. The visit of Lemass to Stormont was followed by the decision of the Nationalist Party to take up the role of **official opposition** in Stormont for the first time in its history.

However, O'Neill's policies also raised expectations, some of which were unlikely to be met given the growing tensions within unionism. There was outrage within Nationalist circles at the decision of the Minister of Development, William Craig, to name the new city linking Portadown and Lurgan, Craigavon, after Northern Ireland's first Prime Minister.

There were also continued accusations that O'Neill's economic policies favoured the Protestant east at the expense of the Catholic west (Source C). As evidence of this a number of points were made:

- With the exception of Derry/Londonderry, all the places earmarked for economic development were in Protestant areas.
- Unemployment was at a higher level west of the Bann.
- Despite significant cross-community protest, Northern Ireland's second university was sited in the mainly Protestant town of Coleraine rather than in the mainly Nationalist Derry/Londonderry, Northern Ireland's second city.

Figure 3.1 Northern Ireland

- No significant attempts were made to increase Catholic membership of various health and education bodies. This fact alone even led the pro-O'Neill *Belfast Telegraph* to argue that a 'nonsense' was being made of attempts at bridge building.

### SOURCE C

*Irish historian Professor J.J. Lee, writing in* Ireland 1912–1985: Politics and Society *(1989), (adapted).*

Catholics could not be convinced that Craigavon and Coleraine were anything but sectarian decisions, designed to deprive the mainly Catholic west from ever catching up with the mainly Protestant east.

## ACTIVITIES

1 Give one reason why some Unionists were unhappy with O'Neill's policies.
2 Give two reasons why not all Nationalists were happy with O'Neill's policies.
3 Explain how and why the following groups differed in their initial reaction to O'Neill's policies:
   - moderate Unionists
   - OUP MPs
   - supporters of Rev. Ian Paisley.
4 How had the Unionist reaction to O'Neill's policies changed by 1967?
5 How did Nationalists initially react to O'Neill's policies? Why did this initial Nationalist reaction to O'Neill's policies change as time went on?
6 Make a copy of the following table:

| Political successes | Political failures |
|---|---|
|  |  |

Using all the information on pages 103–7, fill in the table as appropriate. Now look at your results; would you say that O'Neill's political policies were a success or a failure? Provide evidence to support your answer.

7 Make a copy of the following table:

| O'Neill's policies | Unionist reaction | Nationalist reaction |
|---|---|---|
|  |  |  |

Using all the information on pages 105–7, fill in the table as appropriate. Now look at your results; which of O'Neill's economic and political policies would have been most popular or least popular with each community? Why was this? Provide evidence to support your answer.

## EXTENSION ACTIVITIES

1 Did O'Neill's policies bring about genuine change in Northern Ireland?
2 Would it ever have been possible for O'Neill to satisfy both sides in Northern Ireland with his policies?

### REVISION TIP

O'Neill never had the total loyalty of his party. Make sure you can explain how this would have weakened his position as Prime Minister.

## CIVIL RIGHTS TO ARMALITES: NORTHERN IRELAND 1967–9

### NICRA: Origins and Influences

The Northern Ireland Civil Rights Association (NICRA) was established at the start of 1967. The new group took much of its inspiration from the USA. One of its founder members, Paddy Devlin, later wrote that NICRA was 'inspired by the civil rights campaign to get justice and equality for blacks in the USA'. At the same time there were other sources of encouragement in the period following NICRA's establishment, notably the student demonstrations that took place in France during 1968.

It was not difficult to see why the US movement would have appeared attractive to reformers in Northern Ireland. Martin Luther King Jr's campaign had employed non-violent methods of **civil disobedience** in an effort to achieve equal opportunities for black people. By 1967 a series of marches and protests had led the US **Congress** to pass laws outlawing public discrimination and guaranteeing voting rights. These developments were widely reported in Europe.

Crowds gather for a NICRA march under the watchful eye of the RUC.

### NICRA's Aims

Set up as a non-sectarian movement, NICRA did not seek to end partition; rather it hoped to end what it saw as a number of serious abuses in the existing political system (Source A). In particular it sought to:

- Achieve 'one man, one vote'. This would allow a vote to all people over the age of 18 years of age. It would also remove the right of business owners to cast multiple votes.
- Ensure the fair allocation of council houses. At this time the possession of a vote in council elections depended on being a ratepayer; basically a householder. The fewer the number of Catholics who possessed a property, the fewer the number of Catholics who could vote.
- End gerrymandering, which was the practice of drawing electoral boundaries in a way that would serve to benefit one community over the other. Perhaps the most infamous example of the practice was in the city of Derry/Londonderry where the Unionist-dominated council ruled over a Catholic population of 20,102 compared with a Protestant population of 10,274. (These 1966 figures come from the report of the Cameron Commission set up by O'Neill's government to investigate the disturbances of 1968.)
- Prevent discrimination in the allocation of government jobs. The Cameron Commission found widespread evidence of favouritism towards Protestants in the allocation of jobs (Source B). There was similar evidence of under-representation of Catholics in other areas of government employment including the senior **civil service** and the **judiciary**.
- Remove the operation of the Special Powers Act. Officially known as the Civil Authorities (Special Powers) Act, 1922, this law allowed the government to arrest and detain people without holding a trial to see whether they were guilty or not.
- Disband the B Specials. This group was the sole remnant of the three-pronged Ulster Special Constabulary, which had been established in September 1920 to help fight the IRA during the War of Independence.
- Establish a formal complaints procedure against local authorities to report breaches in the above areas.

## SOURCE A

*Political activist Eamon McCann reflects on NICRA's aims.*

NICRA was a reformist organisation, out for limited change within the North, not an end to the northern state.

## SOURCE B

*An extract from the report of the Cameron Commission into disturbances in Northern Ireland published on 12 September 1969.*

The conclusion at which we arrived ... that certain at least of the grievances fastened upon by NICRA ... were justified in fact is confirmed by decisions already taken by the Northern Ireland government since these disturbances began.

## SOURCE C

*A protestant housewife's view of NICRA.*

It was all the Catholics this, the Catholics that, living in poverty and us lording it over them. People looked around and said 'What, are they talking about us? With the damp running down the walls and the houses not fit to live in.'

## ACTIVITIES

1 Explain where NICRA borrowed some of its tactics and ideas from.
2 Name two of the groups of people who supported the aims of NICRA.
3 What evidence is there to suggest that NICRA was influenced by events in other countries?
4 Why in particular might NICRA have taken inspiration from the civil rights movement in the USA?
5 Construct a spider diagram showing NICRA's main demands.
6 Explain why a new generation of Catholics was emerging at this time and why it was unhappy with its current political leadership.
7 Why did many Unionists react negatively to NICRA? Was this a reasonable interpretation? Explain your answer.

## Support and Reaction

Support for NICRA came from across the community, particularly from a new generation of Catholics, the first to have benefited from free education in the late 1940s. They had seen the growing self-confidence of Catholics elsewhere, not least in the USA where John F. Kennedy had been elected President in 1960. They were also unhappy with their own Nationalist Party, led by Eddie McAteer. Its only policy seemed to be the ending of partition.

However, support also came from other groups including liberal Protestants who sympathised with some of NICRA's demands and believed that making Northern Ireland fairer would undermine demands for a united Ireland. Support also came from communists, academics and trade unionists.

There was much suspicion about the emerging movement from within the Unionist population. Some felt that it was simply intent on causing trouble and was just a front for the IRA, while others believed it was only interested in Catholic rights (rather than rights for all) and would undermine the position of Protestants (Source C). Others thought that NICRA wanted a united Ireland, thus threatening the continued existence of Northern Ireland.

## EXTENSION ACTIVITIES

1 Were NICRA's demands justifiable?
2 Which assessment of the civil rights movement do you think was correct?

## REVISION TIP

Many Unionists saw NICRA as a front for Republicans. Make sure that you are able to explain how this would have had an impact on Unionist attitudes to their demands.

## NICRA'S TACTICS AND O'NEILL'S RESPONSE

### Marching for Houses

The US civil rights movement's tactic of organising peaceful marches to highlight its campaign was first used in Northern Ireland on 24 August 1968. The occasion was a march between the Co. Tyrone towns of Coalisland and Dungannon. This demonstration took place because of the decision of the Dungannon rural district council to give a council house in the village of Caledon to a 19-year-old Protestant woman rather than to a Nationalist family. In response to this decision Austin Currie, Nationalist MP for East Tyrone, **squatted** in the house. After he was evicted, Currie suggested holding a protest march to highlight the situation. Although the demonstration was prevented by the police from reaching its intended destination of Dungannon town square, an alternative rally was organised at the police barricade and the event passed off without incident.

### Violence in Derry/Londonderry

House allocation was also the issue that led to NICRA's second march. In order to highlight what were seen to be inequalities in Londonderry

The RUC moves to break up the NICRA march in Derry/Londonderry on 5 October 1968.

Corporation's housing policy, a march was organised for 5 October 1968. The march was due to travel from the Waterside to the city centre via the Craigavon Bridge. In response the Unionist **apprentice boys** organisation threatened to hold a rival march. The Stormont government responded by banning the holding of any march east of the River Foyle or within the historic city walls. The NICRA march's organisers rejected this ban.

Although the crowd that turned up on 5 October was relatively small, it was accompanied by powerful allies in the shape of four Westminster MPs (including Gerry Fitt, MP for West Belfast) and, even more importantly, an RTE (Irish television) camera crew. That night television pictures beamed across the world showed more clearly than any words the heavy-handed tactics used by the police to break up the rally. It became clear to many on that night that Northern Ireland was on the verge of a crisis that would prove difficult to resolve (Source A).

Further NICRA marches, including in Newry in January 1969, made the situation even worse. Quite often, violence resulted. There were several reasons for this:

- NICRA had been going ahead with marches that had been banned by the government.
- Marches were seen as provocative, especially when they went through Protestant areas.
- NICRA marches were coming into contact with Unionist counter-demonstrations.

## The Five-point Reform Programme

As a result O'Neill, Faulkner and Craig were summoned to Westminster on 4 November to meet with the British Labour Prime Minister Harold Wilson. The outcome of this meeting was the announcement, on 22 November, of a reform programme. The programme included five main proposals, all of which were to be in place by the end of 1971. The proposals were:

- The allocation of council housing on a **points system**.
- The replacement of Londonderry **Corporation** by a Development Commission.
- The removal of parts of the Special Powers Act.
- Reforms within local government including the ending of extra votes for business owners.
- The appointment of an **ombudsman** to investigate complaints.

## Calm before the Storm?

Although O'Neill himself later dismissed this package as too timid, at the time it seemed to point the way towards a better future even if it failed to deliver all of NICRA's demands. However, in the short-term, protests and counter-protests continued and so on 9 December O'Neill appeared on television to hammer home to people the starkness of the position Northern Ireland now found itself in. In particular he appealed to NICRA's leaders to help to restore calm to the province (Source B).

### SOURCE A

*Extract from an article in the October 1988 edition of current affairs magazine* Fortnight *commenting on the NICRA march of 20 years earlier.*

The whole affair was a series of blunders. The violence resulted from inadequate planning and leadership by the organisers of the march, and from stupidity and breakdown of control on the part of the authorities. But the greater share of the blame lies with those who had the greater power – the Minister of Home Affairs and the Royal Ulster Constabulary.

### SOURCE B

*Terence O'Neill broadcasting on television on 9 December 1968.*

Ulster stands at the crossroads ... our conduct over the coming days and weeks will decide our future ... I have made it clear that a Northern Ireland based on the interests of any one section rather than upon the interests of all could have no long-term future ... What kind of Ulster do you want? A happy and respected province in good standing with the rest of the United Kingdom? Or a place continually torn apart by riots and demonstrations and regarded by the rest of Britain as a political outcast?

At first his message seemed to have the desired effect and all further street protests were called off. However, the breathing space O'Neill had won would prove to be very short-lived. While he might have managed to calm the civil rights movement, there were additional problems to deal with:

- The reforms had caused dismay among the Unionist community who opposed concessions to the threat of violence and who now felt that their position was under threat.
- O'Neill faced further opposition from within his own party with Home Affairs Minister William Craig condemning O'Neill's television speech and arguing that the Prime Minister was acting under pressure from the British. Craig was sacked, but even more opposition was appearing on the horizon.

### ACTIVITIES

1 Which issue led NICRA to hold its first two marches?
2 How did the Northern Ireland government react to the events of 5 October 1968?
3 Explain why the issue of housing was so prominent in the earliest NICRA marches.
4 If the Derry/Londonderry march was illegal, why was it that the authorities came out of the events of 5 October worst?
5 Make a copy of the following table:

| NICRA demands | Five-point reform programme |
|---|---|
|  |  |

On the left-hand side list NICRA's demands (see page 108 above). On the right-hand side match O'Neill's reforms (see page 111) with the appropriate demand. Which of NICRA's demands had not been granted?
6 O'Neill later dismissed his five-point reform programme as too timid. Explain why others may not have agreed with him at the time.

### EXTENSION ACTIVITIES

1 Which had the more significant impact on Northern Ireland politics: NICRA or television?
2 Why were all of NICRA's demands not granted at the time of the five-point reform programme?

### REVISION TIP

O'Neill thought the five-point reform programme was not enough. Many Nationalists would have agreed but many Unionists would have believed that they were too much. Are you able to explain why these reforms led to such different reactions?

## THE PEOPLE'S DEMOCRACY MARCH

### A More Radical Movement Emerges

Although NICRA had called for a halt to its campaign of marching its decision was ignored by the recently formed People's Democracy. This group, mainly university students, had emerged out of students' anger at the violence NICRA had faced in October 1968 and their desire to disrupt the Stormont administration. Its leading figures were Michael Farrell and Bernadette Devlin (who was elected Westminster MP for Mid Ulster in April 1969). People's Democracy had developed demands broadly similar to those of NICRA, namely:

- one man, one vote
- fair boundaries
- houses on need
- jobs on merit
- free speech
- repeal of the Special Powers Act (Source A, page 113).

Unhappy with the limited nature of O'Neill's five-point reform programme, People's Democracy announced that they were holding a march between Belfast and Derry/Londonderry, from 1 to 4 January 1969. The march was condemned by NICRA and Nationalist leaders, fearing its impact on an already tense situation.

People's Democracy marchers come under attack at Burntollet on 4 January 1969.

## Ambush at Burntollet

The condemnations were ignored and the demonstration began on schedule. Much of the march was to go through Protestant areas, forcing the police to enforce different routes to avoid confrontation. However, on the third day confrontation took place; the marchers were the target of a violent ambush at Burntollet Bridge, an attack that the police seemed to do little to deflect. Later on the same night, tensions were further raised in Derry/Londonderry when police rampaged through Nationalist areas of the city (Source B). Such events did little to endear the RUC to members of the Nationalist community.

### SOURCE A

*The aims of the People's Democracy march according to Michael Farrell, a People's Democracy leader.*

The march would be the acid test of the government's intentions. Either [it] would face up to the extreme right of its own OUP and protect the march ... or it would be exposed as impotent in the face of sectarian thuggery, and Westminster would be forced to intervene, re-opening the whole Irish question for the first time in 50 years.

### SOURCE B

*An extract from the report of the Cameron Commission into disturbances in Northern Ireland published on 12 September 1969.*

A number of policemen were guilty of misconduct which involved assault and battery, malicious damage to property ... and the use of provocative, sectarian and political slogans.

## PEOPLE'S DEMOCRACY: REACTIONS AND RESIGNATIONS

### Reactions to Burntollet

NICRA had called off its marches in response to O'Neill's reforms; believing now that the events in the north-west indicated that nothing had changed, it started to march again. The first march was held in Newry and again violence resulted. In response, O'Neill established the Cameron Commission to investigate the increasing violence. This led two cabinet members, one of whom was Brian Faulkner, to resign from the government. Faulkner argued that O'Neill was not strong enough to control the situation.

Faulkner's opinion of O'Neill seemed to be gaining support within the OUP with 12 MPs calling for his resignation on 30 January 1969. Instead O'Neill called a general election, which he termed the 'crossroads election', in an attempt to prove that public opinion was behind his efforts to modernise Northern Ireland.

Brian Faulkner (1921–77).

### The 'Crossroads Election'

The election took place on 24 February 1969; however the result was not what O'Neill had wanted:

• There was a reduction in Unionist support and increased divisions of loyalty among the OUP MPs elected.
• There was little or no evidence of the hoped for support from Catholic voters.
• O'Neill, who had never before had to face a challenger in his own Bannside constituency, only polled 1400 votes more than his opponent, Rev. Ian Paisley.

O'Neill struggled on for another two months, but with his party now hopelessly divided and with a further deterioration in the political situation caused by increasing violence and confrontation, he resigned on 28 April 1969 (Source A). The final nail in his coffin was a series of bombings, which at the time appeared to be the work of the

## SOURCE A

*Terence O'Neill, speaking on television on 28 April 1969.*

I have tried to break the chains of ancient hatreds. I have been unable to realise [achieve] during my period of office all that I had sought to achieve.

IRA but which were actually carried out by Loyalists (extreme Unionists) in an attempt to force O'Neill to go. Writing later in his autobiography, O'Neill reflected that the bombs 'quite literally blew me out of office' (Source B). Some historians believe, however, that O'Neill became a victim of the hopes that he raised but was unable to fulfil (Source C).

## SOURCE B

*Terence O'Neill writing in his autobiography.*

As the party would never stand for change, I was really reduced to trying to improve relations between North and South; and in the North itself between the two sections of the community. In this respect I think I can truthfully say that I succeeded. During the period between 1965 and 1968 the Catholics came to realise that I was interested in their welfare. While the South began to take an interest in the North.

## SOURCE C

*The views of historian Jonathan Bardon from his book A History of Ulster (1992).*

Despite his mould-breaking gestures of conciliation, O'Neill eventually created intense frustration within the minority by his inability to deliver thoroughgoing reform, while more and more Loyalists were convinced that he was conceding too much and turned against him.

## A New Leader

In the resulting leadership election O'Neill was succeeded by his cousin, Major James Chichester Clark. Chichester Clark had resigned from the government less than a week earlier in protest at O'Neill's decision to introduce one man, one vote

in time for the next council elections. Then Chichester Clark had argued that the timing of the measure was wrong; now he declared he would continue with O'Neill's reform programme.

James Chichester Clark (1923–2002).

## ACTIVITIES

1 Who won the 1969 general election in Northern Ireland?
2 Who replaced O'Neill as Prime Minister of Northern Ireland?
3 Explain why O'Neill felt he had no choice but to resign as Prime Minister in April 1969.
4 Construct a timeline showing the main times and issues of division 1963–9.
5 O'Neill admitted his failure in various interviews. Using all that you have learnt about O'Neill so far, explain whether you believe that his premiership was either a success or a failure. Provide reasons for your answer.

## EXTENSION ACTIVITY

'O'Neill only had himself to blame for his downfall.' Do you agree?

## REVISION TIP

A number of factors played an important part in O'Neill's decision to resign. You will need to be able to remember them all for the examination.

## Practice Question (Foundation)

### Foundation

Answer all questions

1 (a) Below is a list of questions on relations between Britain, Northern Ireland and the Republic of Ireland in the years 1965–1985.

    (i) The last Prime Minister of Northern Ireland? [1]

    (ii) The first leader of the SDLP? [1]

    (iii) The year that the Battle of the Bogside took place? [1]

    (iv) One of the concessions granted after the end of the 1981 Hunger Strike? [1]

    (v) The first Secretary of State for Northern Ireland? [1]

    (vi) One of the Nationalist reactions to the events of Bloody Sunday? [1]

(b) This question is about the Northern Ireland Civil Rights Association (NICRA).

Study Sources A and B (the photo on page 108 and Source B on page 109) and answer the questions which follow.

    (i) Study Source A (the photo on page 108).

    Using Source A, give two aims of the Northern Ireland Civil Rights Association (NICRA). [4]

    (ii) Study Sources A and B.

    Using Sources A and B, and your own knowledge, describe how the Northern Ireland Civil Rights Association (NICRA) tried to achieve its aims. [10]

(c) This question is about Terence O'Neill.

In what ways did Terence O'Neill try to improve the economy of Northern Ireland in the 1960s? [12]

(d) In this question up to 5 additional marks are available for your use of spelling, punctuation and grammar.

This question is about the Hunger Strikes of 1980 and 1981.

Explain the reaction to the Hunger Strikes of 1980 and 1981.

Use the following three paragraph headings to help you with your answer:

Nationalist reaction
Unionist reaction
Government reaction [18] and [SPaG 5]

# ESCALATION OF POLITICAL AND CIVIL UNREST

## COUNTDOWN TO CHAOS: NORTHERN IRELAND 1969–72

### The Summer of 1969

A change of leadership did not reduce tensions in Northern Ireland. Continuing civil rights protests – now more confrontational than before in the aftermath of Burntollet – were followed by serious rioting in Belfast. As the July–August marching season approached, grave concerns were raised over the likely impact of marches on an already tense situation.

These concerns were evident both within and outside Northern Ireland:

- The Stormont government was worried if the already stretched security forces would be able to cope with a further increase in violence.
- After more or less ignoring Northern Ireland since 1921, the London government had become concerned enough to establish a cabinet committee on Northern Ireland.

- The Dublin government was anxious about the safety of the minority community and sent an intelligence officer to the North to watch what was happening.

To make matters worse, armed groups seemed to be emerging:

- among Loyalists angry at what they saw as concession after concession to Nationalists
- among Republicans who were apprehensive at their own seeming inability to protect Nationalists.

### A Long Hot Summer

In July violence broke out in Belfast, but soon spread to Derry/Londonderry. In Belfast the violence mainly took the form of house burning, mostly by Loyalists, forcing many to leave their homes. However, seven people also lost their lives while 100 were wounded. In Derry/Londonderry the conflict began after the annual **apprentice**

The aftermath of the Battle of the Bogside, August 1969.

boys parade on 12 August. In the middle of intense and frightening violence, centred on the Bogside area, the *Taoiseach*, Jack Lynch, issued a statement outlining his concerns (Source A below) – which, with the accompanying movement of Irish troops and field hospitals to the border, did little to ease tension.

In total the rioting during what became known as the Battle of the Bogside lasted for 50 hours. Finally an uneasy calm was restored by using a small number of troops, as requested by Nationalist politicians, among others. However, violence flared up in several provincial towns and more particularly in Belfast where sectarian conflict was particularly intense (Source B).

The events of August 1969 were later to be seen as a turning point in the development of what became known as 'the Troubles'. They were seen as directly responsible for:

- the deployment of the British army on the streets of Northern Ireland on 15 August in an attempt to restore law and order
- the eventual re-emergence of the IRA.

## ACTIVITIES

1 Give one reason why violence broke out in the summer of 1969.
2 Describe two effects of the violence of this time.
3 Professor Lee describes the situation in Northern Ireland by mid-1969 as a 'time bomb'. What evidence can you find to support this view?
4 How and why would Taoiseach Jack Lynch's statement (Source A on this page) have increased tension in Northern Ireland?
5 Explain the reasons for the introduction of troops on to the streets of Northern Ireland in August 1969.

## EXTENSION ACTIVITY

Could the events of August 1969 have been avoided?

## REVISION TIP

Are you able to understand why August 1969 was such an important month in the emergence of 'the Troubles'?

## REACTIONS (I): WESTMINSTER AND STORMONT

Using the army might help to stop violence, but it would not solve Northern Ireland's problems; new political ideas were also needed. The question now was whether such ideas would come from Stormont or Westminster. London had left the government of the province to the local Parliament for decades without interference; could that now be allowed to continue? More importantly, could Westminster introduce policies that would reconcile Nationalists and reassure Unionists?

### The Downing Street Declaration

On 19 August Chichester Clark travelled to London to meet the British Prime Minister,

British troops on the streets of Belfast, August 1969.

- Following pressure from the British Home Secretary James Callaghan during a visit to Northern Ireland, the Stormont government announced that it was setting up the Scarman **Tribunal** to investigate recent disturbances (Source A below).
- A single housing authority was established, taking over from local councils.
- Measures to prevent discrimination in public employment were announced.
- A Ministry of Community Relations was created.

There were also moves to improve the economy:

- a £2 million programme of work-creating schemes
- increases in investment grants.

> ### SOURCE A
>
> *The views of historian Jonathan Bardon from his book* A History of Ulster *(1992).*
>
> The Scarman Tribunal … reported that in Belfast alone 1820 families fled their homes during and immediately after [the riots]; 1505 of these families were Catholic, making up more than three per cent of all Catholic households in the city.

Harold Wilson. The outcome of this meeting was the publication of the Downing Street Declaration. This declaration aimed to reassure both communities:

- Nationalists were told that 'every citizen of Northern Ireland is entitled to the same equality of treatment and freedom from discrimination as [exists] in the rest of the UK irrespective of political views or religion'.
- Unionists were told that 'Northern Ireland should not cease to be part of the UK without the consent of the people of Northern Ireland'.

### Additional Reforms

Further reforms were announced or introduced in the following weeks:

- The introduction of one man, one vote and an end to gerrymandering.
- A committee on policing was established under Lord Hunt (a British official who had the distinction of leading the first British team to climb Mount Everest).

### Unionist Reactions

However, everyone did not welcome these initiatives. Despite the reassurances of the Downing Street Declaration, many Unionists were concerned at what they saw as continuing concessions to Nationalists (Source B, page 120). The final straw came when the Hunt Report was published. It recommended:

- disarming the RUC
- disbanding the B Specials and replacing them with the Ulster Defence Regiment, a part-time force under army control.

Angered at the proposals, extreme Loyalist violence erupted on Belfast's Shankill Road.

### Nationalist Reactions

Nationalists reacted positively to the reforms, believing that an improved future involving a reformed political system was now within their grasp.

## SOURCE B

*Professor F.S.L. Lyons, writing in* Ireland since the Famine *(1973).*

The government's attempts to walk a tight-rope between the two angry communities was made first difficult and then almost impossible by the publication of the Cameron Report ... in September and of the Hunt Report on the police in October.

## ACTIVITIES

1 Explain two reforms introduced by the British Prime Minister in August 1969.
2 Give two reasons for Unionists' angry reaction to these reforms.
3 Make a copy of the following table:

| Proposals aimed at Nationalists | Proposals aimed at Unionists |
|---|---|
|  |  |

Using the information on page 119, fill in the table as appropriate. Now look at your results; would you say that Nationalists or Unionists would have been more satisfied by the Downing Street Declaration? Explain your answer.
4 Compare the terms of the Downing Street Declaration with NICRA's aims; how would the civil rights leaders have felt about this announcement?
5 How would Nationalists and Unionists have felt about the conclusions of the Cameron Report and the Hunt Report? Use the information in the text to help you with your answer.

## EXTENSION ACTIVITY

James Callaghan, the British Home Secretary, said that 'the only solutions would take 10 years, if they would ever work at all'. What do you think he meant by this?

## REVISION TIP

The Downing Street Declaration was one aspect of the Westminster government's attempt to create stability within Northern Ireland. You need to be able to explain to the examiners how it was viewed by both Unionists and Nationalists.

## REACTIONS (II): MILITARY AND PARAMILITARIES

### Where was the IRA?

'I Ran Away' was the accusation most frequently levelled at the IRA because of its seeming failure to defend Catholics during the violence in 1969. Since the ending of its border campaign in 1962, the IRA seemed to have become more interested in **Marxism**. However, some of its younger members were unhappy with this inaction and wanted to take matters into their own hands, particularly the defence of Nationalist areas.

### Paramilitary Splits

In the final days of 1969 the IRA split into two parts:

- The Official IRA, which continued to focus on establishing a socialist Ireland. At the same time violence was still used until a ceasefire was called in May 1972. In 1974 the movement split again with the emergence of the Irish Republican Socialist Party and the militant Irish Nationalist Liberation Army (INLA).
- The Provisional IRA, which claimed for itself the traditional role of defender of the Nationalist community.

By Easter 1970 the new Provisional movement had declared its objectives; these were:

- civil rights
- defence of the Catholic population
- destroying the Stormont government
- removing 'British **imperialism**' from Ireland.

### The IRA and the British Army

The last aim in particular meant that sooner or later the IRA would come into conflict with the British army. Ironically up to this point the army had been more acceptable to Nationalists – as a source of protection – than it was to the

British troops search for hidden arms as they frisk suspects in Newry as a build up to expected disorder in the area in 1972.

SOURCE A

*Irish historian Professor J.J. Lee, writing in* Ireland 1912–1985: Politics and Society *(1989).*

If the army did nothing but wait, the IRA might gradually acquire the resources to mount an aggressive campaign against it. If it seized the initiative through 'arms searches' it would inevitably foster IRA recruitment among outraged Catholics whose homes it had vandalised ... The 'arms searches' came as a godsend to the IRA.

Unionists. However, although initially welcomed by the Catholic community as preferable to the distrusted RUC, the army was now finding itself in an impossible situation, trying to maintain order while a political solution was imposed (Source A).

As the IRA's campaign began to take off in earnest in the middle of 1970, the British army moved to protect itself from attack. In July it responded to the growing threat by imposing a 34-hour curfew on the Lower Falls area of Belfast while a house-to-house search for weapons was carried out. Although a number of weapons – as well as ammunition and explosives – were discovered, politically the search was a disaster. It damaged the army's previously good relationship with the Nationalist community and helped increase IRA membership (Source B below).

### Protestant Paramilitaries

The Protestant paramilitaries also wanted to see an end to the current Stormont regime, although for different reasons. They sought a return to the old days of Unionist domination. The UVF had grown and prospered against the background of NICRA's campaign and what was seen as O'Neill's **appeasement** of Catholics.

September 1971 saw the formation of the Ulster Defence Association (UDA) to fill a gap in the defences of the Loyalist community. The UDA viewed itself as a defensive grouping that would resist Republican aggression. With over 30,000 members within a year, it was viewed by the authorities as too large to ban.

### Faulkner Replaces Chichester Clark

The levels of violence and destruction shot up during the remaining months of 1970 and on into 1971. The Stormont government demanded a stronger response from Britain's new Conservative government; however little happened, as Westminster did not want to alienate the Nationalist community even more. In despair at London's inaction, Chichester Clark resigned as Prime Minister on 20 March, to be replaced by Brian Faulkner.

While Faulkner appeared to have a better grasp of the situation than his predecessor, he too was unable to reduce the levels of violence (Source C on this page) or the growth of the Provisional IRA. By the time the marching season arrived in July–August 1971, violence was at an all-time high, particularly in Derry/Londonderry. The government's response – in the face of few other options – was the reintroduction of internment: the arrest and detention without trial of those suspected of working for the destruction of the state.

### SOURCE B

*Irish historian Professor J.J. Lee, writing in* Ireland 1912–1985: Politics and Society *(1989).*

If there was a decisive turning point in Catholic attitudes to the army … it was probably the 34-hour curfew … 'In political terms it was a disaster', and Provisional influence increased enormously … Membership mushroomed from about 100 to about 800 in the second half of 1970.

### SOURCE C

*The views of historian Jonathan Bardon from his book* A History of Ulster *(1992).*

The most articulate of all Northern Ireland [Prime Ministers] Faulkner had an air of professionalism which seemed to promise that the government could curb the escalating violence.

### ACTIVITIES

1 Name the two groups the IRA split into in late 1969.
2 Explain how Nationalist attitudes towards the British army changed in the early years of the 1970s.
3 Why did the Provisional IRA emerge in 1970?
4 Explain why the army found itself in a no-win situation in 1970.
5 What impact did the arms searches have on Nationalist attitudes to the army and to the Stormont government?
6 Explain who benefited most from the arms searches of July 1970.
7 Explain the reasons for the growth in Loyalist paramilitary groups.

### EXTENSION ACTIVITY

Who was most responsible for the growth of the IRA?

### REVISION TIP

There are a lot of important issues in this section. You need to understand why the IRA split and how the aims of the two IRA groups differed. You will also need to be able to explain how and why Nationalist attitudes to the British army changed.

# INTERNMENT AND BLOODY SUNDAY

Brian Faulkner was unable to reduce the levels of violence and, facing strong Unionist pressure for firm action to be taken, he reintroduced the previously successful policy of internment – through Operation Demetrius – on 9 August 1971.

Internment failed spectacularly (Source A). The intelligence was entirely out of date. Not one of the 452 men arrested was a leading member of the Provisional IRA. Those really sought, Faulkner himself later admitted, had 'escaped the net'. Moreover, despite the high levels of Loyalist violence, all those targeted for internment were Nationalists or civil rights supporters. The first Loyalists were not interned until February 1973.

## Reactions to Internment

Unionists were happy with the introduction of internment at first although their support decreased when the policy failed to reduce levels of violence. They believed that it had worked in the past and saw it as essential in ending IRA violence, particularly against Protestant businesses. They also believed that internees could help with the location of IRA weapons, something that Faulkner believed did happen. Nationalists, however, saw internment as one-sided in its application and open to substantial abuse. As a result IRA membership increased. In addition, as the British Army was involved in the implementation of internment, its increasingly poor relations with the nationalist community deteriorated even further.

An orgy of violence and destruction followed the introduction of internment in 1971, leaving many dead and thousands from both communities homeless. From then until the end of the year, 143 people lost their lives through bombings and shootings. This was nearly five times as many as died in the first eight months of 1971. Nor was the violence all from the one side; the increasing Republican violence resulted in the establishment of the paramilitary UDA in September 1971. It was responsible for the bombing, on 4 December, of McGurk's Bar in Belfast. Fifteen people lost their lives in this attack, the worst single atrocity of the year.

Violence was not the only response to the introduction of internment. Along with other Nationalist and Republican Labour representatives, the SDLP called for people to withhold payment of rents and rates and for a withdrawal from local government in protest at the policy. Civil rights marches were also organised in protest at the introduction of internment, but the army's response also seemed to be hardening. A protest held at Magilligan Internment Camp on 22 January 1972 was met with baton charges and CS gas from the army.

## Bloody Sunday

In the aftermath of another march in Derry/Londonderry eight days later, a riot developed. In response, troops from the Parachute Regiment were ordered into the Bogside and shot 13 men dead. Thirteen more were injured, one of whom subsequently died of his wounds. An official inquiry headed by Lord Widgery failed to provide a satisfactory conclusion to the events of what became known as Bloody Sunday although it did establish that none of those who died had been carrying a weapon when shot (Source B).

## SOURCE A

*Historian Sabine Wichert writing in her book* Northern Ireland Since 1945 *(1991), (adapted).*

The political consequences of internment were serious; the Unionist government could be seen to have acted with the army against the Catholic population at large, breaking any remaining good will of Catholics towards unionism.

## SOURCE B

*An extract from the Widgery Report into the events of Bloody Sunday.*

There would have been no deaths in Londonderry … if those who organised the illegal march had not thereby created a highly dangerous situation in which a clash between demonstrators and the security forces was almost inevitable … At one end of the scale some soldiers showed a high degree of responsibility; at the other … firing bordered on the reckless … None of the deceased or wounded is proved to have been shot whilst handling a firearm or bomb.

Apart from the immediate outpourings of grief and anger, the events of 30 January 1972 had a number of results:

- Continued support for the government from the Unionist community, which, while regretting the deaths, saw the march as both illegal and provocative. Some in the Unionist community believed that the IRA was involved in the organisation of the march and that some of those killed had been armed.
- Given the belief that all of the victims were innocent and the Parachute Regiment attach unprovoked, Nationalist hostility to the state was increased. This was symbolised by rioting in nationalist areas and by the burning down of the British Embassy in Dublin.
- Britain faced international condemnation for the role it was playing in Northern Ireland.
- IRA membership grew – particularly in Derry/Londonderry – and its bombing campaign intensified (Source C on this page).

The resulting increase in violence and the government's failure to end it led to the formation in February 1972 of the Ulster Vanguard. Headed by William Craig, the former Stormont minister, Vanguard was described as a co-ordinating body for traditional Loyalist groups. One of its largest meetings, in Belfast's Ormeau Park, attracted 70,000 people, a powerful symbol of the levels of Unionist discontent.

By now Westminster had concluded the Northern Ireland government was no longer capable of maintaining law and order. It was also becoming increasingly difficult to justify unionist domination. After 50 years of devolved rule it looked as if the writing was on the wall for Stormont.

### SOURCE C

*An extract from the Irish Press commenting on the events of Bloody Sunday.*

If there was an able-bodied man with Republican sympathies within the Derry area who was not in the IRA before yesterday's butchery there will be none tonight.

The NICRA march which preceded the events of Bloody Sunday, 30 January 1972.

## ACTIVITIES

1 Describe two effects of the introduction of internment.
2 Describe two effects of Bloody Sunday.
3 Explain why internment was always likely to fail.
4 Explain the impact of internment on Northern Ireland's politics.
5 Explain why the events of Bloody Sunday had such an impact on Nationalist attitudes to the government and the army.
6 What impact did these events and the reactions have on the Unionist community?

## EXTENSION ACTIVITIES

1 Was internment the best possible solution in the circumstances?
2 What other policies might have been attempted instead of internment?

## REVISION TIP

The introduction of internment had a major impact on Northern Ireland politics. Are you able to understand why this was the case?

# STORMONT: SUSPENSION AND REACTIONS

## Faulkner Tries to Regain Control

Faulkner now demanded the power to rearm the RUC and re-establish the B Specials. Conservative Prime Minister Edward Heath responded by demanding control of law and order and justice; however Faulkner refused. On 22 March 1972 senior members of the Stormont cabinet travelled to London for what they believed would be top-level talks with the British government about the situation in Northern Ireland. Once there however, Heath informed them that certain changes were being proposed, namely:

- the transfer of security control to Westminster
- the holding of a referendum on the future of the border
- the gradual removal of internment
- the appointment of a Secretary of State for Northern Ireland
- the holding of talks with other parties in Northern Ireland in an attempt to establish a 'community government'.

## The Introduction of Direct Rule

After lengthy negotiations the entire Northern Ireland government resigned, unable to accept the loss of control over security policy (Source A). On 24 March Heath responded by suspending Stormont for a year (later extended) and introducing **direct rule** (Source B). From now on Northern Ireland was to be governed directly by the British government in London, with a team of ministers, led by a **Secretary of State**, taking over the functions of the Stormont cabinet. William Whitelaw was appointed as the North's first Secretary of State.

## Reactions to the End of Stormont

Reactions to the end of 50 years of local government were predictable. Most Unionists were horrified at the removal of Stormont, which they had seen as a barrier against a united Ireland. The last hours of the Parliament were played out on 28 March before a crowd estimated at 100,000. This came in the midst of a series of massive strikes and shutdowns, organised by Ulster Vanguard in protest at the suspension. The strikes were successful at shutting down much of life in Northern Ireland for a two-day period, but they were unable to open Stormont up again. There was also an increase in support for loyalist paramilitaries and a spate of sectarian killings, particularly in Belfast. Meanwhile, support for the DUP and other strongly unionist parties also increased in the aftermath of the introduction of direct rule.

Few tears were shed for Stormont on the Nationalist side, with the SDLP and the Dublin government welcoming the chances for a new beginning. The IRA, although it had achieved one of its aims, stated its opposition to direct rule and announced its determination to continue its struggle to achieve a united Ireland. NICRA stated that its campaign for civil rights would continue.

William Whitelaw (1918–99), Secretary of State for Northern Ireland from 1972 to 1973.

## 1972: The Blackest Year

Despite the introduction of internment and direct rule and the existence of a two-week IRA ceasefire (Source C on this page), 1972 turned out to be the worst year of the Troubles. By the end of the year, 496 people had lost their lives in a series of appalling atrocities including:

- 21 July when the IRA detonated 20 bombs around Belfast in just over one hour. Nine civilians died on a day that became known as Bloody Friday.
- 31 July when, without warning, an IRA bomb exploded in the village of Claudy in Co. Derry/Londonderry. In total nine civilians lost their lives.

The British government responded on 31 July with Operation Motorman. This aimed to allow the army and police to reclaim control of the paramilitary-controlled **no-go areas**, which had sprung up in Belfast, Derry/Londonderry and elsewhere. The success of this operation encouraged the British government to make moves towards a political settlement and, by late 1972, it was holding discussions aimed at establishing a government which could enjoy cross-community support.

### SOURCE A

*An extract from Brian Faulkner's letter of resignation.*

[The transfer of security powers to London] is not justifiable and cannot be supported or accepted by us. It would wholly undermine the powers, authority and standing of this government.

### SOURCE B

*Edward Heath speaking on 24 March 1972.*

The United Kingdom government [believes] that the transfer of [law and order] to Westminster is [vital] for progress in finding a political solution in Northern Ireland. The Northern Ireland government's decision therefore leaves us with no alternative to assuming full and direct responsibility for the administration of Northern Ireland until a political solution to the problems of the province can be worked out.

### SOURCE C

*The views of historian Jonathan Bardon from his book* A History of Ulster *(1992).*

The imposition of direct rule failed to stem the violence and year after year the population endured a wretched cycle of bombings, assassinations and shootings.

The aftermath of one of the bombs detonated on Bloody Friday, 21 July 1972.

## ACTIVITIES

1  Describe what direct rule was.
2  Describe how Unionists and Nationalists reacted differently to the suspension of the Stormont Parliament.
3  Explain the immediate reasons for the suspension of Stormont and the introduction of direct rule.
4  Compare and contrast the attitudes of the British and Northern Irish Prime Ministers (Sources A and B, page 126) to the issue of who should control law and order.
5  Explain how Unionists and Nationalists reacted to the suspension of Stormont. Why were their reactions so different?

## EXTENSION ACTIVITY

Could the British government have considered any other alternatives to the introduction of direct rule?

## REVISION TIP

It is important that you are able to explain why the British government decided to end the Stormont Parliament. You also need to be able to tell the examiner the differences in the Nationalist and Unionist reactions to the suspension.

## Practice Question (Higher)

**Higher**

1 (a) (i) Study Source A (Source B on page 102).

Using Source A, and your own knowledge, describe O'Neill's plans to improve the economy of Northern Ireland. [6]

(ii) Study Source B (the photo on page 108).

Using Source B, and your own knowledge, explain the main demands of the Northern Ireland Civil Rights Association (NICRA). [9]

(iii) Study Source C (the photo on page 121).

Source C suggests that British troops ended up carrying out policing duties in Northern Ireland.

Do you agree with the view that the only reason for the introduction of British troops to Northern Ireland was to do the job of the RUC?

Explain your answer using Source C and your own knowledge. [12]

(b) In what ways did the people of Northern Ireland react to the Hunger Strikes of 1980 and 1981? [6]

(c) In this question 5 additional marks are available for your use of spelling, punctuation and grammar.

How effective was internment in dealing with the political situation in Northern Ireland in the 1970s? [17] and [SPaG 5]

# THE SEARCH FOR A SOLUTION

## A NEW POLITICAL SYSTEM

The year 1973 began as 1972 had ended, with increased levels of violence. Constant Loyalist violence led to the internment in early February. Clearly some form of political progress was crucial but it was not until 20 March 1973 that the British government published its proposals for the future of Northern Ireland.

The plans proposed a new law-making assembly (parliament) elected by proportional representation, but not given control over security or justice. There would also be an executive or government. For the plan to work the British insisted on two other conditions:

- the sharing of power between Catholics and Protestants
- the formal recognition of an 'Irish dimension' – a role for the Republic of Ireland – through the creation of a Council of Ireland, allowing for the discussion of interests common to Belfast, Dublin and London.

### Early Problems

While Nationalist reactions were broadly supportive, Unionism was divided in its reaction to the plans. While some of the OUP remained loyal to Brian Faulkner (who was supporting Secretary of State William Whitelaw's plans) other Unionists – the remainder of the OUP, the DUP and the new Vanguard Unionist Progressive Party (set up by William Craig to oppose power sharing) – joined together to form the United Ulster Unionist Council (UUUC) to oppose the plans. Apart from their opposition to the 'Irish dimension', they saw the proposals as undemocratic and believed that power should not be shared with those disloyal to the Union.

The extent of these splits became clear when the results of the assembly elections were announced at the end of June 1973. The results (see Table 3.1) revealed that the number of anti-power-sharing Unionists elected was greater than the number of Unionists elected who supported power sharing (Source A).

It was clear that the prospects for the success of the new venture were already far from certain (Source B).

### SOURCE A

*Dr Duncan Morrow writing in* Northern Ireland Politics *(1996).*

For Unionists, every attempt to bring anti-Unionists into power, whether in the form of Northern Irish Nationalists or through the formal involvement of the Republic of Ireland, diluted and threatened the Union itself.

### SOURCE B

*Dr Duncan Morrow writing in* Northern Ireland Politics *(1996).*

While there was support in all places for some of the proposals, it was enormously difficult to maintain cross-community support for the package as a whole.

| Party | Pro- or anti-power sharing | Percentage of vote | Number of seats won |
|-------|----------------------------|--------------------|---------------------|
| Faulkner Unionists | Pro | 29.3 | 24 |
| UUUC Unionists | Anti | 32.1 | 26 |
| SDLP | Pro | 22.1 | 19 |
| APNI | Pro | 9.2 | 8 |
| Northern Ireland Labour Party (NILP) | Pro | 2.6 | 1 |

**Table 3.1** Assembly election results

## An Executive is Formed

Nearly five months later, on 21 November 1973, Whitelaw announced that the membership of a power-sharing executive had been agreed. There would be 11 ministries, all of which would go to supporters of power sharing. Six were to be held by Unionists, four by the SDLP and one by the Alliance Party. There would also be four non-voting members of the executive: two SDLP, one Unionist and one Alliance. The OUP's Brian Faulkner would head the executive while the SDLP's Gerry Fitt would be his deputy. See Table 3.2 for the names and positions of the other ministers.

Two of the three elements of the new system were now in place. All that remained was to reach agreement on the form and powers of the Council of Ireland.

| Name | Party | Voting/non-voting member | Portfolio |
|------|-------|--------------------------|-----------|
| Herbie Kirk | OUP | Voting member | Finance |
| Roy Bradford | OUP | Voting member | Environment |
| Basil McIvor | OUP | Voting member | Education |
| Leslie Morrell | OUP | Voting member | Agriculture |
| John Baxter | OUP | Voting member | Information |
| Lloyd Hall-Thompson | OUP | Non-voting member | Chief Whip |
| John Hume | SDLP | Voting member | Commerce |
| Austin Currie | SDLP | Voting member | Housing, Development and Local Government |
| Paddy Devlin | SDLP | Voting member | Social Security |
| Ivan Cooper | SDLP | Non-voting member | Community Relations |
| Eddie McGrady | SDLP | Non-voting member | Planning and Co-ordination |
| Oliver Napier | APNI | Voting member | Office of Law Reform |
| Bob Cooper | APNI | Non-voting member | Manpower Services |

**Table 3.2** Ministers in the new assembly

### ACTIVITIES

1 Explain who won the elections to the new power-sharing assembly.
2 Name the two main leaders of the new power-sharing system.
3 Explain how the proposed political system was going to work.
4 What were the main weaknesses in the new proposals?
5 What were the attitudes of Northern Ireland's voters to the British government's proposals? Use the information in the text and in Table 3.1 to help you with your answer.

### EXTENSION ACTIVITIES

1 How democratic was the power-sharing system devised by Whitelaw?
2 Was it a mistake to withhold control over law and order from the new system?

### REVISION TIP

The most important thing that you need to understand about the power-sharing assembly is the reaction of Unionist voters to it and how this weakened its chances of success.

## SUNNINGDALE

The discussions about the Council of Ireland began on 6 December 1973 at Sunningdale in Berkshire. The meeting brought together a powerful assortment of politicians from Britain, Ireland and Northern Ireland as Table 3.3 shows.

| Representing | Politicians | Position |
|---|---|---|
| UK | Edward Heath<br>Francis Pym | Prime Minister<br>Secretary of State |
| Republic of Ireland | Liam Cosgrave<br>Garret FitzGerald | *Taoiseach*<br>Foreign Minister |
| OUP | Brian Faulkner | Chief Executive Designate |
| SDLP | Gerry Fitt | Deputy Chief Executive Designate |
| Alliance | Oliver Napier | Office of Law Reform |

Table 3.3 The Sunningdale participants

There were, however, no anti-power-sharing politicians present; the Irish government and other local parties had argued that they would disrupt the negotiations. At one stage Rev. Ian Paisley (DUP leader) and William Craig (Vanguard Unionist Progressive Party leader) were asked to attend but only to give their views. Unsurprisingly this offer was rejected.

### Terms of the Agreement

After several days of negotiations, agreement between the parties was finally secured on 9 December. The Sunningdale Agreement contained the following elements:

- London agreed not to oppose Irish unification if a majority of the Northern Ireland population desired it.
- Dublin accepted that Irish unity could only ever be achieved peacefully and with the consent of the majority of the people of the North.
- A Council of Ministers with 14 members was to be established. The powers were vague but it was agreed it would help with the development of co-operation between North and South and would eventually be given decision-making powers (Source A).

The discussions at Sunningdale, December 1973.

*Historian Sabine Wichert writing in her book* Northern Ireland Since 1945 *(1991).*

The insistence on the Irish dimension ruined whatever chance Faulkner had of persuading even a majority of Official Unionists to accept the executive as a genuine attempt to achieve a lasting settlement in the North.

- A 60-member Consultative Assembly would be elected by the Dáil and the assembly at some future date.
- Also at some future date control over internal security issues would be returned to the assembly at Stormont.
- Approval of the decisions made at Sunningdale was to take place at a future conference.

## Problems for the Future

On the surface the agreement looked promising; the problem was, however, that the Unionist and Nationalist representatives involved believed that they had agreed to something entirely different (Source B):

- The SDLP saw the agreement as paving the way towards the creation of closer ties between North and South.
- Faulkner saw it as a mere token, which he had agreed to as a means of getting Dublin to accept the position of Northern Ireland as part of the UK.

**SOURCE B**

*Comment by Paul Bew and Gordon Gillespie from* Northern Ireland, A Chronology of the Troubles *(1993) (adapted).*

The flaw in the Sunningdale Agreement was that those involved in it had completely different views of what it involved. Faulkner saw the Council of Ireland as an advisory body. Some members of the SDLP had a different opinion of what the Council of Ireland would mean. The British government failed to define clearly the areas which the Council of Ireland would control and which it would not.

When these different interpretations became clear they would have a significant impact on the chances of success for power sharing. Republicans were also lukewarm in their response, seeing the new system as proposing substantially less than what they sought.

In the shorter term, however, Faulkner faced more serious problems. On 10 December 1973 Loyalist paramilitaries announced the formation of an Ulster Army Council to resist any significant 'Irish dimension'. Nor did the IRA seem any more satisfied, setting off a series of bombs in London in the week before Christmas. It seemed as if the power-sharing experiment was facing a very uncertain future as the date for the handover of power approached.

## ACTIVITIES

1 Explain why the main Northern Ireland politicians went to Sunningdale in December 1973.
2 Name two of the things agreed at the Sunningdale meeting.
3 Why were anti-power-sharing Unionists excluded from the Sunningdale negotiations?
4 Construct a spider diagram showing the main points agreed at Sunningdale.
5 What were the main problems with what had been agreed at Sunningdale?
6 How did the paramilitaries react to the Sunningdale Agreement?

## EXTENSION ACTIVITIES

1 Was Sunningdale a good idea given the results of the election to the power-sharing assembly?
2 Would it have been better to invite all of Northern Ireland's parties to the Sunningdale negotiations?

## REVISION TIP

Sunningdale was unlikely to work because those involved had different understandings as to what they had agreed. You will need to be able to explain how and why this was the case.

# THE EXECUTIVE IN OPERATION

## A House of Cards?

The executive took up office on 1 January 1974 but almost immediately its future was plunged into doubt (Source A). A meeting of the OUP's ruling body, the Ulster Unionist Council, on 4 January voted to reject the Sunningdale Agreement (Source B). Faulkner immediately resigned as party leader and was replaced by Harry West. However, Faulkner retained the support of 19 of the 21 OUP Assembly members and so was able to remain as Chief Executive of the power-sharing executive. It was clear, however, that he was isolated within Unionism.

Unfortunately for the new system events across the water provided further problems. A general election for the Westminster Parliament was called for 28 February. A struggle for the hearts and minds of Unionist voters followed between the pro-Faulkner candidates and the anti-Sunningdale UUUC.

### SOURCE A

*Historian Sabine Wichert writing in her book* Northern Ireland Since 1945 *(1991).*

When the new power-sharing executive took office ... it looked on the surface as if ... the Protestants appeared to have accepted a compromise, the Catholics seemed to have voted for constitutional politics, violence had declined considerably ... and there appeared to be a prospect of working out a political solution.

Almost a third of the electorate, however, had given its vote to non-Faulknerite unionism ... Neither Protestant or Catholic paramilitaries had been nor could be defeated, and new fuel was added to the sectarian smouldering by the introduction of the 'Irish dimension', which enraged Loyalists but did not appease extremist Nationalists.

Members of the power-sharing executive meeting *Taoiseach* Liam Cosgrave (1920–) (third from left) and other members of the Irish government.

**SOURCE B**

*The judgement of historian Patrick Buckland from
A History of Northern Ireland (1989).*

The insistence on the Irish dimension ruined
whatever chance Faulkner had of persuading
a majority even of Official Unionists to accept
the executive as a genuine attempt to achieve a
lasting settlement in the North.

**SOURCE C**

*The views of historian Jonathan Bardon from his
book A History of Ulster (1992).*

The February election was in effect a referendum
on the Sunningdale Agreement, now decisively
rejected by 51 per cent of the electorate. It was
quite clear that the assembly, where the executive
could still command a majority, no longer reflected
the wishes of most people in Northern Ireland.

## The 1974 Westminster Election: Results and Impact

The outcome was almost a landslide for the
UUUC. With 80 per cent of the vote, 11 of the
12 Northern Ireland constituencies were won by
anti-Sunningdale candidates. The only exception
was Gerry Fitt who retained his West Belfast seat
for the SDLP. Closer examination of the results
revealed that pro-agreement Unionists won just
over 94,000 votes compared to just under 367,000
for their UUUC opponents (Source C). Naturally
enough there were calls from the UUUC for new
assembly elections but none took place.

The UUUC had portrayed the election as a
referendum on the Sunningdale Agreement. The
results clearly indicated that a majority of the
population of the province were opposed to what
had been agreed. It could justifiably be argued that
the assembly was no longer a true reflection of
public opinion in the North.

The election also resulted in a change in
government in London with Labour returning to
power under Harold Wilson. In local terms
Merlyn Rees replaced Francis Pym (who had
replaced William Whitelaw) as Secretary of State,
but a small Labour majority in Westminster meant
that he was forced to spend more time in London
than was good for the already ailing system.

These political developments took place against
a background of continuing violence coupled
with regular public protests against the
Sunningdale Agreement. Although the British
government continued to insist that there was no
alternative to the agreement, it was clear that
within Unionism there was a determination that
the system would fail. Since nothing else
attempted seemed to have worked, the weapon
chosen to destroy Sunningdale would be a massive
strike.

### ACTIVITIES

1 Explain the reasons for the resignation of Brian
   Faulkner as leader of the OUP in January 1974.
2 What did the results of the 1974 general
   election to the Westminster Parliament show?
3 What were the positive points and negative
   points of the situation the executive found
   itself in at the start of January 1974?
4 Using the information in the text explain what
   happened in January and February 1974 that
   reduced the chances of the assembly and
   executive working.
5 Why did the UUUC want new elections to be
   held for the power-sharing assembly?

### EXTENSION ACTIVITIES

1 How did the British general election of February
   1974 make things worse in Northern Ireland?
2 Why was the existence within Northern Ireland
   of a majority in favour of power sharing not
   enough for the success of the system?

### REVISION TIP

You need to understand and be able to explain to
the examiner how and why Faulkner's position was
so weak by the time the Ulster Workers' Council
strike began.

# THE STRIKE

## The Shutdown Begins

On the evening of Tuesday 14 May 1974, shortly after the assembly had voted to continue its support for the Sunningdale Agreement, a general strike began. The strike was organised by the Ulster Workers' Council (UWC), a group of Protestant trade unionists who had gained substantial amounts of political and paramilitary support. Its aim was to show the levels of Unionist opposition to the Sunningdale Agreement.

Initially support for the strike was limited, but UDA intimidation and improved co-ordination by the UWC ensured that by the end of the week much of Northern Ireland had come to a standstill. Industries had closed down, there were regular electricity blackouts, fuel supplies were strictly controlled and there were hundreds of roadblocks – making travel almost impossible. Attempts by some of Northern Ireland's trade unions to organise a back-to-work demonstration on 21 May met with little support – only 200 people turned up.

The tension in the province was further heightened by the news on 17 May that car bombs, believed to have been planted by Loyalists, in Dublin and Monaghan, had claimed 27 lives (five more of the injured later died of their wounds). This was the worst single day's death toll during the entire period of the Troubles.

British troops keeping a petrol station open during the UWC strike.

## Wilson's Fatal Intervention

Although there were by now 17,500 soldiers in the province, the army was hesitant about taking on the strikers, arguing that the strike was political and not a terrorist action. The British Prime Minister however, was losing patience with the situation and appeared on television on 25 May to denounce the strike and call its organisers 'spongers' (Source B on page 136). This speech infuriated Unionists and more than anything else, ensured that the strike continued (Source A).

Although the British government was not prepared to use the army to break the strike, it was prepared to use it to maintain fuel supplies. When the army was ordered in to take over fuel supplies the UWC ordered a total shutdown across Northern Ireland. Seeing no obvious solution and with the British and SDLP still refusing to negotiate with the UWC, Faulkner resigned as Chief Executive on 28 May (Source C on page 136). The other Unionist members of the executive resigned with him thus ending power sharing. Having achieved its goal, the UWC ended the strike on 29 May. The assembly was suspended on 30 May and, after 5 months absence, direct rule was reintroduced.

It is impossible to know if power-sharing could have worked if it had been given more time to establish firm roots. It seems clear that many of those involved in the power-sharing initiative were not as fully committed to its success as was needed. This lack of commitment – coupled with intense opposition from some quarters – was enough to ensure the failure of this attempted solution – and the continuation of political unrest.

### SOURCE A

*The views of historian Jonathan Bardon from his book* A History of Ulster *(1992).*

[Wilson's] speech rallied Protestant feeling behind the strikers to such an extent that Glenn Barr [UWC chairman] said they thought of making Wilson an honorary member of the UWC.

# DEVELOPMENTS 1975–80

During the rest of the 1970s and the early years of the 1980s successive British governments attempted, without success, to solve the Northern Ireland problem. At the same time, although the levels of violence lessened due to improved security measures, the IRA launched a campaign of violence in Britain, exploding bombs in cities such as Guildford and Birmingham.

## New Security Policies

Following the collapse of the power-sharing executive, the Secretary of State Merlyn Rees and his successor Roy Mason pursued policies of Ulsterisation and criminalisation. The former involved reducing the strength of the army in Northern Ireland while increasing the size of the RUC and UDR. The latter saw the end of **special category status** for those convicted of terrorist offences.

Introduced in 1972, special category status had allowed those who claimed that they had broken the law for political reasons to live as prisoners of war (POWs). Its removal meant that those convicted after March 1976 would be treated in the same way as other criminals. They would be housed in a new prison consisting of H-shaped blocks, which had been built at the Maze outside Belfast.

Although the numbers of deaths as a result of violence began to decrease in the latter years of the 1970s, there were still some appalling incidents such as the IRA firebombing of the La Mon House Hotel outside Belfast, resulting in the deaths of 12 people.

The H blocks.

## SOURCE A

*Pope John Paul II speaking at Drogheda, 30 September 1979.*

To all of you who are listening, I say: do not believe in violence, do not support violence ... On my knees I beg of you to turn away from the paths of violence and to return to the ways of peace. You may claim to seek justice ... But violence only delays the day of justice. Violence destroys the work of justice.

## SOURCE B

*The IRA's response to Pope John Paul II's address at Drogheda, 2 October 1979.*

Force is by far the only means of removing the evil of the British presence in Ireland ... we know also that upon victory, the [Catholic] Church would have no difficulty in recognising us.

## ACTIVITIES

1 Describe two new policies introduced by the British government in the late 1970s.
2 Why did the IRA begin a campaign of violence in Britain?
3 Explain the policies of Ulsterisation and criminalisation.

## EXTENSION ACTIVITY

1 How did the approach of the British government to the Northern Ireland question change in the second half of the 1970s?

## REVISION TIP

The new security policies introduced in the late 1970s would prove important later on. Make sure you know what these policies were.

## THE HUNGER STRIKES

### The 1980 Hunger Strike

IRA prisoners – who saw themselves as soldiers fighting for Ireland's freedom – detested the policy of criminalisation. From the time of the ending of special category status in 1976 the scene was set for a confrontation between prisoners and the British government. That confrontation was to reach its climax with the 1981 hunger strikes.

The initial reaction of Republican prisoners to the removal of special category status was to refuse to wear prison clothes, instead covering themselves with blankets. This blanket protest was followed in 1978 by the dirty protest, when prisoners smeared their cell walls with excrement rather than having to slop out. By late 1980 over 340 of the 837 Republican prisoners were involved in the protest.

Public demonstrations in support of the protests met with little success. Even a series of attacks on prison warders proved ineffective as the new Conservative Secretary of State, Humphrey Atkins, refused to compromise with the prisoners. Therefore, in late 1980, the IRA began a group hunger strike as a last method of achieving their demands. This historically successful tactic was called off in December, however, without anything having been achieved although the prisoners had believed that they had agreed a deal on the wearing of their own clothes.

## The 1981 Hunger Strike

On 1 March 1981 a second hunger strike began, led by Bobby Sands, the IRA inmates' Officer Commanding. Unlike the previous strike, this time prisoners would join the protest at intervals. This would make the strike last longer and so maximise its impact. However, although the hunger strike gained huge publicity and the sympathy of many in the nationalist community, it did not change government policy (Source A). Therefore, when Frank Maguire, the Independent MP for Fermanagh–South Tyrone died, Republicans saw their chance to increase pressure on the British and put Sands up as a candidate. On the fortieth day of his strike Sands, standing as an anti-H-block candidate, was elected to Westminster.

### SOURCE A

*Margaret Thatcher speaking about the hunger strikes in the House of Commons on 20 November 1980.*

Let me make one point about the hunger strike in the Maze Prison ... There can be no political justification for murder or any other crime. The government will never concede political status to the hunger strikers.

The funeral of Bobby Sands, 7 May 1981.

Despite huge amounts of international pressure on both sides, neither side would compromise and on 5 May Sands died. His funeral was attended by an estimated 100,000 mourners. The strike continued until 3 October 1981 by which time nine other prisoners had died. In the same period 61 people died as a result of the violence that erupted in reaction to the deaths inside the prison.

## Concessions Granted

No concessions were made during the hunger strike. However, within a week of the strike's end James Prior, the new Secretary of State, announced that a number of the concessions that the prisoners had sought would be granted. These included:

- Prisoners would be allowed to wear their own clothes at all times.
- The 50 per cent reduction in length of sentence lost by those involved in protests would be restored.
- More prison visits would be permitted.
- More association among prisoners would be allowed.

These concessions resulted in the protests in favour of special category status all but ending by late October 1981.

## Aftermath

Politically this was a difficult time for the British government. In the aftermath of the hunger strikes new problems were emerging:

- Increased Nationalist alienation from the state, resulting from what they saw as Prime Minister Margaret Thatcher's heavy-handed approach to the hunger strikers whose cause they saw as reasonable (Source B).
- Rising support for Republicans.
- Unionists, while glad that the government had not given into the demands of the hunger strikers, who they saw as murderers and criminals, were increasingly voicing their anxieties at the growth in support for the IRA (as demonstrated by the huge numbers attending the funerals of Bobby Sands and other hunger-strikers) and seeming weaknesses of the province's security provisions which allowed IRA violence to continue (Source C).
- The Irish government was pushing for the introduction of a new political initiative to end the Troubles.

## SOURCE B

*Irish historian Professor J.J. Lee, writing in* Ireland 1912–1985: Politics and Society *(1989).*

The British handling of the whole H-block situation was inept … the hunger strike and the authorities' response did more to unite Catholic opinion than any other single event since internment in 1971 or Bloody Sunday in 1972.

## SOURCE C

*Politics lecturer Paul Dixon writing in* Northern Ireland, The Politics of War and Peace *(2001).*

Unionists tended to interpret the election of Sands and the turnout at his funeral as implying widespread Catholic support for terrorists who had murdered members of their community.

## ACTIVITIES

1 Explain why IRA prisoners began a hunger strike in March 1981.
2 Describe two concessions made by the British government after the hunger strike ended.
3 Explain why the IRA prisoners began their campaigns of protest in 1976. How did their tactics develop over the next few years?
4 Why was the British government not prepared to concede special category status to the prisoners again?
5 Using the information in the text explain the significance of Sands' victory in the Fermanagh–South Tyrone by-election.
6 Was the hunger strike a success or a failure for the Republican movement? Explain your answer.
7 Explain the attitude of the Unionist community to these events.
8 Explain the new problems emerging in the aftermath of the hunger strike.

## EXTENSION ACTIVITY

Why do you think the British government only granted most of the IRA prisoners' demands after the hunger strike ended?

## REVISION TIP

Make sure that you understand and can explain why the hunger strike began and what it achieved.

## THE RISE OF SINN FÉIN

Sands' victory in Fermanagh–South Tyrone was hugely significant. It showed the Republican movement that there was much to gain from involvement in the political process at a time when the British government was enjoying increasing success in its undercover campaign against Republicans. That Sands' victory was not a fluke was proved when his election agent, Owen Carron, won the seat at the **by-election** following Sands' death.

The official adoption of this policy came at the 1981 Sinn Féin *Ard Fheis*. At this the delegates approved the movement's plan of contesting elections while also continuing to use extra-constitutional methods to achieve its aims (Source A below).

## SOURCE A

*Danny Morrison, speaking at the Sinn Féin Ard Fheis, 31 October 1981.*

Who here really believes we can win the war through the ballot box? But will anyone here object if, with a ballot box in one hand and the Armalite in the other, we take power in Ireland?

The results of following elections clearly revealed the growth in support for Sinn Féin among Nationalist voters. The party was soon winning an increasing number of local council seats. Then in the June 1983 Westminster general election the party's President, Gerry Adams, defeated Gerry Fitt for the West Belfast seat. The British government was growing increasingly concerned that Sinn Féin might even replace the SDLP as the main Nationalist party in the province. This prospect also worried the SDLP (Source B). The party, led since 1979 by John Hume, was looking more and more to Dublin for support.

Now with both governments co-operating ever more closely in the face of Sinn Féin's growth, there was the possibility that the SDLP might again have a significant input into the future direction of the province.

## SOURCE B

*Irish historian Professor J.J. Lee, writing in* Ireland 1912–1985: Politics and Society *(1989).*

It was not so much that Sinn Féin secured the allegiance of previous SDLP voters, but that it mobilised previous non-voters and first-time young voters, who saw no prospect of any sort of fulfilling life within the Northern Ireland they knew.

At the same time the levels of violence – while lower than the 1970s – still gave considerable cause for concern. On 6 December 1982 17 people, 11 of whom were soldiers, died when an INLA bomb exploded in Ballykelly. The INLA had emerged in 1975 from a split in the Official IRA (see page 120).

Gerry Adams (1948–)

## ACTIVITIES

1 Explain the new policy introduced by Sinn Féin in 1981.
2 Explain why Sinn Féin decided to become involved in the political process.
3 Explain the reasons for the growth in support for Sinn Féin in the 1982 and 1983 elections.
4 How did the SDLP react to the political growth of the Republican movement?

## EXTENSION ACTIVITIES

1 Why did the SDLP seem to be in trouble by the early 1980s?
2 What would Sinn Féin have seen as the advantages of following the 'ballot box and Armalite' strategy?

## REVISION TIP

You need to be able to explain how and why Nationalist politics began to change in the aftermath of the 1981 hunger strike.

# THE ANGLO-IRISH AGREEMENT (I): TERMS

## Origins of the Agreement

Faced with such violence and growing support for Sinn Féin, the British and Irish governments decided to work more closely together. The outcome was the Anglo-Irish Agreement which was signed by Thatcher and *Taoiseach* Garrett FitzGerald on 15 November 1985. Historians have provided different reasons as to why it was signed:

- Constitutional Nationalists in Ireland and the British government were afraid that Sinn Féin might overtake the SDLP and become the principal Nationalist party in the North. This would make the chances of agreement within the North more difficult, could worsen the security situation and could threaten the stability of Ireland.
- Margaret Thatcher's main reason for signing the Anglo-Irish Agreement was security. The IRA's attempt to kill her at the 1984 Conservative Party Conference in Brighton has brought the problem particularly into focus. Thatcher realised that unless she dealt with Nationalist alienation in Northern Ireland, she would not be able to improve the security situation.
- FitzGerald hoped that reduced Nationalist alienation and reform of the security forces in Northern Ireland would undermine the minority's toleration of the IRA.

What was different from earlier attempted solutions, however, was that no assembly or executive were established; it was purely an agreement between the two governments. In this way, it was reasoned, institutions that did not exist could not be pulled down.

## What was Agreed?

The key terms of the agreement were:

- The establishment of an intergovernmental conference, headed by the Secretary of State and the Irish Foreign Minister. This would deal with issues such as security, legal matters, political questions and improving cross-border co-operation.
- A permanent **secretariat** made up of northern and southern civil servants would provide administrative support to the conference.
- Devolution would only occur if there was agreement on the sharing of power.

Put simply, the agreement clearly recognised that the Republic had a role to play in the government of the North (Source A). At the same time the Republic accepted that a united Ireland was a long-term goal that would only happen with a majority agreement (Source B below). Britain was

Garrett FitzGerald (1926–2011) shakes hands with Margaret Thatcher (1925–2013) following the signing of the Anglo-Irish Agreement.

hoping that the agreement would lead to better security and co-operation while Dublin hoped to persuade Nationalists to accept the Northern Ireland state. Dublin believed that if this happened, support for Sinn Féin would collapse.

### SOURCE A

*The views of historian Jonathan Bardon from his book* A History of Ulster *(1992) (adapted).*

There was no doubting the historic importance of the agreement. For the first time since the partition of 1920–1 a Westminster government had clearly recognised that the Republic had a role to play in the governing of Northern Ireland.

### SOURCE B

*Historian Sabine Wichert writing in her book* Northern Ireland Since 1945 *(1991).*

In political terms the Anglo-Irish Agreement was an extraordinary achievement for Britain. Without conceding anything except the obvious, namely that the Republic's government had an interest in the North, the British government had enrolled Dublin's support for its policy in the province.

### ACTIVITIES

1 Give two reasons for the signing of the Anglo-Irish Agreement.
2 Name three terms of the Anglo-Irish Agreement.
3 Explain the various reasons provided for the signing of the Anglo-Irish Agreement.
4 What were the main terms of the Anglo-Irish Agreement?
5 Why would it be harder for Unionists to destroy the Anglo-Irish Agreement than it had been to destroy the 1974 power-sharing executive?

### EXTENSION ACTIVITY

Who had most to be satisfied about after the signing of the Anglo-Irish Agreement?

### REVISION TIP

It is essential that you are able to explain to the examiner what the main parts of the Anglo-Irish Agreement were.

## THE ANGLO-IRISH AGREEMENT (II): REACTIONS

While the agreement passed through both Westminster and the Dáil without any real problems, it met with a variety of reactions within Ireland, north and south.

### Northern Ireland

#### Unionists

Unionists of all shades and opinions were appalled by the agreement (Source A). They felt that they had been abandoned by their own government and believed that they were now in a process that would eventually result in a united Ireland.

What annoyed them the most however was the fact that they had been kept in the dark during the negotiations leading up to the agreement while it looked as if the SDLP had been at least consulted in the process. Only the Alliance Party did not condemn the agreement outright.

---

**SOURCE A**

*Rev. Ian Paisley speaking in his church in the aftermath of the Anglo-Irish Agreement.*

We pray this night that thou wouldst deal with the Prime Minister of our country … O God, in wrath take vengeance upon this wicked, treacherous lying woman: take vengeance upon her O Lord, and grant that we shall see a demonstration of thy power.

---

#### Nationalists

The SDLP had been given more of a role in the creation of the agreement than any other party in the North. It was therefore able to view the accord as an opportunity to create a better way of life for all those living in the province (Source B).

#### Republicans

Sinn Féin condemned the agreement, arguing that rather than bringing a united Ireland closer, it actually made the division of Ireland more permanent since in the agreement the Irish government was recognising the existence of Northern Ireland (Source C) and accepting that a united Ireland was a long-term aim that would only happen with the consent of a majority in Northern Ireland.

---

**SOURCE B**

*John Hume, speaking in the House of Commons on 26 November 1985.*

This is the first time that we have had a real framework within which to address the problem … There is no road towards a solution to this problem that does not contain risks. The road that has been chosen by both governments is the road of maximum consensus and is, therefore, the road of minimum risk.

---

**SOURCE C**

*Gerry Adams, speaking on 16 November 1985.*

This deal does not go anywhere near bringing peace to this part of Ireland. On the contrary it reinforces partition because Dublin is recognising Northern Ireland.

---

### Republic of Ireland

While the agreement was clearly acceptable to the Fine Gael and Labour parties that made up the Republic's **coalition** government, the Fianna Fáil opposition party led by Charles Haughey condemned it. Like Sinn Féin, Fianna Fáil was dismayed at the recognition being given by Dublin to Britain's right to be in Northern Ireland. A prominent Irish Labour Party Senator, Mary Robinson, resigned from her party because the

Mary Robinson (1944–).

agreement was unacceptable to the Unionist community (Source D).

## SOURCE D

*The views of Irish Labour Party Senator Mary Robinson.*

I do not believe that [the agreement] can achieve its objective of securing peace and stability within Northern Ireland or on the island as a whole.

## Britain

The agreement enjoyed overwhelming cross-party support at Westminster but individual members of the British Parliament were not so happy. Ian Gow, the Prime Minister's former Parliamentary Private Secretary and now a Treasury Minister, resigned from his position in the government. He argued that the agreement was won by violence and would make the situation in the province worse rather than better (Source E).

## SOURCE E

*Conservative MP Ian Gow reflecting on the agreement.*

The involvement of a foreign power in a consultative role in the administration of the province will prolong, and not diminish, Ulster's agony.

Ian Gow (1937–90).

# THE ANGLO-IRISH AGREEMENT (III): CAMPAIGN OF OPPOSITION

## The Unionist Campaign of Opposition

Where could Unionists look for support in their campaign against the agreement? The two main groups opposing the agreement apart from themselves, Fianna Fáil and Sinn Féin, would not have been the Unionists' first choice for support. It seemed that they would have to look to their own community for ways of making their sense of despair and betrayal clear.

Unionist politicians decided that the best way of opposing the Anglo-Irish Agreement was by a campaign of non-cooperation with the British government (Source A). However, they were also keen to demonstrate, by strength of number, the depth and breadth of Unionist opposition to what they termed the 'Dublin **diktat**'.

### SOURCE A

*The views of historian Jonathan Bardon from his book* A History of Ulster *(1992).*

Ulster Loyalists were firm in their resolution to 'derail' the 'sell-out'. Their problem, however, was how to achieve this without imperilling the Union they held so dear.

The campaign against the agreement took a variety of forms:

- Bonfires burning effigies of Margaret Thatcher, Irish Foreign Minister Peter Barry and other members of the Dublin government.
- Marches to the headquarters of the new Anglo-Irish Secretariat. On a number of occasions the marches degenerated into violence.
- A huge protest rally was held at Belfast's City Hall on 23 November 1985, attended by an estimated 100,000 people. (Some historians put the figure as high as 250,000.) The crowd was addressed by the OUP leader, James Molyneaux, and the DUP leader, Rev. Ian Paisley.
- All 15 Unionist MPs resigned their seats at Westminster on 17 December but then stood for them again in the resulting by-elections. The aim was to show the strength of Unionist opposition through the total number of votes the candidates received.

  The results of these by-elections, held on 23 January 1986, were extremely interesting. The Unionists gained a total of over 420,000 votes but lost one of their seats to the SDLP. Significantly, Sinn Féin's share of the Nationalist vote fell from nearly 42 per cent to just over 35 per cent. This suggested that one of the key aims of the architects of the agreement – the destruction of Sinn Féin – might be achievable.
- A Unionist 'day of action' was arranged for 3 March 1986. Although much of the province was brought to a standstill using peaceful protest, in a number of places the protests resulted in violence.

Aerial view of the crowd protesting against the Anglo-Irish Agreement at the City Hall, Belfast, 23 November 1985.

- The launching of a campaign of civil disobedience with measures including the shunning of British ministers, the refusal to set rates in Unionist council areas and a **boycott** of Westminster.

At the same time a more sinister response was becoming evident. Loyalist paramilitaries engaged in a campaign of violence and intimidation against the RUC who were seen as essential to the success of the agreement. In addition, in November 1986, Ulster Resistance, a paramilitary organisation whose aim was the destruction of the agreement, was formed.

### Results of the Campaign

By and large, however, these tactics failed to have any impact on the British government's determination to stick by the agreement. The absence of 14 MPs out of over 650 was not noticed at Westminster and since local councils had little power as it was, the refusal to use this power made little or no difference. By September 1987, when the Unionist leaders agreed to talk to British ministers again, it was clear that the campaign to destroy the agreement had failed (Sources B and C).

| SOURCE B |
|---|
| *The views of historian Jonathan Bardon from his book* A History of Ulster *(1992).* |
| In most respects the Unionist plan was a miserable failure. The absence of Unionist MPs from Westminster was hardly noticed ... Local authorities in Northern Ireland exercised very limited powers ... [And] many Unionists were uncomfortable with abstention tactics, which seemed rather too similar to those applied by Sinn Féin for decades. |

| SOURCE C |
|---|
| *Historian Sabine Wichert writing in her book* Northern Ireland Since 1945 *(1991).* |
| The Unionist protest ... gradually modified its demands from scrapping the agreement to suspending it, after which, they said, they would be willing to talk to the SDLP about devolution and power sharing. |

## ACTIVITIES

1 Describe two of the ways in which Unionists showed their opposition to the Anglo-Irish Agreement.
2 Explain whether or not the Unionists were successful in their opposition to the Anglo-Irish Agreement.
3 Explain the difficulty the Unionists faced in opposing the Anglo-Irish Agreement.
4 Construct a spider diagram showing the tactics used by Unionists against the Anglo-Irish Agreement.
5 Make a copy of the following table:

| Unionist tactics against the Anglo-Irish Agreement | Reasons tactics were successful | Reasons tactics were unsuccessful |
|---|---|---|
| | | |

Using the information on pages 144–5, fill in the table as appropriate. Now look at your results. Using the information in your table and in the text, decide whether or not the Unionists' campaign against the agreement was a success or a failure. Provide evidence to support your answer.

## EXTENSION ACTIVITIES

1 Did the Unionists' campaign against the Anglo-Irish Agreement achieve anything?
2 Why did the Unionists' campaign against the Anglo-Irish Agreement fail?

## REVISION TIP

It is important that you are able to explain the ways in which Unionists opposed the Anglo-Irish Agreement and why their campaign was a failure in the end.

# The Cold War 1945–91

## CHAPTER 4

## FROM ALLIES TO ENEMIES

### A CLASH OF IDEOLOGIES? COMMUNISM VERSUS CAPITALISM BEFORE 1945

#### The Origins of the Cold War

Although historians usually date the beginning of the Cold War to 1945, its origins actually go back much further. In October 1917 **Bolsheviks**, led by V.I. Lenin, seized power in Russia. This revolution greatly worried most Western countries, which were **capitalist democracies**. This was because Bolsheviks believed in **communism** and wanted to destroy the capitalist system that they operated (Source A). Table 4.1 outlines the main differences between the two systems.

At first the Bolsheviks did not control all of Russia and in 1918 a **civil war** broke out between the Bolsheviks, who were nicknamed the Reds, and their opponents who were called the Whites. Because of their fear of communism Britain,

> ### SOURCE A
>
> The views of historian Allan Todd in his book Democracies and Dictatorships: Europe and the World 1919–1989 (2001).
>
> The Bolshevik revolution in [October] 1917 alarmed most European states and consequently communist Russia was increasingly **boycotted** … Many European states placed restrictions on trade and economic relations with the new workers' state. It was hoped that these would bring down the communist government.

France, Japan and the USA sent soldiers to help the Whites in the conflict. In the end the Whites lost the war but the Bolsheviks (now known as communists) never forgot the fact that the capitalist nations had tried to destroy them.

| Capitalist democracies | Communist countries |
|---|---|
| *Political system*<br>Free and regular elections where people vote for candidates from a wide range of parties and viewpoints. | *Political system*<br>Elections – if they are held at all – have no choice; all candidates are for the same party. Only the government party's ideas are heard. |
| *Media*<br>Freedom of the press and of speech is protected. People are free to disagree with the political system. | *Media*<br>No freedom of speech. The media is only allowed to print and say what the government allows it to. |
| *Wealth*<br>Individuals own the different industries. They are free to keep the profits that they make. | *Wealth*<br>All industry is under the control of the government. Individuals are not allowed to make a profit. |

Table 4.1 The main difference between capitalist and communist systems

Тов. Ленин ОЧИЩАЕТ землю от нечисти.

Soviet propaganda cartoon: Comrade Lenin sweeps away the world's dirt.

This mutual suspicion continued and deepened throughout the 1920s and 1930s. The distrust was made clear in a number of ways:

- Russia was not invited to the 1919 **Paris Peace Settlement**.
- Russia was not allowed to join the **League of Nations**.
- It was not until 1924 that the British government officially recognised the Communist regime as Russia's government. (The USA followed suit in 1933.)
- During the later 1930s Britain and France refused to form an alliance with Russia against Nazi Germany.

Joseph Stalin succeeded Lenin as leader of Russia (now called the USSR or the Soviet Union). He was well aware of the West's desire to destroy communism. The policies that he followed aimed to ensure that the USSR would be able to protect itself if the capitalist countries attacked:

## SOURCE B

The views of historian Allan Todd in his book *Democracies and Dictatorships: Europe and the World 1919–1989* (2001).

It was … the reluctance of France and Britain to negotiate seriously with the USSR which left Stalin little choice but to … make a deal with Nazi Germany in order to buy time for the **Red Army** to prepare itself for a fight with the **Wehrmacht**.

- Stalin began a series of Five-Year Plans to ensure that the Soviet economy would be ready to fight a war against the West.
- When Britain and France failed to agree an alliance with the USSR against Hitler, Stalin signed a non-aggression pact with the Nazis in August 1939 (Source B). Stalin knew that Hitler wanted to destroy communism, but it suited him to delay the war for a while until the USSR was ready to fight.

### Fighting a Common Enemy

Stalin and the **Allies** joined together when Germany invaded Russia in June 1941. However, Stalin remained suspicious of the West, claiming that they delayed **D-Day** until June 1944 to see if Germany and the USSR would wear each other out.

Stalin was determined to ensure his country could never be invaded again. He therefore sought the creation of a buffer zone of communist countries between Western Europe and Russia as a way of protecting the Soviet Union from attack.

## ACTIVITIES

1 What are the main differences between capitalism and communism?
2 Why did capitalism and communism fear each other so much? Use the information in the text and in Source A to help you with your answer.
3 What evidence is there to suggest that capitalist nations wanted communism to fail? Use Source B and the text to help you with your answer.
4 Why did the USSR and Germany sign a non-aggression pact in 1939 when they hated each other so much?

## EXTENSION ACTIVITY

'Capitalism and communism were never going to get along.' Discuss.

## REVISION TIP

It is essential that you understand and are able to explain the reasons why capitalist and communist countries feared each other so much.

## RENEWING DIVISION: THE EVENTS OF 1945

### Yalta

In February 1945 the leaders of Britain (Winston Churchill), the USA (Franklin D. Roosevelt) and the USSR (Stalin) – known as the 'Big Three' – met at Yalta in the Ukraine. Although the war was not yet over it was clear that the Allies were going to win and so the aim of the meeting was to reach agreement on what would happen in post-war Europe.

Each leader was hoping to achieve something different from the meeting:

- *Churchill* wanted to ensure the survival of the British Empire; however he also saw the USSR as a danger to the West that had to be stopped. This was because as the Red Army was pushing the Germans back into Western Europe it was gaining control of countries such as Poland and Hungary.
- *Roosevelt* was not so keen on a revival of the British Empire. He sought the creation of a free world that would be protected by the United Nations (UN), a new peace-keeping body. He wanted the USSR to join the UN and was prepared to work with Stalin to ensure that this happened (Source A).

## SOURCE A

*The views of Harry Hopkins, Roosevelt's closest aide, speaking after the Yalta conference.*

We really believed in our hearts that this was the dawn of the new day we had all been praying for ... There wasn't any doubt in the minds of the President or any of us that we could live with [the Soviets] and get along with them peacefully for as far into the future as any of us could imagine.

The 'Big Three' meeting at Yalta, February 1945.

149

- *Stalin* sought the creation of a 'buffer' zone between Western Europe and Russia as a way of protecting the Soviet Union from attack. To ensure that the countries making up this zone would be friendly towards the USSR, Stalin wanted them to be controlled by communist governments.

## Agreements made at Yalta

Despite these differences, agreement was reached in a number of areas at Yalta. These included:

- Germany and Berlin would be divided into four zones to be occupied by the armies of Britain, France, the USSR and the USA.
- Germany would pay **reparations**.
- The UN would be established.
- The USSR would declare war on Japan in August, three months after Germany's surrender.
- Agreement over new borders for Poland (although no agreement was reached on the type of government Poland would have).
- An agreement that Eastern Europe would come under the influence of the USSR. However, it was also agreed that there would be democratic elections in these countries to allow the people of Eastern Europe to choose their own governments.

## Potsdam

By the time the 'Big Three' met again at Potsdam in Germany in July 1945, several important changes had taken place:

- The war in Europe had ended and Hitler was dead.
- Soviet troops were spread throughout Eastern Europe.
- Plans were being made to return most US troops home.
- Roosevelt had died in April 1945 and was replaced by Harry Truman. Truman did not like Stalin and was suspicious of the USSR's aims. Truman's advisers were also urging him to take a harsh line against Stalin.
- Labour's Clement Attlee replaced Churchill as Britain's Prime Minister during the conference at Potsdam.
- US and British attitudes towards the USSR were hardening as they watched Germany being

stripped of resources and saw **puppet governments** being set up in several of the countries now under Soviet control.

The meeting at Potsdam was, therefore, much less friendly (Source B). In addition, Stalin's fear of the West increased when he was told that the USA had developed an atomic bomb, and that the Americans would not share the technology with the Soviets.

## Potsdam Decisions

At Potsdam the following was agreed:

- How Germany was to be divided and occupied. Each power could take reparations from their own zone, although not so much as to endanger the lives of ordinary Germans. The USSR could also take some reparations from the British and US zones in return for providing supplies of food, fuel and raw materials.
- How Austria was to be divided and occupied.
- Changes to Germany's border with Poland. This border was moved westwards to the Oder and

**Figure 4.1** The new borders for Germany and Poland after the Potsdam Agreement.

Niesse rivers. This created a natural border between the two countries. All former German territory to the east of the new border became part of Poland and all Germans still living within this area were expelled. At the same time the USSR's border with Poland was also moved to the west.

In general, however, there was considerable disagreement about the future shape of Europe. Now that the common enemy of Nazism was defeated the wartime alliance was breaking up. The suspicions and tensions of Potsdam marked the first 'drop in temperature' of what would become the Cold War.

# THE EXPANSION OF COMMUNISM IN EASTERN EUROPE

## USA–USSR Suspicions

The world at the end of 1945 was very different than it had been just six years earlier:

- The USSR and the USA were both far stronger than any other nation.
- Each feared that the other wanted to spread their influence.
- Each believed that the other wanted to destroy them. In particular, the USSR feared the atomic bomb, which the USA had used to such devastating effect against Japan in August 1945. In turn, the USA was concerned at the huge size of the Red Army.
- Each was suspicious of the reasons behind the other's actions and began to act defensively against the other.

## Churchill's Fulton Speech

It was Winston Churchill who most clearly expressed the West's suspicion of the USSR in a speech he gave in Fulton, Missouri, USA in March 1946 (Source A, page 152). In this speech Churchill condemned Stalin's attempts to control Eastern Europe and demanded an Anglo-American alliance to stop the spread of communism. It was in this speech that the phrase 'Iron Curtain' was popularised.

Winston Churchill (1874–1965) preparing to speak at Fulton, March 1946.

Stalin reacted angrily to the speech (Source B). He felt that his actions were necessary; he argued that the way in which the USSR suffered during the war made the protection of his country from invasion only natural.

### The Emergence of the Buffer Zone

What made Churchill speak out so strongly against his former ally? In particular it was the communist take-over of Eastern European countries that worried him most. Between 1945 and 1947 elections were held in a number of states, each resulting in the election of governments friendly to Moscow. The West suspected that the elections were rigged; however the USSR denied this. Yet, by 1947 the following countries were ruled by communists:

- Albania
- Bulgaria
- Hungary
- Poland
- Romania.

In addition, communists held power in Yugoslavia, although its leader, Tito, was less inclined to do what Stalin told him. Tito had been a war hero in his own country and had enough support to stand up to the USSR. However, as far as the West was concerned Yugoslavia was just another communist state.

British cartoon showing Churchill peeping under the Iron Curtain.

### The Steps to Communism

Although the take-over of each country (apart from Yugoslavia) differed to some degree, certain trends were common to each. For example:

- Russian pressure to ensure that communists – many of whom had been trained in Moscow – obtained key positions (such as control of law and order) in the temporary governments set up after the war.
- Suggesting radical changes to help economic recovery. This helped gain the communists popularity.
- Controlling elections to ensure a communist victory.

By the end of 1947 only Czechoslovakia remained free from communist control in Eastern Europe.

### How these Events were Interpreted

Each side viewed these events in different ways and this was one of the main reasons for the huge increases in international tension:

- In particular the USA's view of the USSR's actions was influenced by the ideas of George Kennan, an American diplomat based in Moscow. Kennan argued that communism demanded the spread of revolution worldwide and so the two **superpowers** could never live in peace. He recommended that the USA would have to act to contain the USSR's aggression in the future (Source C). President Truman took him at his word and the policy of containment was born. Where possible, the USA would act to stop the further spread of communism.

**SOURCE C**

Extract from an article, 'The sources of Soviet conduct' written by George Kennan, July 1947.

The main element of any United States policy towards the USSR must be that of a long-term, patient but firm … containment.

**Figure 4.2** The Iron Curtain in Europe.

• At the same time the USA failed to understand that the USSR was obsessed with its own security. By seeing everything that the USSR did as evidence of the communists' desire to control Europe, the suspicion, fear and hostility that were the hallmarks of the Cold War were increased.

## ACTIVITIES

1 Give three reasons why the USA and USSR were suspicious of each other by 1945.
2 Study Source A. Explain why Churchill's speech might have played a part in the development of the Cold War.
3 Were the elections held in Eastern European countries as free as Stalin had promised at Yalta (see page 150)? Use Source B to help explain your answer.
4 Explain the origins and meaning of containment. Use the information in the text and in Source C to help you with your answer.
5 Who do you believe was responsible for the emergence of the Cold War? Use the information in the text and in the sources to help you fill in a copy of the following table:

| Reasons why the Cold War was the fault of the USA | Reasons why the Cold War was the fault of the USSR |
| --- | --- |
|  |  |

## EXTENSION ACTIVITY

'The USSR was more to blame than the USA for the increases in post-war tension.' Discuss.

## REVISION TIP

Both sides in the Cold War blamed the other for starting it; this is because each side interpreted the actions of the other as aggressive and their own actions as defensive. A good examination answer will be able to explain why each side felt that they were in the right.

# THE SPREAD OF COMMUNISM IN EUROPE 1945–9

## Events in Greece

After the end of the Second World War the Allies had agreed to help train and equip the Greek army, which was engaged in a civil war with Greek Communists. In March 1947 the British government announced that it could no longer afford to continue funding the Greek forces. This worried Truman, who feared that if Greece became communist, so too would neighbouring countries and the oil-rich Middle East.

## The Truman Doctrine

Truman decided to ask **Congress** for help (Source A). He told Congress that rather than remain isolated – as it had done between the First and Second World Wars – it would now be the USA's policy to use military or economic means to stop countries falling to communism either from external invasion or internal revolution. This policy became known as the Truman Doctrine and has remained one of the main parts of US foreign policy. Congress released $400 million, which provided enough support and equipment to end the communist threat in Greece.

Truman believed that communism spread more easily if countries were poor. He thought that if economic recovery took place in such countries:

• communism would fail to take control
• these countries would be able to trade with the USA, helping its economy.

Harry Truman (1884–1972) announcing the Truman Doctrine to Congress, March 1947.

## SOURCE A

*Extract from a speech delivered by President Truman to the US Congress, 12 March 1947.*

I believe it must be the policy of the US to support free peoples who are resisting attempted subjugation [conquest] by armed minorities or by outside pressures ... The seeds of totalitarian [dictatorial] regimes are nurtured [fed] by misery and want. They spread and grow in the evil soil of poverty and strife. They reach their full growth when the hope of a people for a better life has died. We must keep that hope alive ... If we falter in our leadership we may endanger the peace of the world – and we shall surely endanger the welfare of our own nation.

A cartoon from *Punch* magazine commenting on the importance of Marshall Aid for Western European recovery.

US **Secretary of State**, General George Marshall, agreed. He had toured Europe in April 1947 and saw that many countries were in danger of economic collapse and a communist take-over. Marshall proposed a massive investment of $13.3 billion into Europe over a four-year period (Source B). The money would be offered to all countries as long as they opened their markets to Western goods and made their economic records available for inspection. The investment became known as the Marshall Plan or Marshall Aid.

Initially Congress was unconvinced; however the communist take-over of Czechoslovakia in February 1948 changed its mind. Sixteen countries, particularly Britain and the Allied parts of Germany, benefited from the Marshall Plan, which was overseen by the Organisation for European Economic Co-operation (OEEC).

### Reactions to the Marshall Plan

Stalin described the Marshall Plan as 'dollar diplomacy'. He argued that the USA would use its investment to gain influence over countries by controlling their economies (Source C).

## SOURCE B

*Extract from a speech delivered by US Secretary of State George Marshall, 5 June 1947.*

It is logical that the United States should do whatever it is able to do to assist in the return of normal economic health in the world, without which there can be no political stability and no assured peace. Our policy is directed not against any country or doctrine but against hunger, poverty, desperation and chaos.

## SOURCE C

*Extract from a speech delivered at the United Nations, 18 September 1947, by the USSR's Deputy Foreign Minister, Andrei Vyshinsky.*

It is becoming more and more evident to everyone that the implementation of the Marshall Plan will mean placing European countries under the economic and political control of the United States ... This plan is an attempt ... to complete the formation of a bloc of several European countries hostile to the interests of the democratic countries of Eastern Europe and most particularly to the interests of the Soviet Union.

He rejected the offer of finance and made sure that all the countries he controlled did the same by:

- Establishing the Communist Information Bureau (Cominform). This aimed to ensure communist nations worked together more closely and effectively.
- Setting up the Council for Mutual Economic Assistance (Comecon). It was a Soviet version of the Marshall Plan, which encouraged economic co-operation among Iron Curtain states.

### Impact of the Truman Doctrine and Marshall Plan

Both the Truman Doctrine and Marshall Plan mark a significant development in the Cold War, in both a positive and negative sense: see Table 4.2.

| Positive | Negative |
|---|---|
| The USA was indicating its intent to remain involved in European affairs. | Political and economic divisions between East and West were deepened. |
| The economies of many European countries recovered rapidly. | The USSR strengthened its grip over the Iron Curtain countries with the establishment of Cominform and Comecon. |
| The US economy developed rapidly. | |

Table 4.2 Impact of US involvement in Europe after the Second World War

The Marshall Plan played a vital part in the economic reconstruction of Europe. However, it might also be seen to have played a central part in the ongoing destruction of East–West relations (Source D). It is interesting that 1947 was the year in which the phrase 'cold war' was first used to describe the relationship that now existed between East and West.

### SOURCE D

*The view of historian John W. Mason in his book* The Cold War, 1945–1991 *(1996).*

The Marshall Plan caused a crisis in Soviet–Western relations. The Soviet Union ... refused to participate and its subsequent denunciation of the plan sealed the economic and political division of Europe.

### ACTIVITIES

1 Explain the part events in Greece played in the emergence of the Truman Doctrine.
2 What was Truman's explanation for increasing the USA's involvement in European affairs? Use the text and the information in Source A to help you with your answer.
3 Study Sources B and C. Use the information in them to explain the differences in the US and Soviet attitudes towards the Marshall Plan.
4 'The Marshall Plan made the Cold War worse.' Using the information in the text and in Source D, explain whether or not you agree with this judgement.

### EXTENSION ACTIVITY

'The Truman Doctrine and the Marshall Plan were designed to benefit the USA more than anyone else.' Discuss.

### REVISION TIP

The introduction of the Truman Doctrine and the Marshall Plan were important turning points in the development of the Cold War. You need to be able to explain why these policies were introduced and what impact they had.

## CONFRONTATION AND CONTAINMENT

### Causes of the Berlin Blockade

More than two years after the end of the Second World War the former Allies still had not agreed on the long-term future of Germany. This issue caused the first major crisis of the Cold War.

### Divisions over the Future of Germany

At the Allied conferences held at Yalta and Potsdam (see pages 150–1) it had been agreed that Germany would be divided into four zones each to be administered separately by the British, Americans, Soviets and French. Berlin was also divided, but as it was located over 100 miles inside

**Figure 4.3** The division of Germany and Berlin.

the Soviet zone, the Allies had to travel through the Soviet area to get to the city.

However, that was as far as agreement had gone since both sides had completely different opinions about Germany's future:

- The Western powers wanted Germany to recover so it could be both a barrier against the further spread of communism and a cornerstone of European economic recovery. Therefore, significant resources were invested in Germany including over $1300 million of Marshall Aid.
- The USSR wanted Germany to remain weak since Germany had invaded Russia twice since 1914.

By 1948 the Western zones of Germany were on the road to economic recovery, mainly because of Marshall Aid. The same could not be said of the Soviet zone; during the same period the USSR had removed a significant amount of resources from the East to compensate for war damage. As a result, living conditions in the East were much poorer than those in the Western zones.

### Introducing a New Currency

By June 1948 the Western zones (US, British and French) had been merged and the Allies decided to introduce a new currency – the *Deutschmark* –

into the region. They believed that this was essential for economic recovery. Stalin was not consulted about this decision and was unhappy about it:

- He saw it as the first stage in the reconstruction of a Germany that would again threaten Russia.
- Even worse, this recovery would be obvious to the poor people of East Berlin who were living so close to their Western neighbours. This could cause problems as discontent at lower living standards in the communist zone might develop.

Therefore, on 24 June 1948, and in violation of what had been agreed at Potsdam, Stalin ordered the closure of all road, rail and canal links with West Berlin (Figure 4.3). The official reason given for the closures was 'technical difficulties' (Source A).

### SOURCE A

*A Russian viewpoint on the Berlin Blockade.*

The crisis was planned in Washington, behind a smokescreen of anti-Soviet propaganda ... The conduct of the Western powers risked bloody incidents.

Why did Stalin take this risk? It is unlikely that he expected his actions to lead to war; instead he probably hoped that he could force the West to abandon Berlin and thus leave it under Soviet control. Berlin only had enough supplies to last it for a maximum of six weeks.

Of course, there was no way that the USA could allow this to happen; Berlin had become a powerful symbol of the struggle for supremacy in Europe between capitalism and communism. Any sign of weakness would undoubtedly result in the collapse of American influence over the rest of Europe. Action had to be taken (Source B).

---

## SOURCE B

*President Truman, writing in his* Memoirs *(1955).*

When we refused to be forced out of Berlin, we demonstrated to Europe that we would act when freedom was threatened.

---

A cartoon from *Punch* magazine showing Stalin 'guarding' Berlin from the airlift.

## The Berlin Airlift

Although several options were open to the USA, most had to be scrapped because of the risk of war. General Clay, who was the Governor of the US zone, pushed for the breaking of the blockade by force, but Truman rejected the idea. It was decided that airlifting supplies to West Berlin would be the best way of breaking the blockade. It was felt that Stalin was unlikely to shoot planes down, as that would be seen as an act of war.

For almost a year, therefore, up to 13,000 tons of supplies were flown in each day with planes landing, on occasion, at two-minute intervals. The airlift had not been expected to work and for long periods the two million citizens of West Berlin had to endure severe rationing, yet by mid-1949 Stalin was forced to admit defeat and on 12 May the blockade was lifted. Over two million tons of supplies had been airlifted in; 101 men had died, mostly as a result of plane crashes, but war had been avoided and Berlin had been saved from communism.

## Results of the Berlin Blockade

The breaking of the Berlin Blockade was a huge propaganda triumph for the West and a setback for the USSR. It was also a significant turning point in the Cold War (Source C) and had several important consequences:

- The policy of containment could be seen to have worked as communism had failed to spread into West Berlin.
- In April 1949, even before the end of the blockade, 12 Western nations set up the **North Atlantic Treaty Organisation (NATO)**. The reason was to ensure that the West could co-operate to prevent future Soviet aggression. NATO was based around the principle that an attack on one of its members would be considered as an attack on all.
- Although NATO was established as a defensive organisation, the Soviets refused to accept that it was anything other than an aggressive alliance. This opinion seemed to be confirmed when West Germany was allowed to join NATO in 1955. Again the Soviet fear of a strong Germany was revived. In response the Warsaw Pact was established in May 1955. It was basically a communist version of NATO with all countries in the Soviet sphere of

influence agreeing to defend each other if one was attacked. The pact was dominated by the USSR however.

- All hopes for the reunification of Germany were now gone. In May 1949 the Federal Republic of Germany (known as West Germany) was established. In October the USSR renamed its zone the German Democratic Republic (East Germany).

## SOURCE C

*Extract from Steve Phillips,* The Cold War: Conflict in Europe and Asia *(2001).*

The Berlin crisis ... marked the first major flashpoint of the Cold War. Relations between the USA and the USSR ... reached such a low position of distrust and suspicion that it became difficult to have any meaningful dialogue, let alone agreement.

## ACTIVITIES

1 Explain how the former allies differed in their ideas about what should happen to Germany and Berlin.
2 Create a timeline of the events of the Berlin Blockade.
3 Study Sources A and B. Using the information in the text and in these sources, explain how and why the US and Soviet explanations for the blockade were different.
4 Are Sources A and B equally reliable and useful to an historian investigating the Berlin Blockade? Explain your answer.
5 Using the information in the text and in Source C, assess the impact of the Berlin Blockade on the development of the Cold War.
6 Create a spider diagram showing the main results of the Berlin Blockade.

## EXTENSION ACTIVITIES

1 'Stalin was justified in the actions he took.' To what extent do you agree?
2 Were Stalin's policies concerning Germany and Berlin a mistake?

## REVISION TIP

Many of the questions in your GCSE exam will ask you to comment on the usefulness of sources (see Question 4). To answer this type of question you must think about how useful the source is in helping you find out about a particular event. Remember that a biased source is not necessarily useless to the historian!

## CHALLENGES TO THE CONTROL OF THE USSR: HUNGARY AND BERLIN

### USSR: A New Leader and New Policies

Joseph Stalin died in March 1953. For a while the USSR had a collective leadership but by 1955 Nikita Khrushchev had emerged as the country's overall leader. People wondered whether this would mean a thaw in the Cold War. For a time the policies pursued by Khrushchev suggested it might.

In particular a positive tone seemed to be set by some of the things that the new leader did:

- In 1955 Khrushchev visited Yugoslavia and apologised for the way in which Stalin had treated the country.
- In the same year he agreed to meet the leaders of the West in Geneva, the first such meeting for over a decade.
- In February 1956 Khrushchev delivered an historic speech at the Communist Party's Twentieth Party Congress. In his address – known as the Secret Speech – Khrushchev denounced the policies that Stalin had followed and urged the development of 'peaceful co-existence' with non-communist nations.
- Khrushchev began a policy aimed at ending the influence of the dead leader over the USSR. This was known as destalinisation.
- The new Soviet leader also ordered the dissolution of Cominform.

Khrushchev's Secret Speech was not just welcomed by the West; it was also listened to with great interest within other Iron Curtain countries. There, people decided that Khrushchev's unheard of criticism of Stalin also meant disapproval of Stalin's policies, particularly those involving the satellite states. They began to believe that a more relaxed system of government might emerge in their countries, one that would provide economic prosperity and a better standard of living. Indeed Khrushchev himself spoke of there being 'different roads to socialism'.

## The Emergence of Opposition

Resentment at the negative impact of a decade of communist rule emerged first in Poland in July 1956. There protests were held against the economic hardships being experienced by the people. Although Soviet tanks crushed the opposition, Khrushchev followed force with concession by agreeing to the appointment of a moderate communist, Wladyslaw Gromulka, as leader and to the introduction of a number of reforms. However, he insisted that Poland remain within the Warsaw Pact.

## Hungary

The biggest revolt emerged in Hungary in October 1956. Here, years of bitterness at the hardships of communist rule spilled over into a full-blown rebellion. Hungarians had much to be angry about; under communist rule their religion had been oppressed, their economy ruined and their freedoms crushed.

Figure 4.4 Hungary.

Bodies in Budapest: the aftermath of the 1956 Hungarian rising.

## Events of the Rebellion

The rebellion developed as follows:

| | |
|---|---|
| 23 October | Hungarian students followed the Polish example and took to the streets demanding reforms. |
| 26 October | As unrest grew Imre Nagy, a moderate communist, was appointed as leader in place of the hardline Matyas Rakosi. |
| 1 November | Nagy announced that Hungary would hold free multi-party elections and would withdraw from the Warsaw Pact. |
| 4 November | Over 6000 Russian tanks crossed the border to put down the revolt. Pleas were made for the West and UN to intervene. In the fierce fighting that followed the invasion, 30,000 died and a quarter of a million fled westward. Nagy fled to the Yugoslav Embassy but was later arrested and executed. He was replaced by Janos Kadar and communist control was reasserted. At that stage some reforms were introduced. |

Russia's response indicated that it could not take the risk of a member of the Warsaw Pact leaving the organisation since it might result in:

- The opening of a gap in the Iron Curtain leaving Russia exposed to attack.
- The collapse of the Iron Curtain; if one country was allowed to break free then all the others might follow suit.

## The Reaction of the West

Throughout the crisis the people of Hungary had hoped for assistance from the West; however nothing arrived except words of support (Source A). There were a number of reasons for this:

- The Western powers were preoccupied and divided by the Suez Crisis. Here Britain and France had attacked Egypt over the decision of Egypt's President Nasser to **nationalise** the Suez Canal to provide funds for economic development.
- The USA was in the middle of a Presidential election campaign.
- The West felt that it would be much more risky to confront Russia in Eastern Europe, which it now accepted as a Soviet sphere of influence, than it was to confront communism in Asia.

More than anything, the events of 1956 suggested that Khrushchev's criticism of Stalin did not mean any change in Russia's attitude to its defence. Khrushchev might speak of peaceful co-existence, but this seemed to mean keeping things as they were. Events in Berlin further proved this to be the case.

### SOURCE A

*US Secretary of State Dulles commenting on events in Hungary, October 1956.*

To all those suffering under communist slavery, let us say: you can count on us.

## Berlin: Reasons for Difficulties

The Hungarian experience confirmed that it was impossible for Eastern European nations to break free from communist control. In Berlin however, the same was not true for individuals. Although a divided city, it was still possible for people to flee to the West using West Berlin as their point of exit.

Why did they want to go? Due to substantial US investment West Berlin was like a living advertisement for the benefits of capitalism and many Eastern Europeans wanted to buy into the lifestyle that it seemed to promise.

It is estimated that by 1962 over two million people – many of whom were highly skilled – had slipped through the Iron Curtain in this way. Even when barbed wire and other barriers were erected the flow of people still continued.

These statistics worried the USSR for a number of reasons:

- It meant a significant loss of workers.
- It implied that people preferred to live under capitalism rather than under communism.

Khrushchev was also concerned that West Berlin was being used as a 'listening post', enabling the West to gather information about activities behind the Iron Curtain.

## Khrushchev's Response

Khrushchev hoped to pressure the West into leaving Berlin; in 1958 he attempted to force the West to withdraw by threatening to give East Germany control of access points to the city; however he failed. In 1960 he attended a **summit** meeting in Paris, again hoping to persuade the West to leave, but the meeting collapsed when Khrushchev revealed that Russia had shot down a U2 spy plane flying over its territory.

## The Berlin Wall

The events during the 1960 summit meeting increased tensions even further and a new wave of people fled through West Berlin causing labour shortages in the east of the city. Khrushchev decided that he could not allow this to continue and so in August 1961 he ordered the erection of a massive wall that made permanent the division of the city (Source B, page 162). Armed guards patrolled the wall and those attempting to cross it without permission ran the risk of being shot. The river of defections dwindled to a trickle.

The USA protested but did nothing, unwilling to risk war (Source C, page 162). On a visit to the city, the new US President, John F. Kennedy, called himself a Berliner, but this did not get rid of the feeling that the USSR had won this round of the Cold War. This 'Concrete Curtain' became a powerful symbol of the ideological, social and economic divisions that now existed between East and West.

## SOURCE B

*Russian reasoning behind the permanent division of Berlin, August 1961 (adapted).*

The Western powers use Berlin as a centre of rebellious activity against East Germany.

## SOURCE C

*President Kennedy speaking about the permanent division of Berlin, August 1961.*

If the Russians wanted to attack us ... they wouldn't be putting up barbed wire ... I'm not going to get het up [annoyed] about it.

Berlin divided! The Berlin Wall snakes its way through the divided city. In the background can be seen the famous Brandenburg Gate.

## ACTIVITIES

1 What evidence is there to suggest that at the start Khrushchev seemed to be a different style of leader from Stalin?
2 Explain the background to events in Poland and Hungary in 1956.
3 Examine the Hungarian Rebellion under the following headings:
   * reasons
   * events
   * results.
4 Study Source B. The source and the text provide different reasons for the division of Berlin in 1961:
   * Explain how and why they are different.
   * Does this mean that Source B is of no use to an historian?
5 Examine the building of the Berlin Wall under the following headings:
   * reasons
   * results.
6 Study Sources A and C. Explain the difference between the US government attitudes expressed in Sources A and C.
7 Explain the reasons why the USA offered only words of support during the Hungarian and Berlin crises.

## EXTENSION ACTIVITIES

1 Was Khrushchev any different than Stalin?
2 'The West let the people of Hungary and East Berlin down.' Discuss.
3 Was the USSR winning the Cold War by 1961?

## REVISION TIP

Events in Hungary and Berlin were the first main internal challenges that the USSR faced to its control of Eastern Europe. Make sure you understand why these events happened and why Khrushchev responded in the way that he did.

# SPRINGTIME IN EUROPE? THE 1968 CZECH RISING

## USSR's New Leader

The communist leadership in Moscow removed Khrushchev in 1964 due to dissatisfaction with parts of his domestic and foreign policies. He was replaced by the more hardline Leonid Brezhnev. The first major test of his leadership came with the Czech crisis of 1968.

## Leadership Changes in Czechoslovakia

In January 1968 Czechoslovakia's hardline leader Antonin Novotny was replaced by the more moderate Alexander Dubček. The immediate cause of Novotny's resignation was a series of demonstrations. These were directed against the lack of civil rights and the appalling standard of living that had resulted from two decades of communist rule.

Dubček wanted Czechoslovakia to remain communist but he also knew that if that were to happen reforms would have to be carried out (Source A). To achieve 'socialism with a human face' he introduced a series of political and economic reforms that included:

- freedom of speech and of the press
- less centralised economic control
- development of foreign trade
- removal of restrictions on travel abroad
- reduction in the powers of the secret police.

These reforms were greeted with widespread public approval. The new atmosphere produced by the reforms was christened the 'Prague spring'.

## Reactions to Dubček's Policies

Dubček's reforms were less enthusiastically greeted in Moscow. Brezhnev feared that the reforms would be copied by other Eastern European countries and would ultimately result in the destruction of the Iron Curtain. The communist leaders of Poland and East Germany expressed similar fears. In July the leaders of these two countries along with Hungary, Bulgaria and the USSR wrote to Czechoslovakia to express their concern. Dubček assured them of his commitment to socialism and guaranteed that Czechoslovakia would remain in the Warsaw Pact.

---

## SOURCE A

*Alexander Dubček speaking in early 1968.*

We want to set new forces of socialist life in motion in this country, allowing a fuller application of the advantages of socialism.

---

Despite Dubček's guarantees Brezhnev ordered 400,000 troops into the country on 20 August 1968. He claimed that senior Czech communists had invited them in (Source B below). Although it was officially a Warsaw Pact operation with troops from Bulgaria, East Germany, Hungary, Poland and Russia, in reality it was mainly a Soviet force.

## Response to Invasion

Dubček realised that continued opposition would be pointless and urged his people not to resist the invasion with violence. Instead he urged the people to show their opposition through **passive resistance** (Source C below). By and large this was the case although there were isolated examples of violent resistance to the Soviet forces.

Dubček was summoned to Moscow; on his return to Prague he announced to the people that the 'Prague spring' had ended. He resigned a few months later and was replaced by the much more hardline Gustav Husak.

---

## SOURCE B

*Statement issued by Tass (the Official Soviet news agency), 21 August 1968.*

The leaders of the Czechoslovak Socialist Republic have asked the Soviet Union and allied states to render the Czechoslovak people urgent assistance.

---

## SOURCE C

*Alexander Dubček speaking after the Warsaw Pact invasion.*

How could they do this to me? My entire life has been devoted to the Soviet Union.

---

## The Brezhnev Doctrine

In November 1968 Brezhnev justified the actions that he took in Czechoslovakia. He argued that it was the duty of communist countries to act together to prevent another communist state from turning to capitalism. This became known as the Brezhnev Doctrine (Source D).

As with Hungary 12 years earlier, the West responded to the events of 1968 with little more than words of sympathy. The USA in particular was too caught up with its own problems in a war in Vietnam and – as with Hungary – accepted that there was no point in trying to intervene in events behind the Iron Curtain. It was also keen not to damage the recent improvement in relations between East and West that became known as détente (after the French word for relaxation).

### SOURCE D

*Extract from Steve Phillips,* The Cold War: Conflict in Europe and Asia *(2001).*

There was no doubt that the USSR was willing to take action when it felt the interests of socialism were threatened. From a Soviet viewpoint their actions were successful ... There was to be little serious unrest in the region until the early 1980s.

A Warsaw Pact tank in Prague 1968.

**Figure 4.5** Czechoslovakia.

## ACTIVITIES

1 How and why did Dubček try to reform Czechoslovakia?
2 Using the information in Sources A and C, explain whether or not it was Dubček's intention to break free from communism.
3 Why was the USSR so concerned about Dubček's actions?
4 How reliable and useful would Source B be as evidence to an historian investigating why the USSR invaded Czechoslovakia? Use the information in the text to help you with your answer.
5 Make a copy of the following table and fill it in to show the similarities and differences between the Hungarian and Czechoslovakian risings:

| Area | Hungary | Czechoslovakia |
|---|---|---|
| Origins | | |
| Events | | |
| Reaction of USSR | | |
| Results | | |

6 Were the USSR's actions in Czechoslovakia worthwhile? Use the information in the text and in Source D to help you with your answer.

## EXTENSION ACTIVITY

Should Dubček have realised that Russia would not allow his reforms to go ahead?

## REVISION TIP

There are many similarities between what happened in Czechoslovakia in 1968 and what took place in Hungary in 1956. Make sure that you are able to explain the similarities and differences between these two attempts to introduce reforms to communist rule.

## *DÉTENTE*

### Origins

For part of the 1960s and most of the 1970s there seemed to be an improvement in relations between East and West. This improvement became known as *détente* and resulted in the signing of a number of treaties and agreements. These imposed limitations on arms and aimed to improve both trade and human rights.

*Détente* emerged for a number of reasons, including the strained relations that existed between the USSR and China by the late 1960s. Part of the US reasoning behind *détente* was its desire to take advantage of these tensions. The USA believed that if it could create better relations with China this would put significant pressure on the USSR. The USA also believed that both countries might help it end the Vietnam War (see pages 183–7) by putting pressure on North Vietnam to negotiate a settlement.

### Background: Sino-Soviet Relations

Initially China and the USSR got on well together as indicated by the signing of a Treaty of Friendship in 1950. However, relations had deteriorated thereafter for a number of reasons, mostly concerned with arguments over what was the best form of communism:

- Both differed over the best methods of agricultural development (Source A).
- China believed the USSR wanted to dominate it.
- The USSR refused to share nuclear technology believing that the Chinese were too offhand about its dangers. China went on to develop its own nuclear capability by 1964.
- China was against the public criticism of Stalin in Khrushchev's Secret Speech of 1956.

### SOURCE A

*Soviet response to China's economic policies, 1958.*

A road of dangerous experiment, a road of disregard for the experience of other socialist states.

- Although officially neutral, India was supplied with aircraft engines by the USSR during a 1962 border dispute with China.
- China believed peaceful co-existence was a betrayal of the ideas of Karl Marx (the founder of communism) and Lenin. They thought Khrushchev was being too soft with the West.
- China condemned the Soviet climb down over Cuba (see pages 179–82).
- In 1969 a border dispute between the two powers resulted in the deaths of a number of military personnel.

Basically the Chinese believed that they were true communists who wanted to spread revolution worldwide whereas the USSR only used communism to make itself stronger (Source B). By the late 1960s relations between the two states were at an all time low and because of the propaganda each spread about the other the rest of the world knew about it.

### SOURCE B

*Comment in Beijing's* People's Daily *on China's attitude to the USSR, June 1967.*

Throughout the past year scarcely a day has passed without Brezhnev ... attacking China's great revolution. A tragedy has taken place in international communism. Its creators are the scabs – Khrushchev [and] Brezhnev.

### Reasons for Improving Relations

The USA had been hostile to China since the communist victory in 1949 and US suspicion of Chinese involvement in various Asian conflicts had done little to improve the relationship. This suspicion had resulted in the formation of SEATO (the South East Asian Treaty Organisation). This was a defensive organisation covering parts of Australasia and was similar in intent to NATO.

In turn China had been left feeling isolated by US policies such as the refusal to recognise its communist government and the refusal to allow China to sit on the **Security Council** of the **United Nations**. Nevertheless, by the late 1960s both sides began to realise that there could be benefits from an improved relationship. In particular:

- Economic advantages such as the opening of new markets to both countries and, in China's case, the possibility of the investment of capital and technological knowledge.
- Military benefits, in that the USA wanted China to put pressure on North Vietnam to negotiate an end to the Vietnam War. At the same time China saw the USA as a possible ally against an increasingly powerful USSR.
- Diplomatic benefits that meant each country could use the other in their ongoing power struggles with the USSR.

In 1971 the US table-tennis team was invited to visit China. This was followed by China's entry into the UN in 1971 and President Nixon's visit to China in February 1972. In the same year both countries signed a Friendship Treaty, which spelt out their position over issues such as control of South-east Asia. The US finally granted China full diplomatic recognition in 1978.

President Nixon (1913–94) being greeted by Chairman Mao (1893–1976).

### The Impact on the USSR

The USSR was concerned about the improvement in US–Chinese relations and what this might mean for its own position. The Soviet Union's desire to keep China isolated was one of their main reasons for wanting to improve relations

with the USA, but there were other issues for both sides including:

- The realisation that they had come too close to nuclear war in the 1960s over Cuba (see pages 179–82) and that new understandings needed to be reached.
- The need to cut back on military spending due to the fact that both countries were facing severe economic problems.
- The USA needed new export markets and the USSR badly needed foreign supplies of grain as its harvest had failed in 1972.

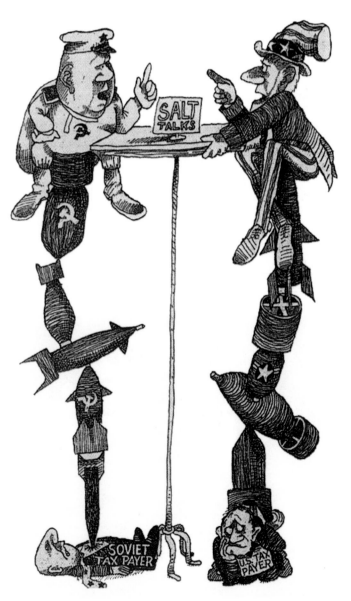

Cartoon suggesting the real reasons behind the Strategic Arms Limitation Talks (SALT) agreements.

## *Détente:* the Key Agreements

A series of summit meetings were held between the USSR and the USA throughout the 1970s; as a result the key agreements shown in Table 4.3 were made.

## Conclusions

As Table 4.3 shows, *détente* was far from perfect, but the 1970s was one of the decades during the Cold War that had the least East–West confrontation (Source C). Issues that had previously caused tension – such as the division of Germany – ceased to be as contentious as *détente* emerged in the relationship between West Germany, East Germany and the USSR (known as *Ostpolitik*). The USSR recognised West Germany as a country and permitted some movement of relatives from West to East Berlin. In addition, the USSR benefited significantly from Western grain imports. It seemed as if the Cold War might become slightly less chilly on a permanent basis (although Sino-Soviet relations remained strained). Yet relationships were thrown back into the deep freeze with the Soviet invasion of its neighbour Afghanistan in 1979. Moscow's aim was to install a government loyal to the USSR.

> ### SOURCE C
>
> *The view of historian John W. Mason in his book The Cold War, 1945–1991 (1996).*
>
> [*Détente*] was not intended to end the arms race, eliminate Soviet–American rivalry ... or provide the instrument of reform within the Soviet Union ... Its purpose was rather to work with the Soviet Union in order to prevent differences between the two superpowers from exploding into dangerous crises.

| Date | Name of agreement | Key details | Limitations |
|------|-------------------|-------------|-------------|
| 1972 | Strategic Arms Limitation Talks (SALT) I | Limited the number of certain types of weapons. | Only certain types of weaponry were included; many more powerful missiles were left out. |
| 1975 | Helsinki Agreement | Acceptance of existing borders in Europe by USA. Agreement to improve human rights by USSR. | Human rights did not really improve behind the Iron Curtain. |
| 1979 | SALT II | Further limitations on weaponry. | Never approved by the US Congress because of the USSR's invasion of Afghanistan in December 1979. |

**Table 4.3** The key agreements from US–Soviet talks 1972–9

President Jimmy Carter (1924–) meeting General Secretary Leonid Brezhnev (1906–82).

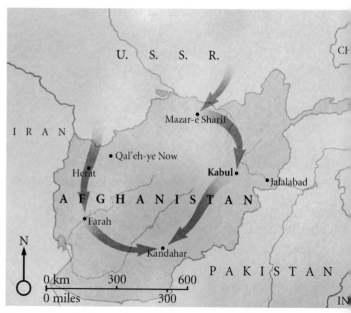

**Figure 4.6** The location of Afghanistan in relation to the USSR.

## ACTIVITIES

1 Explain what is meant by *détente*.
2 Study Sources A and B. Using the information in the text and in these sources, explain why there was a worsening in Sino-Soviet relations in the 1950s and 1960s.
3 Draw up a list of the reasons China, the USA and the USSR had for pursuing the policy of *détente*. Prepare a table in the following format:

| China | USA | USSR |
|-------|-----|------|
|       |     |      |

Now look at your results: which country had the most need of *détente*? Explain your answer.
4 Who benefited most from *détente*?
5 '*Détente* was a failure.' Using the information in the text and in Source C, explain whether or not you agree with this assessment.

## EXTENSION ACTIVITY

Was *détente* a policy of choice or necessity?

## REVISION TIP

*Détente* happened for a lot of different reasons; make sure that you can explain the different motives behind each country's pursuit of the policy.

## THE COLLAPSE OF COMMUNISM AND THE END OF THE COLD WAR

### A New US President

The November 1980 US presidential election was won by Ronald Reagan. Reagan served two terms as President (1981–9). During this time the Cold War descended to new depths of tension and then reached new heights of co-operation, heights that had been almost unimaginable up to that point.

### 'Star Wars'

Reagan was passionately anti-communist and therefore an opponent of *détente*. In 1983 he famously called the USSR the 'evil empire' and made clear his determination to ensure that the USA would never be destroyed by communism (Source A). To this end he began to spend huge amounts of money on new defence systems. A range of up-to-date missiles was introduced and a significant number of missiles were based in Europe to the annoyance of peace groups such as **Campaign for Nuclear Disarmament (CND)**.

Even more impressively, Reagan supported the development of the Strategic Defence Initiative (SDI), a laser defence system that would effectively create a shield around the USA, which could not be penetrated by Soviet missiles. Perhaps not surprisingly it was nicknamed 'Star Wars'. Tensions increased to the point where the USSR boycotted the 1984 Olympic Games, which were being held in Los Angeles (Source B).

### SOURCE A

*President Reagan's judgement on the USSR, 1983.*

An evil empire … the focus of evil in the modern world … I believe that communism is another sad, bizarre chapter in human history whose last pages even now are being written.

### SOURCE B

*Soviet response to Reagan's policies, 1984.*

[The Reagan administration is] pushing mankind to the brink of disaster.

### Economic Problems

'Star Wars' cost billions of dollars and before long the US economy was in difficulty. However, the situation was even worse in the USSR. As Moscow tried to keep up with US technological advances the already crumbling Soviet economy came close to total collapse. Both countries needed to reduce costs as a matter of urgency.

The state of the Soviet economy particularly concerned Mikhail Gorbachev, the third new Soviet leader in three years, who took over in March 1985. He was the first Soviet leader not to have been politically associated with the Stalinist era. Gorbachev knew that the USSR could not afford to spend money in a vain attempt to keep up with US defence spending. This was because:

- Living standards were appallingly low.
- There were significant levels of corruption within the Communist Party and as a result money was being wasted.
- Millions were on the verge of starvation because of the poor performance of the country's agricultural sector.
- Many of the USSR's main industries were in dire need of modernisation.
- Technologically, the USSR was decades behind the West.
- The war in Afghanistan was draining billions from the economy.

## Gorbachev's Foreign Policy

Gorbachev knew that economic reform in the USSR would have to be preceded by huge cuts in defence spending. Cuts in defence spending would require a better relationship with the West. In 1986 he signalled a major change in Soviet foreign policy when he indicated the USSR's desire to get rid of all nuclear weapons. He also indicated his willingness to abandon previous Cold War policies, such as peaceful co-existence and the Brezhnev Doctrine, in favour of ensuring the survival of the USSR.

## Arms Limitation Talks

In an attempt to reach agreement Reagan and Gorbachev held a series of summit meetings. At first little was achieved, but after some intensive negotiations both sides agreed to a reduction in weaponry. Their agreement was contained in the 1987 Intermediate Nuclear Forces (INF) Treaty, which ensured the removal of nearly 4000 nuclear warheads and the halting of the 'Star Wars' programme. It also allowed teams of inspectors to oversee the destruction of the weapons. A year later Gorbachev announced the withdrawal of Soviet forces from Afghanistan and a huge reduction in the size of the Soviet armed forces. Troops were also withdrawn from other Iron Curtain countries.

Under Reagan's successor, George H. Bush (elected in November 1988), the changes continued. The new President was particularly impressed by the political changes that Gorbachev

Mikhail Gorbachev (1931–) and Ronald Reagan (1911–2004) meeting in Iceland 1986.

was introducing behind the Iron Curtain. Bush met Gorbachev in Malta in 1989 and both leaders declared that the Cold War was over (Source C below). In July 1991 the Warsaw Pact was dissolved, removing one of the key symbols of East–West divisions.

### SOURCE C

*Mikhail Gorbachev speaking about the end of the Cold War.*

I do not regard the end of the Cold War as a victory for one side. The end of the Cold War is our common victory.

### ACTIVITIES

1 Create a timeline showing the developments in US–Soviet relations in the 1980s.
2 Study Source A. Using the information in the text and in this source, explain:
   - What was Reagan's initial attitude to the USSR?
   - What policies did he introduce because of his attitude?
3 Study Source B. Using this source and the text, explain how the USSR reacted to Reagan's policies in the early 1980s.
4 What factors led Gorbachev to seek the end of the Cold War?
5 Study Source C. Looking at the evidence presented in this chapter, do you think Gorbachev's opinion in Source C is correct? Provide evidence to support your answer.

## EXTENSION ACTIVITY

Who deserves the credit for ending the Cold War: Reagan or Gorbachev?

## REVISION TIP

You need to decide here whether the Cold War began to end because of the influence of individuals, or whether the poor state of the Soviet economy meant that change would have taken place anyway.

# FINAL THAW: USSR AND THE SATELLITE STATES

## Glasnost and Perestroika

Gorbachev knew that the USSR had to change completely, both politically and economically, if it was to survive. The first step was to end the arms race so that money could be invested in the Soviet economy. However, Gorbachev also began to encourage the Soviets to offer constructive criticism of the communist system as a way of helping it to modernise and improve.

Gorbachev stated that his reforms would revolve around the ideas of *perestroika* and *glasnost*:

- *Perestroika*: restructuring of the Soviet economy through the introduction of more Western-style policies (Source A).
- *Glasnost*: openness. In other words there would be freedom to debate, freedom for the media, freedom from government control.

In March 1985 Gorbachev announced the end of the Brezhnev Doctrine (Source B). The thinking behind this was simple: his decision to end the Cold War meant that the Eastern European buffer zone was no longer needed. Now there would be no attempt to hold countries back if they sought their freedom (Source C). To show that he meant what he said, Gorbachev began to withdraw Soviet troops from Eastern Europe (Source D).

## Reactions Behind the Iron Curtain

The people of the other Iron Curtain countries – fed up with years of repression and economic decline – had been watching the changes in the USSR with great interest. Gorbachev's decision to loosen the bonds that tied them to the USSR and his refusal to demand that countries remain communist meant that similar freedoms were now within their own grasp. It was in 1989 that most countries broke free. Unlike the experiences of 1956 and 1968, nothing was done to oppose them.

## SOURCE A

*Mikhail Gorbachev explaining his new domestic policy ideas in* Perestroika *(1987).*

Perestroika means overcoming stagnation [decline]. *Perestroika* is the development of democracy … It is a thorough renewal of every aspect of Soviet life.

## SOURCE B

*Mikhail Gorbachev outlining his new foreign policy ideas to the United Nations, December 1988.*

Force, or the threat of force, neither can, nor should be instruments of foreign policy … The principle of freedom of choice is vital.

## SOURCE C

*USSR Foreign Minister Gennady Gerasimov explaining Moscow's replacement for the Brezhnev Doctrine, 1989 (adapted).*

The new doctrine is in place which is the Frank Sinatra doctrine. Frank Sinatra doctrine has a very popular song, 'I did it my way'. So Hungary, Poland, any other country does it its own way. They decide which road to take. It's their business.

## SOURCE D

*Extract from Steve Phillips,* The Cold War: Conflict in Europe and Asia *(2001).*

The Cold War came to an end when the USSR lost its will for empire. It could not sustain the resources needed to pursue an empire it no longer felt it needed, to secure itself against its enemies.

## The Opening of the Iron Curtain

In each country the search for freedom took a slightly different path as Figure 4.7 shows.

## Freedom for All?

However, not all people obtained the freedoms that they sought. In China things were very different. A wave of student demonstrations between April and June 1989 ended in disaster in Beijing's Tiananmen Square when government forces crushed the opposition movement.

## Crisis in Russia

Nor was all well in Russia; the economy was still in crisis and society seemed to be in a state of collapse. Russia was divided between those who

**POLAND**
**1980.** Solidarity was set up as the first free trade union within the Iron Curtain. It emerged as a result of opposition to Poland's economic and political decline. Solidarity soon has 9 million members.
Government recognised Solidarity.
**1981.** Under pressure from Moscow, Poland's leader, General Jaruzelski, declared martial law. Solidarity was declared illegal but continued to exist underground, supported particularly by the Catholic Church and its Polish leader Pope John Paul II.
**1989.** April: Solidarity was legalised again after a wave of strikes.
Workers were granted the right to strike.
June: Solidarity won Poland's elections.
August: A non-communist government was installed.
December: Lech Walesa became President of Poland and the first non-communist leader in Eastern Europe for 4 decades.

**BALTIC STATES**
Initally even Gorbachev resisted the demands of Latvia and Lithuania for freedom, as he feared that it would lead all the other republics that made up the USSR to seek the same.
**1991.** Estonia, Latvia and Lithuania declared their independence.

**EAST GERMANY**
**1989.** October: Gorbachev visited East Berlin and encouraged people to push for democracy.
October: East Germany's leader, Erich Honecker resigned.
November: The Berlin Wall – the symbol of East-West division – was opened, allowing freedom of movement between East and West Berlin.
**1990.** October: Germany was reunified.

**CZECHOSLOVAKIA**
**1989.** May: Huge protest rallies were organised to demand change.
November: After some initial resistance the communist regime was overthrown with almost no loss of life. This became known as the 'Velvet Revolution'.
December: The Chairman of the newly elected federal parliament was Alexander Dubček. Playwright Vaclav Havel became President.
**1993.** Czechoslovakia split into Czech Republic and Slovakia.

**ROMANIA**
**1989.** December: After authorizing the killings of large numbers of people protesting for food, dictator Nicolae Ceausescu fled. Later he was caught and executed by the army.

**HUNGARY**
**1988.** Hard line leader Janos Kadar was sacked and Imre Nagy given a state funeral.
**1989.** January: Opposition parties were allowed.
March: Demonstrations were held against Soviet troops.
May: Fences cutting off the Border with Austria were removed. As a result many East Germans went through Hungary and Austria into West Germany.
October: A non-communist government was set up.

**YUGOSLAVIA**
**1980.** Death of Tito.
**1990.** Emergence of four different regimes within Yugoslavia.
**1991–95.** A series of wars was fought among the various ethnic groups in the region.

**BULGARIA**
**1989.** February: Free trade union established.
November: Communist leadership resigned.

**Figure 4.7** The collapse of Communism in Eastern Europe.

A lone protestor trying to halt government tanks in Tiananmen Square 1989.

and he was soon reinstated. Yet within four months the Communist Party had been outlawed in Russia and the USSR had ceased to exist; all 15 member republics had declared their independence. Three of the largest states, Russia, the Ukraine and Belorussia, formed a new union called the Commonwealth of Independent States.

Gorbachev's decision to end the Cold War and reform the USSR had resulted in the end of communist control. The last leader of the USSR was now a President without a country and he resigned on Christmas Day 1991.

thought there had been too much change and those who felt that there had not been enough. One of the latter was Boris Yeltsin who was elected leader of Russia in 1990. Russia was the largest of the different Republics that together made up the USSR.

In August 1991 an attempt was made to overthrow Gorbachev by army hardliners. The **coup** was defeated by troops loyal to Gorbachev

## ACTIVITIES

1 Create a timeline showing the key developments in Eastern Europe 1985–91.
2 Study Source A. Using the information in the text and in this source, explain the meaning of and the thinking behind:
   • *glasnost*
   • *perestroika*.
3 Study Sources B–D. Using the information in the text and in these sources, explain:
   • The reasons for the removal of the Brezhnev Doctrine.
   • The Soviet reaction to the collapse of the Iron Curtain.
4 Create a spider diagram explaining the reasons for the collapse of the USSR in 1991.

## EXTENSION ACTIVITIES

1 Did the USA win the Cold War or did the USSR lose it?
2 Why did the people of Eastern Europe reject communism?

## REVISION TIP

You need to understand that the collapse of the USSR was not Gorbachev's aim, but was more than likely given the policies that he introduced.

East German soldiers greet a West German woman through a gap in the Berlin Wall 1989.

## THE SPREAD OF COMMUNISM IN ASIA 1945–75 (I)

### China

Although by the late 1940s communism seemed to have been contained in Europe, it was soon establishing itself elsewhere. Since the 1920s Chinese communists, led by Mao Zedong, had been engaged in a civil war with Chiang Kai-shek's Nationalist Kuomintang (KMT). They temporarily joined forces in an attempt to defeat the Japanese in the Second World War, but before long the conflict was renewed. Despite significant US support for the KMT it had grown out of touch with the people and the communists were eventually victorious (Sources A and B). On 1 October 1949, Mao Zedong announced the establishment of the People's Republic of China. Chiang Kai-shek fled to the nearby island of Formosa (later renamed Taiwan).

### USSR's Reaction to the Communist Take-over

The USSR was delighted that China was now communist. Stalin had never expected the communists to win the war; now that they had, he was determined to establish a link with his new communist neighbour. Therefore in 1950 a Treaty of Friendship was agreed between the two powers which committed the USSR to supporting China's economic, technological and military development.

### USA's Reaction to the Communist Take-over

Not surprisingly the USA was severely concerned by these developments; China was a vast country with a massive population and huge resources; its fall to communists turned the Cold War into a worldwide struggle. The USA (wrongly) suspected that the fall of China was part of Stalin's scheme to spread communism across the world (Source C). Even more worryingly its fall came shortly after the USSR successfully exploded its first atomic bomb. Truman's regime came under massive criticism at home for its failure to stand up to the communists more forcefully.

Since it regarded Mao Zedong as little more than Stalin's puppet, the US government:

- Refused to recognise the new regime as China's legitimate government.
- Tried its best to ignore communist China and continued to support Chiang Kai-shek's right to represent China in the UN.

Stalin's attempts to obtain the Chinese seat at the UN for the communists were rejected; in response the Soviet delegation to the UN staged a walkout.

### The Threat to Asia

What did the communist take-over in China mean for Asia (Source D)? Would China's neighbours follow suit? Would Japan be a target?

---

### SOURCE A

*Extract from Steve Phillips,* The Cold War: Conflict in Europe and Asia *(2001).*

[Mao's success in China] was hardly surprising. The Nationalists had been corrupt and out of touch with the needs of the majority of the Chinese people … Even the anti-communist US General Stilwell described the Nationalist government as 'corruption, chaos, neglect, taxes, words and no deeds' and acknowledged that in comparison the communists 'raise production and standards of living. Practise what they preach.'

### SOURCE B

*A Chinese army marching song.*

Speak politely.
Pay fairly for what you buy.
Return everything you borrow.
Pay for any damage.
Don't strike or swear at people.
Don't damage the crops.
Don't take liberties with women.
Don't mistreat captives.

## SOURCE C

*Extract from Steve Phillips,* The Cold War: Conflict in Europe and Asia *(2001).*

Mao's declaration of a Communist People's Republic of China ... sent shockwaves across the USA ... The Communist take-over was seen as evidence of Stalin's work in spreading world communism ... the forces of freedom and capitalism seemed, to many Americans, to be under threat.

## SOURCE D

*Comment by Nationalist China's Representative at the United Nations, 1948.*

The fate of the entire Far East is linked to that of China. Because the Chinese Communists will help communism in all the Far East. Against this tide, you have built up in the West a solid dyke. But now, this tide will overflow in another direction.

The USA's fear of a series of neighbouring countries becoming communist one after another became known as the **domino theory**. To stop this happening containment would have to become a worldwide policy – not just a European one. The first test of the USA's determination to oppose the spread of communism in Asia came almost immediately. This time the country involved was China's neighbour – Korea.

## ACTIVITIES

1 Study Sources A and B. Using the information in the text and in these sources, explain why the Communists were more popular with the Chinese people than the Nationalists.

2 Study Sources C and D. Using the information in the text and in these sources, explain why the fall of China to the Communists worried the US so much.

3 How did the American government react to the fall of China to communism? What impact did this reaction have on relations with Communist China?

## EXTENSION ACTIVITY

Did the USA's reaction to events in China make things better or worse?

## REVISION TIP

It is very important that you understand that the spread of communism to China turned the Cold War into a worldwide issue.

# THE SPREAD OF COMMUNISM IN ASIA 1945–75 (II)

## Korea

It was in Korea that the Cold War became a lot hotter for the first time. In 1945 Korea was liberated from Japanese control by Soviet soldiers who moved into the north of the country and by US troops who landed in the south. The country was partitioned along the 38th parallel of latitude until elections could be held and the country reunited.

## The Emergence of Two States

Unfortunately the two superpowers could not agree what kind of a country Korea should become:

- The USSR was keen to see the election of a government sympathetic to communism.
- The USA sought the establishment of a regime that would ensure the introduction of a capitalist democracy.

By the time the Soviet and US forces had left Korea in 1949, two separate governments had been established to run the country:

- In the north a communist regime was set up under Kim Il Sung. The new state was called the Korean People's Democratic Republic but was more commonly known as North Korea.
- In the south a capitalist dictatorship was established led by Syngman Rhee. Officially this state was christened the Republic of Korea; more commonly it was called South Korea.

## The Start of the War

Both states sought the reunification of the country and on 25 June 1950 North Korea acted out its aim by invading the South. Within days the capital Seoul had been captured by North Korean forces (Figure 4.8). The USA believed that Stalin had encouraged the invasion. They also feared that a domino effect would soon begin by which one country after another would fall to communism (Source A). For these reasons the USA asked the United Nations to intervene to stop the attack. In fact, evidence shows that the driving force behind the invasion was Kim himself; Kim believed that Rhee was unpopular because of the dictatorial manner in which Rhee was running the country and believed that the people of South Korea would welcome the North Koreans. The UN however agreed with the US interpretation; first it condemned the attack; then it began to put together a military force to stop the invasion.

### SOURCE A

*President Truman commenting on events in Korea, 1950.*

The attack upon Korea makes it plain beyond all doubt that communism has passed beyond the use of subversion [rebellion] to conquer independent nations and will now use armed invasion and war.

## UN Response

The USSR was unable to use its **veto** to object to the UN's actions as it was then boycotting the UN. This was in protest at the USA's refusal to allow communist China to sit on the UN Security Council. The UN force – which was mainly US and led by American General Douglas MacArthur – landed at Inchon in September 1950 (Figure 4.9). Before long it had pushed the North Korean forces back over the 38th parallel (Figure 4.10).

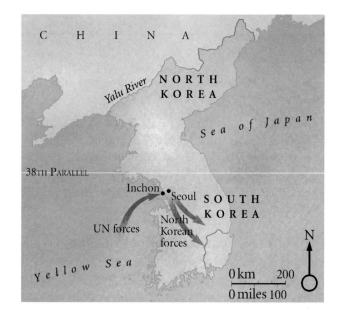

Figure 4.9 Korea, September 1950.

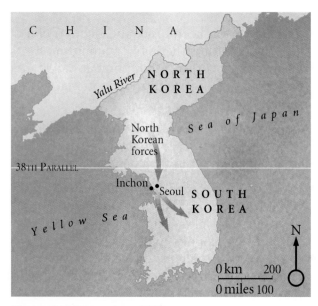

Figure 4.8 Korea, June 1950.

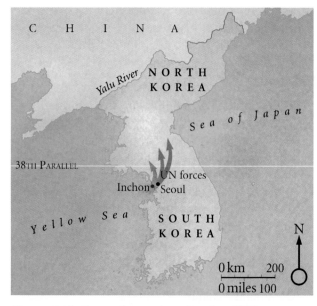

Figure 4.10 Korea, September–October 1950.

Crossing the 38th parallel meant that the UN force was now exceeding its UN orders. However, MacArthur's intention (with Truman's agreement) was to reunite the whole country. This considerably worried North Korea's neighbour China, which was still being ignored by the USA. The Chinese government was afraid that the USA would take the opportunity to invade China and restore Chiang Kai-shek and his Nationalists. As a result Mao Zedong issued a warning to the UN about the consequences of its actions.

## China's Response

China's fears seemed to be confirmed when MacArthur pushed on as far as the Yalu river, North Korea's border with China (Figure 4.11). Fearing the worst, over 250,000 Chinese troops (called 'volunteers' rather than soldiers so that war would not have to be declared) invaded North Korea in November 1950 and pushed the UN forces back over the 38th parallel. (Figure 4.12). What had begun as a war between North and South Koreans had turned into an open conflict between the USA and China.

MacArthur now pleaded with Truman to allow an attack that would lead to the destruction of communism in China; he even urged the use of the atomic bomb (Source B). Truman, however, had decided on containment rather than confrontation; he refused to consent to an escalation of the conflict fearing direct Soviet

> ### SOURCE B
>
> *General MacArthur speaking about the importance of the Korean War.*
>
> Asia is where the communist conspirators have elected to make their play for global conquest. If we lose this war to communism in Asia, the fall of Europe is inevitable. There is no substitute for victory.

intervention. Furthermore, in April 1951 he sacked MacArthur after the General had openly criticised the President's policies.

The war dragged on back and forth across the 38th parallel until the middle of 1951 when both sides dug in. The war then took to the skies where US and Soviet pilots (the latter dressed in Chinese uniforms and flying planes with Chinese markings) fought for a further two years with the loss of over 6000 planes. The aerial battles were kept secret from the US population in case they demanded all-out war with the USSR.

## The End of the War

Peace talks had begun in June 1951 but were unable to find a solution acceptable to all sides. In 1953 a change in the leadership of the USSR and the USA offered the opportunity for an end to the war. Dwight D. Eisenhower succeeded Truman and

**Figure 4.11** Korea, October 1950.

**Figure 4.12** Korea, November 1950.

Stalin died, eventually leaving Nikita Khrushchev in control. The new leaders sought peace and a ceasefire was agreed at Panmunjom in July 1953. Possibly Eisenhower's threat to use nuclear weapons against China assisted the conclusion of negotiations! Although a peace treaty was never signed, the agreement saw the creation of a permanent border – slightly north of the 38th parallel – and a demilitarised zone (DMZ) between the two states (Figure 4.13).

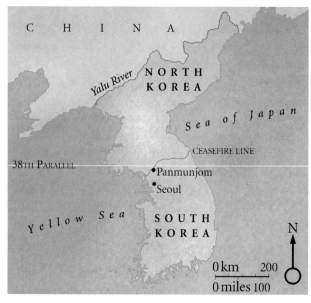

Figure 4.13 Korea, July 1953.

## Results of the Korean War

This was the situation at the end of the war:

- Over two million people had died, which resulted in a border little different to where it was before the war began.
- Containment had worked: communism had not spread into South Korea.
- The relationship between North and South Korea remained tense and bitter.
- US–Chinese relations deteriorated further, particularly as the USA continued to recognise Chiang Kai-shek's regime as China's rightful government.
- Realising the importance of preventing Japan falling to communism, the USA signed a peace treaty, ended military occupation and invested heavily in the Japanese economy.
- The US signed agreements with the Philippines, Australia and New Zealand, which

confirmed its position as the protector of the region.
- NATO was changed from a mainly political association into a full-blown military alliance.

Put simply, the Korean War indicated that the USA was now committed to pursuing a policy of containment anywhere in the world if its interests were felt to be under threat, even if this meant committing troops to combat situations.

### ACTIVITIES

1 How did the USA and USSR get involved in Korea?
2 Why were elections not held in Korea as had been intended?
3 Study Sources A and B. Why did the USA start fighting in Korea? Use the information in these sources and in the text to help you with your answer.
4 Explain why China became involved in the Korean War.
5 Using the information in the text, make a copy of the following table and fill it in:

| Positive results of the war | Negative results of the war |
|---|---|
|  |  |

Now look at your results; was the Korean War a success or a failure for US foreign policy? Explain your answer.

### EXTENSION ACTIVITY

'The Korean War was a waste of time.' Do you agree?

### REVISION TIP

Korea was where the Cold War became hot for the first time. Examiners will expect you to be able to explain why fighting broke out and what the main results of the conflict were.

# THE 1962 CUBAN MISSILE CRISIS

Perhaps the closest the two superpowers came to all-out war with each other was over the Caribbean island of Cuba, a small landmass just 90 miles off the Florida coast. For most of the twentieth century Cuba had exported its main crop, sugar, to the USA while American companies controlled most of the island's industry.

## Fidel Castro

Since 1959 Cuba had been led by Fidel Castro. Castro had overthrown the previous leader, the dictator Fulgencio Batista. At first Castro was not a communist; however, he was a **nationalist** who wished to ensure Cuba's independence from the influence of other countries. Once in power Castro began to nationalise industries, many of which were owned by US businesses; naturally this upset the Americans. As US hostility to Cuba grew, trade between the two nations declined. Castro turned elsewhere for assistance; in 1960 the USSR and Cuba agreed to trade oil and sugar for machinery. Before long the USSR had become Cuba's main trading partner. Then, in 1961, Castro announced that he had become a communist.

## The Bay of Pigs

In January 1961 John F. Kennedy took over as US President; at 43 years of age he was the youngest man to be elected to the position. Shortly after he took over, the **Central Intelligence Agency (CIA)** informed Kennedy that they were planning an invasion of Cuba with the assistance of anti-Castro Cuban exiles. Kennedy approved the invasion but it went totally wrong. It became known as the Bay of Pigs disaster after the bay in Cuba on which the 1500 invaders landed. The main problem was the bad military intelligence available to the invaders. This had led them to hugely overestimate the amount of support that they would receive from Cubans when they invaded. The invasion made Kennedy look inexperienced and turned Castro into a hero in Cuba.

## Missiles Arrive

Castro was deeply concerned by the American attempts to overthrow him. More and more he began to turn to the USSR for assistance. This

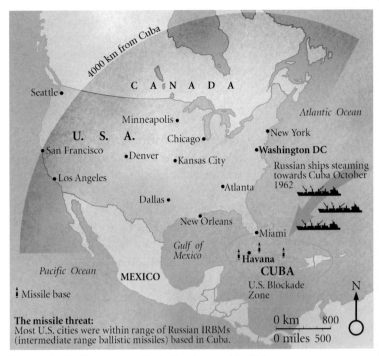

**Figure 4.14** The range of missiles located in Cuba.

resulted, in August 1962, in the arrival of equipment required to establish nuclear missile bases in Cuba. Missiles in Cuba would be able to reach most US cities (Figure 4.14) and would provide a counterbalance to the American missiles that had been installed in countries such as Turkey (because of their proximity to the USSR).

The US intelligence services obtained convincing proof of the missile bases by 14 October 1962. It also revealed that Soviet ships were en route to Cuba with further supplies. Kennedy was determined that he would not be made to look foolish again; he would stand firm against the threat being posed by the USSR.

## The Missile Crisis

Throughout the crisis, ExComm, a committee of the **National Security Council**, advised Kennedy. One of the key members was **Attorney General** Robert Kennedy, the President's brother. ExComm considered a range of options available to the USA including:

- an invasion of Cuba
- a **naval blockade** of Cuba
- air attacks on the missile bases
- a nuclear attack on Cuba
- allowing the missile bases to be erected.

Each of the options had good and bad points. Eventually, on 22 October, Kennedy decided on a naval blockade of Cuba. On the same day he revealed the unfolding crisis in a television broadcast (Source A). The remainder of the crisis played out as follows:

23 October — The USSR condemned the USA's actions as piracy and argued that it was only helping Cuba to improve its defences.

24 October — Beginning of the US naval blockade. Plans for an American invasion of Cuba were drawn up.
US Air Force planes began to fly over Cuba.
On reaching the naval blockade the Soviet ships were either stopped or turned away.
Evidence from U2 spy planes suggested that the missile sites were nearing completion.

26 October — On the same day that tensions were increased with the shooting down of a U2 spy plane over Cuba, Kennedy received a telegram from Khrushchev, which stated that the USSR would remove the missiles if the USA agreed to end the blockade and undertook not to invade Cuba.

27 October — A second telegram arrived from Khrushchev (Source B). This stated that the USSR would only remove its missiles from Cuba if the USA removed its missiles from Turkey.
A U2 spy plane violated Soviet airspace.
Against a background of advisers recommending an air strike, Kennedy took his brother's advice and decided to ignore Khrushchev's second telegram since he was not prepared to bargain with the USSR. Instead, he would send a reply to the first telegram. In this he agreed to remove the blockade and not invade the island in return for the removal of Soviet missiles. He added that if he did not receive a reply by 29 October an invasion of Cuba would begin.

28 October — Khrushchev agreed to Kennedy's offer and the removal of the missiles began.

U2 spy plane photograph of a missile base on Cuba.

A cartoon showing the battle for supremacy between Khrushchev and Kennedy.

## SOURCE A

*President Kennedy speaking on television, 22 October 1962.*

Any missile launched from Cuba against any nation in this hemisphere would bring a full retaliatory response upon the USSR.

## SOURCE B

*Extract from Khrushchev's second telegram to Kennedy, 27 October 1962.*

Our purpose has been to help Cuba develop as its people desire. You want to relieve your country from danger. Your rockets are stationed in Turkey … Turkey lies next to us!

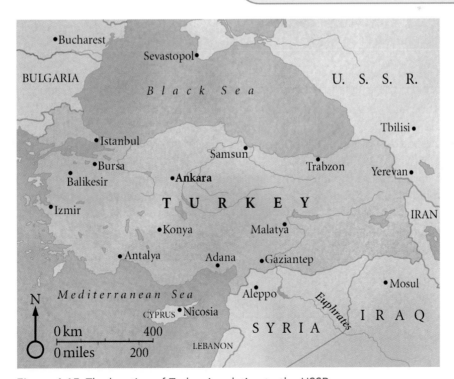

**Figure 4.15** The location of Turkey in relation to the USSR.

## Results of the Crisis

After 13 days of **brinkmanship** nuclear war had been avoided. In public it looked like a great victory for Kennedy; in reality however the result was not so clear-cut. Kennedy had agreed secretly, on 27 October, to remove the missiles in Turkey. This was not a great sacrifice as the missiles were old and out of date. Shortly after the crisis ended, the USA began to dismantle some of its missiles from various bases in Europe including Turkey. Within six months the US missiles were gone; Castro, however, remained in place (Source C).

Several valuable lessons were learnt during the Cuban missile crisis. In particular both sides agreed that such a confrontation should be avoided in the future. To assist with this a telephone hotline between Washington and Moscow was set up. A direct phone line would be much more helpful than other and slower methods of communication. They also agreed to begin talks designed to reduce the number of nuclear weapons each side had. As a result, the **Partial Test Ban Treaty** was signed in 1963.

Both leaders seemed to have reached an understanding that might have signified a better future. However, within two years both were gone: Kennedy had been assassinated and Khrushchev overthrown.

> ### SOURCE C
>
> *Extract from S.R. Gibbons, (1986).*
>
> The Chinese were furious that the Russians had 'backed down' over Cuba … Castro was also furious: the deal to withdraw the missiles had been made over his head … Khrushchev later claimed that he had 'won' all he wanted: the American promise not to invade.

### ACTIVITIES

1 Explain how and why Fidel Castro annoyed the US government.
2 What made Castro develop closer relations with the USSR?
3 Make a copy of the following table and fill it in:

| Option | Positive aspects | Negative aspects |
|---|---|---|
| An invasion of Cuba.<br>A naval blockade of Cuba.<br>Air attacks on the missile bases.<br>A nuclear attack on Cuba.<br>Allowing the missile bases to be erected. | | |

What would be the positive and negative aspects of each option? Why do you think Kennedy chose the option that he did?
4 Study Source A. What do you think were Kennedy's reasons for making the threat that he did in this source?
5 Study Sources B and C. Using the information in these sources and in the text, who you think won or lost the Cuban missile crisis: Kennedy, Khrushchev or Castro? Explain your answer.

### EXTENSION ACTIVITY

How real was the threat of war during the Cuban missile crisis?

### REVISION TIP

The Cuban missile crisis was portrayed as a great triumph for Kennedy, but you need to decide if it was really a US victory or whether Khrushchev seemed to be doing one thing he did not expect to get away with (putting missiles in Cuba) really to get something else as compensation (US missiles out of Turkey).

# THE SPREAD OF COMMUNISM IN ASIA 1945–75 (III): THE VIETNAM WAR

## Background: War with France

Since the nineteenth century Vietnam had been part of a French Empire in Asia known as Indochina (also made up of Cambodia and Laos). During the Second World War the Japanese replaced the French as occupiers. However, the Japanese were no more welcome and found themselves under attack from a Vietnamese nationalist army known as the Vietminh. This army was led by the communist Ho Chi Minh.

After the end of the Second World War the Vietminh declared Vietnam independent. This did not suit France as it had hoped to regain control of Vietnam. When the French forces moved back in, they too found themselves being resisted by the Vietminh. Initially the USA opposed French actions as **colonialism**, but by 1950 it began to provide support for the French. This was because it began to see the war as yet another part of the ongoing struggle against communism.

Despite US support the French suffered a humiliating defeat at Dien Bien Phu in 1954. This was followed by an **armistice** in which Vietnam was temporarily divided along the 17th parallel of latitude. The northern part would be under Vietminh control while the anti-communist Ngo Dinh Diem would control the South. It was agreed that after elections were held the country would be reunited.

The elections never took place since the South Vietnamese government – supported by the USA – were afraid that the communists would win. Once again the USA saw the possibility of the domino theory coming into play; if all of Vietnam fell to communism then neighbouring countries might follow suit. This could create a new communist power bloc based around China, something that would not suit US interests (Source A).

> ### SOURCE A
>
> *Senator John F. Kennedy, speaking in 1956.*
>
> Vietnam represents the cornerstone of the Free World in South-east Asia.

## Increased US Involvement

As a result President Eisenhower provided support for the South Vietnamese government in the form of money, weapons and military advisers. The aim was once more to contain the spread of communism. Eisenhower's successor, John F. Kennedy, increased the levels of aid. All this came at a time of increasing **guerrilla** attacks against the South's army by the National Liberation Front or Vietcong. This group had been set up in South Vietnam in 1960 to reunite the country under communist control. It was supported by Ho Chi Minh.

Unfortunately for the USA, Ngo Dinh Diem was not a popular leader. His regime was both brutal and corrupt and the government was made up of mostly Catholic landowners and was out of touch with its people, the majority of whom were Buddhist peasants. The Vietcong gained more and more support and control in the South. In November 1963 Diem was overthrown and assassinated by the Vietcong. Shortly after, Kennedy himself was killed; by then there were 16,000 US military advisers in Vietnam.

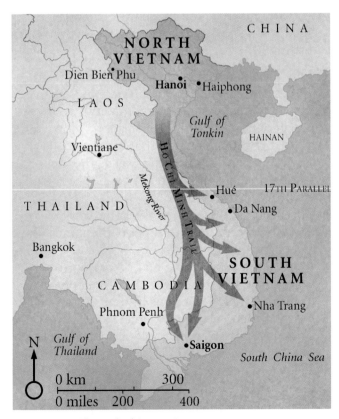

**Figure 4.16** The Indochina region.

A Buddhist monk sets himself on fire in protest at Diem's corrupt regime.

*Comment made by President Johnson in 1964.*

I am not going to be the President who saw South-east Asia go the way China went.

Rolling Thunder) against the Vietcong. In particular, the USA used chemicals such as napalm (a petroleum jelly) and Agent Orange (made up of, among other things, dioxin, which can damage the brain and the central nervous system) in their bombing raids. The former burned civilians indiscriminately; the latter cleared the forests of foliage. This enabled the Americans to see their enemy from the air; however it also destroyed the land and wounded countless civilians.

## Reasons for the USA's Difficulties

With over 500,000 troops in Vietnam by 1968 the USA should have had no difficulty in defeating its enemy. Even though it was receiving limited support from China and the USSR, the Vietcong was numerically inferior and significantly less well equipped. As the war went on the expected victory did not happen; indeed the opposite seemed to be the case. In many ways this was not surprising:

- The Vietnamese had already seen off foreign armies in the shape of the French and Japanese.
- The US army was made up of many inexperienced soldiers (**conscripts**). Moreover, it was fighting an enemy that used guerrilla tactics, dressed in the same way as the Vietnamese peasantry and knew the country well (Source C, page 186).
- The Vietcong developed a vast network of underground tunnels to support their guerrilla campaign (see Figure 4.17).
- The Vietnamese people had no reason to support the US forces, which seemed prepared to harass and kill civilians in their efforts to root out the Vietcong (Source D, page 186). The most notorious example of this was the My Lai massacre of March 1968 when nearly 350 Vietnamese villagers were massacred by a company of US troops. The platoon leader, Lieutenant William Calley, was imprisoned for life but later pardoned by President Nixon.

## The Tonkin Resolution

In August 1964 the North Vietnamese attacked a US destroyer, *USS Maddox*, in the Gulf of Tonkin. Kennedy's successor Lyndon B. Johnson believed that this attack provided the excuse for massive American involvement in Vietnam (Source B). The US Congress agreed and passed the Tonkin Resolution, allowing the President to fight a war as he saw fit.

Johnson took Congress at its word. Over the next three years massive numbers of troops were landed in the country and the US Air Force launched repeated bombing raids (Operation

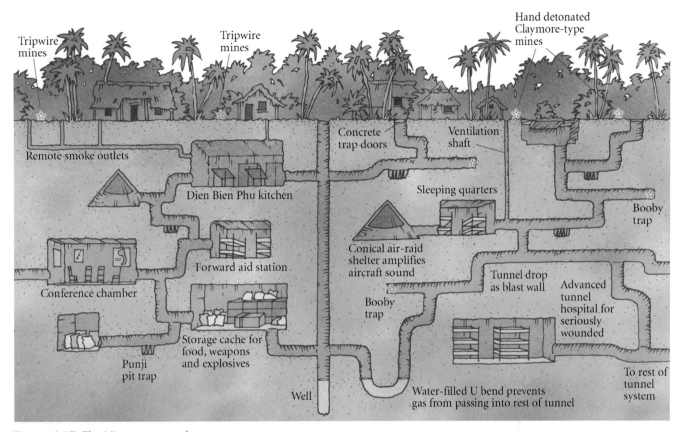

**Figure 4.17** The Vietcong tunnel system.

The My Lai massacre, March 1968.

## The Beginning of the End

In January 1968 the Vietcong launched a massive counteroffensive (known as the Tet Offensive as it started at the time of the Vietnamese New Year [Tet] celebrations) against the US forces. Vietcong troops got as far as the South's capital, Saigon, before they were driven back. Although ultimately a failure militarily, the Tet Offensive had an even more significant political impact: it made Americans feel that they could not win this war.

The same feelings were beginning to emerge back in the USA. Television pictures brought home to people the full horror of a war that many Americans did not understand. More and more young Americans were being drafted (conscripted) and more and more US troops were being brought home in body bags. Complaints were heard about the cost of the war. Students protested against the US government's policies. More and more of those being called up burned their **draft cards**. Johnson himself became so unpopular that he decided not to run for re-election in 1968 (Source E). The demonstrations continued after Richard M. Nixon became President; in one such protest the National Guard killed four students during a protest at Kent State University, Ohio. Even serving soldiers began to object about the job they had been sent to do.

Nixon was determined to remove the USA from the Vietnam War, but he wanted to do it in a way that did not make the USA look as if it had lost. To this end he:

- Increased the levels of bombing against North Vietnam and its capital Hanoi.
- Ordered secret bombing raids against the neighbouring countries of Cambodia and Laos in 1970. This was because they were being used as supply routes by the Vietcong (the so-called Ho Chi Minh trail). In total up to 10 million tons of bombs were dropped by the USA on Vietnam.
- Introduced the policy of Vietnamisation. By this US troops would be withdrawn and South Vietnamese forces would do the fighting.

## Peace Talks

In 1973, after several years of extended negotiations a peace treaty was signed in Paris. The terms of the treaty allowed for the withdrawal of the US forces and the return of US prisoners of war. It also allowed the Vietcong to remain in the South and put off a decision on the country's political future until a later date.

Nixon felt able to argue that he had achieved his aim of 'peace with honour' but within two years it was doubtful if this was the case. By 1975 all of Vietnam was in the hands of the communists; US involvement seemed to have achieved very little at an immense cost (Source F).

## Results of the Vietnam War

Here are some of the outcomes of the Vietnam War:

- There were huge military and civilian losses (see Table 4.4).
- Many of the US veterans suffered severe mental damage as a result of their experiences.
- Vietnam was devastated by the war, economically, socially and geographically.
- Cambodia and Laos also became communist; although no other neighbouring country did the policy of containment seemed to have failed.
- The USA spent at least $120 billion on the war.
- The war proved that an enemy that used suitable tactics could humble the USA.

| Country | Military dead | Military wounded | Civilian dead |
|---|---|---|---|
| North Vietnam | 900,000 | 2,000,000 | 1,000,000 |
| South Vietnam | 250,000 | 600,000 | |
| USA | 58,132 | 300,000 | |

Table 4.4 Deaths during the Vietnam War

### ACTIVITIES

1 Create a timeline of the key events in Vietnam 1945–75.
2 Study Sources A and B. Using the information in the text and in these sources, explain the factors that led the USA to support first the French and then the South Vietnamese government.
3 Study Sources C and D. Using the information in these sources and in the text, create a spider diagram showing all the reasons why the US campaign failed in Vietnam.
4 How reliable and useful would Sources C and D be as evidence to an historian investigating why the US campaign failed?
5 Study Sources E and F. What impact did the Vietnam War have on US politics? Use the information in the text and in these sources to help you with your answer.
6 Did the USA achieve 'peace with honour' in the Vietnam War? Explain your answer.

### EXTENSION ACTIVITIES

1 Was the Vietnam War justified?
2 How similar were the wars in Korea and Vietnam?

### REVISION TIP

In the exam you may be asked to comment on how successful the USA was in Vietnam. Think about what its original reasons were for getting involved and compare these with the situation at the end of the conflict.

## Practice Question (Foundation and Higher)

Source Materials: The Spread of Communism in Eastern Europe after the Second World War

### Source A
*Stalin replying to Churchill's address,
13 March 1946.*

[The USSR's] loss of life has been several times
greater than that of Britain and the USA …
So what is surprising about the Soviet Union,
anxious for its own future safety, trying to
see that loyal governments should exist in
these countries?

### Source B
*President Truman, writing in his Memoirs (1955).*

When we refused to be forced out of Berlin,
we demonstrated to Europe that we would act
when freedom was threatened.

### Source C
*US Secretary of State Dulles commenting on
events in Hungary, October 1956.*

To all those suffering under communist slavery,
let us say: you can count on us.

### Source D
*Extract from Steve Phillips, The Cold War:
Conflict in Europe and Asia (2001).*

There was no doubt that the USSR was willing
to take action when it felt the interests of
socialism were threatened. From a Soviet
viewpoint their actions were successful … There
was to be little serious unrest in the region until
the early 1980s.

## Foundation

### Section A
Answer all of this section

1 This question is about the spread of communism in Eastern Europe after the Second World War.

(a) Study Source A.

Give two reasons from Source A to explain the actions of the USSR in Eastern Europe after the Second World War. [4]

(b) Study Source B.

Give three reasons from Source B to explain what happened during the Berlin Airlift. [6]

(c) Study Source C.

How useful is Source C in telling us how the West reacted following the Soviet invasion of Hungary? [10]

(d) Study Sources A, B, C and D.

Using Sources A, B, C and D, and your own knowledge, explain why there are different views of the reasons for the development of the Cold War in Eastern Europe after the Second World War. [15]

### Section B
Answer one question

In this question up to 5 additional marks are available for your use of spelling, punctuation and grammar.

2 Explain the ways relations changed between the USA and the USSR in the years 1945–1962.

Use the following three paragraph headings to help you with your answer:

The Berlin Blockade
Hungary
The Berlin Wall [15] and [SPaG 5]

3 Explain the ways the USA reacted to the spread of communism in the years 1948–1973.

Use the following three paragraph headings to help you with your answer:

The Truman Doctrine
Korea
Vietnam [15] and [SPaG 5]

**Higher**

Section A
Answer all of this section

1  This question is about the spread of communist control in Eastern Europe after the Second World War.

  (a)  Study Source A.

  What does Source A tell us about why the USSR spread communism to the countries of Eastern Europe after the Second World War?  [4]

  (b)  Study Sources A and B.

  How far does Source B support the view in Source A about the actions of Stalin and the USSR after the Second World War?  [6]

  (c)  Study Source C.

  How useful is Source C in telling us how the West reacted following the Soviet invasion of Hungary?  [9]

  (d)  'The USSR had to keep control over Eastern Europe for its own safety'.

  Using Sources A, B, C and D, and your own knowledge, explain whether you agree with this interpretation of the actions and policies of the USSR in Eastern Europe after the Second World War.  [15]

Section B
Answer one question

In this question up to 5 additional marks are available for your use of spelling, punctuation and grammar.

2  How and why did events in Berlin in the period 1945–1961 cause tensions to develop between the USA and the USSR?  [16] and [SPaG 5]

**or**

3  How and why did relations between the USA and the USSR change in the period 1960–1991?  [16] and [SPaG 5]

# USEFUL WEBSITES

## Germany

Useful material on personalities and events. Includes facts, documents, other sources and illustrations.
www.spartacus.schoolnet.co.uk/Germany.htm

BBC Bitesize revision website. Includes revision material, examination advice and online tests.
www.bbc.co.uk/schools/gcsebitesize/history/mwh/germany/

Some useful basic information on Nazi Germany.
www.historylearningsite.co.uk/Nazi%20Germany.htm

Some excellent interactive resources and downloadable materials.
www.activehistory.co.uk/Miscellaneous/menus/GCSE/Weimar_Germany.htm and www.activehistory.co.uk/Miscellaneous/menus/GCSE/Nazi_Germany.htm

Wide range of excellent resources and materials for downloading.
www.johndclare.net/Weimar1.htm

Useful revision material, activities, quizzes, downloadable materials, etc.
www.schoolhistory.co.uk/revision/germany.shtml
Also includes: www.schoolhistory.co.uk/lessons/riseofhitler/index.htm which has some excellent materials available.

Examples of various types of Nazi propaganda.
www.calvin.edu/academic/cas/gpa/

## Northern Ireland

Some basic information on Irish history up to 1922.
www.historylearningsite.co.uk/ireland_1848_to_1922.htm

A State Apart is an interactive chronicle covering the 30 years of conflict in Northern Ireland.
www.bbc.co.uk/northernireland/education/stateapart/

This site contains information and source material on 'the Troubles' in Northern Ireland from 1968 to the present.
http://cain.ulst.ac.uk/

BBC Bitesize revision website. Includes revision material, examination advice and online tests.
www.bbc.co.uk/schools/gcsebitesize/history/mwh/ni1965_85/

Through a series of articles, media clips and photographs, 'the Troubles' website takes you through Northern Ireland's turbulent history.
www.bbc.co.uk/history/recent/troubles/the_troubles_article_01.shtml

## Cold War

Useful material on personalities and events. Includes facts, documents, other sources and illustrations.
www.spartacus.schoolnet.co.uk/ColdWar.htm

Some excellent interactive resources and downloadable materials.
www.activehistory.co.uk/Miscellaneous/menus/GCSE/Cold_War.htm

Website on answering source questions.
www.schoolhistory.co.uk/gcselinks/source.html

Internet Modern History Sourcebook: Eastern Europe since 1945.
www.fordham.edu/halsall/mod/modsbook50.html

Internet Modern History Sourcebook: Western Europe since 1945.
www.fordham.edu/halsall/mod/modsbook49.html

BBC Bitesize revision website on Cold War. Revision activities and tests.
www.bbc.co.uk/schools/gcsebitesize/history/mwh/ir2/

Wide range of excellent resources and materials for downloading.
www.johndclare.net/cold_warA1.htm
www.johndclare.net/cold_warB1.htm

# GLOSSARY

| | |
|---|---|
| **Abdicate** | To give up the position of King or Queen of a country. |
| **Abdication crisis** | The time in 1936 when Britain's King Edward VIII abdicated so that he could marry a divorced American woman, Wallis Simpson. |
| **Alliance Party of Northern Ireland** | Launched in April 1970, led by Oliver Napier. Although broadly unionist, the Alliance Party welcomed supporters from all denominations. It hoped to achieve the not yet introduced parts of Prime Minister Terence O'Neill's reforms. |
| **Allies** | The name given to Britain, France, the USA and the USSR (Russia) during the First and Second World Wars. |
| **Anderson air raid shelter** | A particular model of air raid shelter designed to accommodate six people. |
| **Anschluss** | The annexation (takeover) of Austria by Germany (German – union). |
| **Anti-Semitism** | Anti-Jewish ideas. |
| **Appeasement** | The policy of making concessions to an opponent in the hope that they will stop making demands. |
| **Apprentice Boys** | A loyalist club set up to remember the group of apprentices who closed the gates of Derry/Londonderry against the armies of King James II in 1689. |
| **Ard Fheis** | Annual Party Conference (Irish). |
| **Armistice** | A truce or ceasefire. |
| **ARP** | Air Raid Precautions. An organisation set up to protect civilians from the dangers of air raids. |
| **Aryan** | The master race in Nazi Germany, made up of individuals of northern European descent and excluding those of a Semitic background. |
| **Attorney General** | The politician in charge of justice in the USA. |
| **Autarky** | A self-sufficient economy. |
| **Backbencher** | An MP who is a member of the government party but who does not have a job in the government. |
| **Barrage Balloon** | Large balloons attached to steel cables (which were attached to the ground) which forced enemy aircraft to fly higher (to avoid contact with the cables) thus limiting their bombing accuracy. |
| **Barter economy** | When goods rather than money are given in exchange for a service or other goods. |
| **Battle of Britain** | 1940 aerial campaign between the RAF and Luftwaffe to gain control of the skies above the Channel and Great Britain. |
| **Battle of the Atlantic** | The naval campaign fought between the Allies and Germany 1939–45. |
| **Bolshevik** | Russian communist. |
| **Boycott** | To cut off connections with a person, group or organisation. |
| **Brinkmanship** | Practice of almost, but not quite, going to war with the aim of gaining concessions off an opposing country. |
| **British Commonwealth** | An association of countries that were formerly colonies of Great Britain. |
| **By-election** | An election for an individual parliamentary seat held between general elections. |

| | |
|---|---|
| Capitalist | An economic system (or a person supporting it) which believes in private ownership and the making of profits. |
| Censorship | Prevention of the publication of unwanted viewpoints. |
| CIA | Central Intelligence Agency. A US government body set up in 1947 to collect information on foreign groups and governments. |
| Civil disobedience | Protesting peacefully against alleged injustice. |
| Civil service | A government's administrative support. |
| Civil war | A war between members of the same nation. |
| CND | Campaign for Nuclear Disarmament. A pressure group set up in Britain to oppose the possession and use of nuclear weapons. |
| Coalition | A government made up of different political parties. |
| Collective leadership | Leadership of a country by more than one person. |
| Colonialism | The belief that rich countries should control or rule poorer countries. |
| Comintern | Communist International. Set up in Moscow in 1919 to help spread Communism throughout the world. |
| Communism | The ideas of Karl Marx who supported a system of rule where industries were run by the government for the good of the people. |
| Concentration camp | Detention camp for political prisoners. |
| Congress | The US Parliament. |
| Conscription/conscripts | Compulsory military service and those that serve. |
| Constitution | A document setting out the rules by which a country is to be run. |
| Constitutional parties | Political parties which operate completely within the democratic system. |
| Constitutional monarchy | A system where power is shared between a monarch and a Parliament. |
| Convoy | Group of merchant ships sailing together with a military escort. |
| Corporation | Town or city council. |
| Coup (coup d'état) | Violent seizure of power (French). |
| D-Day | The Allied invasion, on 6 June 1944, of Western Europe. |
| Demilitarise | Ensure an area does not have a military presence. |
| Democracy | System whereby the people freely elect a government on a regular basis. |
| Democratic Unionist Party | Originally known as the Protestant Unionist Party, this party emerged in September 1971. Led by Reverend Ian Paisley, it aimed to defend Northern Ireland's constitution while reforming its economy and society. |
| Détente | Easing of Cold War tensions (French). |
| Devolved/devolution | A political system where local parliaments are given some powers by the central parliament. |
| Diktat | A dictated peace (German). |
| Direct rule | The system by which Northern Ireland was ruled directly from Westminster and not by its own local parliament. |
| Dominion | A self-governing colony. |
| Domino theory | Idea that political change in one country will lead to political change in other countries (like a row of dominos falling). |
| Draft card | Letters informing individuals they are liable to be conscripted into the army. |
| Duties | Taxes on imports. |

| | |
|---|---|
| Ecumenism | Theory which seeks the unification of Christian churches. |
| *Ersatz* | A German word meaning substitute or replacement. |
| Family allowance | Money paid to a family by the government to help cover expenses. |
| Federal | A political system with a central and local parliament each with their own areas of responsibility. |
| General election | An election held for all the seats in a parliament. |
| Gerrymandering | The practice of drawing electoral boundaries in a way that benefits one particular group at the expense of another. |
| Governor General | Representative of the monarch in a dominion. |
| Guerrilla | A conflict where one side tends to use hit-and-run tactics against a superior enemy. |
| Home rule | Self-government. |
| Hyperinflation | Massive increases in prices. |
| Imperialism | The idea of a country having colonies. |
| Imports | Goods brought in to one country from another. |
| Indoctrination | Process of imposing beliefs (political/racial) on an individual or group of people. |
| Intern/internment | Imprisonment without trial. |
| Iron Cross | German military award. |
| Jehovah's Witnesses | A branch of Christianity founded in the US in the late nineteenth century. |
| Judiciary | The system of judges and courts. |
| League of Nations | A body established by the Paris Peace Settlement in 1919 in an attempt to provide a place where leaders could talk together and so avoid wars. |
| Lundy | An insulting term within unionism, meaning 'traitor'. Lieutenant Colonel Robert Lundy was the Governor of Derry/Londonderry during the siege of 1688–1689. Lundy recommended surrender rather than defence of Derry/Londonderry against King James II. |
| Lutheran (Church) | The main Protestant Church in Germany. |
| Marxism | The ideas of Karl Marx (see communism). |
| Merchant shipping | Ships carrying goods/produce. |
| Middle class | Social group between the lower/working and upper classes, traditionally including professional and business workers and their families. |
| Moderator | The leader of a church (usually Presbyterian). |
| Mutiny | Refusal by military personnel to obey orders. |
| National Assistance (Act) | Act which gave local authorities the responsibility to provide accommodation and services to people with disability or mental health problems. |
| National Security Council | A group which advises the US President on foreign policy issues. |
| Nationalise/nationalisation | To bring industries under the ownership/control of the nation. |
| Nationalist | A person who seeks to protect the interests of a particular nation. |

| | |
|---|---|
| Naval blockade | Blocking of area by military ships. |
| No-go areas | Areas of Northern Ireland that were policed by Republican paramilitaries and which were not accessible to the RUC or British army. |
| Non-aggression pact | Agreement between two or more countries not to go to war against each other. |
| Non-contributing pensions | Pensions not involving contributions from workers. Instead the pension is fully funded by the employer. |
| North Atlantic Treaty Organisation (NATO) | Established in 1949, a military alliance initially set up to oppose the spread of communism/Soviet aggression. |
| Official opposition | The second largest party in a parliament. |
| Ombudsman | An official who deals with complaints from the public. |
| Paris Peace Settlement | The name given to a number of treaties drawn up at the end of the First World War. |
| Partial Test Ban Treaty | A 1963 agreement between the USA and USSR which banned all test detonations of nuclear weapons except those taking place underground. |
| Partition/partitioning | The artificial division of a country. |
| Passive resistance | To oppose a group without using violence. |
| Planter | An individual (or his/her descendant) who took part in the colonisation of Ireland in the 1600–1700s. |
| Plebiscite | A type of referendum. A special vote where all the people of a country decide on a particular issue. |
| Points system | A system for determining council house allocation. A certain number of points were needed to gain a house and points were awarded for a variety of reasons. |
| Privy Council | Part of the British judicial system. |
| Propaganda | Political advertising. |
| Proportional representation | A system of voting designed to create a result more in line with the way in which people voted. |
| Puppet government | A government that is under the control or influence of another state. |
| Radar | System for detecting aircraft, etc. based on radio waves. |
| Rates/ratepayer | A payment made by householders to their local council/person who makes such a payment. |
| Red Army | The national army in the USSR. |
| Reichstag | The German Parliament. |
| Reparations | The fine placed on Germany at the end of the First World War. A general term for a fine imposed by one country on another. |
| Republic | A form of government with no monarch. |
| Republican | Believer in a republic. |
| Reserved occupations | Job from which an individual will not be taken to serve in the armed forces. |
| Satellite state | A country that is under the influence of another state. |
| *Schutzstaffel* (SS) | Hitler's personal bodyguard, established in 1925. |
| Secretariat | A group of civil servants supporting the work of the Anglo-Irish Agreement. |

195

| | |
|---|---|
| Secretary of State | In the UK a politician who is in charge of a government department and who is usually a member of the Cabinet. In the US the term refers specifically to the Foreign Minister. |
| Sectarian | Religious-based bias or hatred. |
| Security Council (UN) | The part of the UN which works to maintain international peace and security. |
| Social Democratic and Labour Party | Established in August 1970 and led by Gerry Fitt. They sought political reforms within Northern Ireland and the eventual re-unification of Ireland. The SDLP immediately became the main opposition party in Stormont, replacing the old Nationalist Party (led by Eddie McAteer). |
| Socialist | Individual who believes that the state should own and control the means of production and distribution in a country. |
| Special category status | The recognition that those convicted of crimes connected with 'the Troubles' had acted for political and not criminal reasons. |
| Squatter/squatted | An individual who occupies a house that he or she does not own or pay rent on/act of squatting. |
| Stormont | The name given to the Northern Ireland Parliament building opened in 1932. |
| Summit | A meeting between leaders of different countries. |
| Superpower | Extremely powerful nation. |
| *Taoiseach* | Irish Prime Minister (Irish for chief/leader). |
| TD | Member of Dáil Éireann (Teachta Dála – Deputy to the Dáil). |
| Third Reich | Germany under the Nazis (German for empire). |
| Totalitarian | A political system where all power is held by one person or by a small group of people. |
| Trade deficit | When a country spends more money on importing goods than it makes from exporting goods. |
| Trade union | Organisation set up to protect the rights of workers. |
| Treaty of Rapallo | 1922 treaty between Germany and the USSR. In it the two countries agreed to give up demands for reparations from each other and renewed diplomatic relations. |
| Tribunal | A body set up to reach a decision on a particular issue. |
| Unionist | A person who wishes the political union between Great Britain and Northern Ireland to continue. |
| United Nations | An international organisation set up in 1945 to enable nations to co-operate in all areas and to achieve world peace. |
| UVF | Ulster Volunteer Force. A paramilitary group originally set up in 1912 to oppose the introduction of Home Rule to Ireland. |
| Veto | The right or ability to prevent or forbid an action or decision taking place. |
| Viceroy | The representative of the monarch. |
| Victoria Cross | The highest British military award for bravery. |
| *Wehrmacht* | The German army, 1935–45. |
| Welfare State | A system where the government provides educational and health facilities for the people of a nation. |
| Western approaches | An area of the Atlantic Ocean off the western coast of Britain. The majority of shipping to and from Britain made use of this route. |

# ACKNOWLEDGEMENTS

The publishers would like to thank the following individuals, institutions and companies for permission to reproduce copyright illustrations in this book: p.3 © Ullstein Bild/TopFoto; p.4 AKG-images; p.9 AKG-images; p.10 Popperfoto/Getty Images; p.11 AKG-images; p.12 AKG-images/Ullstein bild; p.15 AKG-images; p.16 Ullstein Bild; p.17 AKG-images; p.19 © BPK; p.20 l AKG-images; p.20 r © Austrian Archives/CORBIS; p.22 l AKG-images; p.22 r © Bettmann/CORBIS; p.24 AKG-images; p.25 t © Hulton-Deutsch Collection/CORBIS; p.25 b Punch Ltd; p.28 AKG-images/Ullstein Bild; p.30 AKG-images; p.31 © BPK; p.32 David Low, *Evening Standard*, 3 July 1934/British Cartoon Archive, University of Kent; p.33 Süddeutsche Zeitung Photo/Scherl; p.34 AKG-images; p.35 AKG-images; p.36 © BPK; p.38 AKG-images; p.39 l © Hulton-Deutsch Collection/CORBIS; p.39 r AKG-images; p.41 Ullstein Bild; p.42 AKG-images; p.43 © Bettmann/CORBIS; p.45 t AKG-images; p.45 b AKG-images/Ullstein Bild; p.46 AKG-images; p.49 Ullstein Bild; p.50 AKG-images; p.52 AKG-images; p.53 © BPK; p.54 © Bettmann/CORBIS; p.55 t Punch Ltd; p.55 b © Bettmann/CORBIS; p.57 Punch Ltd; p.58 l Photograph by NMI, Camera Press London; p.58 r Crawford Municipal Art Gallery; p.59 Courtesy of the National Library of Ireland; p.60 © Bettmann/CORBIS; p.61 Hulton Archive/Getty Images; p.62 l © Hulton-Deutsch Collection/CORBIS; p.62 r Punch Ltd; p.65 © Windows To Ireland; p.67 Keystone/Getty Images; p.68 © Hulton-Deutsch Collection/CORBIS; p.73 © Hulton-Deutsch Collection/CORBIS; p.75 © Hulton-Deutsch Collection/CORBIS; p.77 Hulton Archive/Getty Images; p.78 r Photograph by J. J. Brown, Camera Press London; p.79 © CORBIS; p.81 © National Museums and Galleries of Northern Ireland; p.82 Haywood Magee/Getty Images; p.83 © Belfast Telegraph; p.85 Ulster Museum; p.88 t Leslie Gilbert Illingworth, *Daily Mail*, 9 November 1940/British Cartoon Archive, University of Kent; p.88 b © British Library/Colindale; p.92 People's History Museum; p.95 l Linenhall Library; p.96 © Bettmann/CORBIS; p.97 t © Bettmann/CORBIS; p.98 t © Popperfoto/Getty Images; b © Geray Sweeney/CORBIS; p.99 © The Irish Image Collection/Corbis; p.102 © Belfast Telegraph; p.105 © Hulton-Deutsch Collection/CORBIS; p.108 Bentley Archive/Popperfoto/Getty Images; p.110 AP Images/PA Photos; p.113 © Belfast Telegraph; p.114 © 2003 Topham Picturepoint; p.115 © Bettmann/CORBIS; p.117 © Hulton-Deutsch Collection/CORBIS; p.119 © Topfoto; p.121 © Topfoto; p.124 © Belfast Telegraph; p.126 © Bettmann/CORBIS; p.127 Popperfoto/Getty Images; p.131 © Hulton-Deutsch Collection/CORBIS; p.133 © Belfast Telegraph; p.135 © Belfast Telegraph; p.137 ©2003 Topham/PA; p.138 © Bettmann/CORBIS; p.140 © Peter Turnley/CORBIS; p.141 AP Photo/Peter Kemp; p.142 © DURAND PATRICK/CORBIS SYGMA; p.143 © Topfoto; p.144 © Topfoto; p.148 © David King Collection; p.149 © Bettmann/CORBIS; p.151 © Bettmann/CORBIS; p.152 Leslie Gilbert Illingworth, *Daily Mail*, 6 March 1946/British Cartoon Archive, University of Kent; p.154 Al Fenn/Time Life Pictures/Getty Images; p.155 Punch Ltd; p.158 Punch Ltd; p.160 © Bettmann/CORBIS; p.162 © Bettmann/CORBIS; p.164 © Topfoto; p.167 l © CORBIS; p.167 r Ranan Lurie; p.168 © Wally McNamee/CORBIS; p.170 © Peter Turnley/CORBIS; p.173 t JEFF WIDENER/AP/PA Photos; p.173 b © Peter Turnley/CORBIS; p.180 © Bettmann/CORBIS; p.181 Leslie Gilbert Illingworth, *Daily Mail*, 29 October 1962/British Cartoon Archive, University of Kent; p.184 © Bettmann/CORBIS; p.185 b Ronald S. Haeberle/Time Life Pictures/Getty Images; p.188 Punch Ltd.

The publishers would also like to thank the following for permission to reproduce material in this book: Blackstaff Press for extracts from *A History of Ulster* by Jonathon Bardon, 1992, reproduced by permission of Blackstaff Press on behalf of the author; Pearson Longman for extracts from *Northern Ireland Since 1945* by Sabine Wichert, 1991.

The publishers would like to acknowledge use of the following extracts: Addison Wesley for extracts from *Northern Ireland Politics* by Dr. Duncan Morrow, 1996; Cambridge University Press for extracts from *Democracies and Dictatorships: Europe and the World 1919–1989* by Allan Todd, 2001; Cambridge University Press for extracts from *Ireland 1912–1985: Politics and Society* by J.J. Lee, 1989; Collins Educational for an extract from *The Cold War 1945–1989* by Fiona MacDonald and Richard Staton, 1996; Harcourt Education for extracts from *The Cold War: Conflict in Europe and Asia* by Steve Phillips, 2001; Rupert Hart-Davis for an extract from *Terence O'Neill's Autobiography*, 1972; Holmes and Meier for extracts from *A History of Northern Ireland* by Patrick Buckland, 1981; Palgrave Macmillan for an extract from *Northern Ireland: The Politics of War and Peace* by Paul Dixon, 2001; Palgrave Macmillan for an extract from *Twentieth Century Ireland* by Dermot Keogh, 1994; Routledge for extracts from *The Cold War, 1945–1991* by John W. Mason, 1996; The Scarecrow Press, Inc. for an extract from *Northern Ireland: A Chronology of the Troubles* by Paul Bew and Gordon Gillespie, 1993; Scribner for an extract from *Ireland since the Famine* by F.S.L. Lyons, 1973; *The Times* for an extract from *Gustav Stresemann's obituary*, October 1929.

# INDEX

1931 Statute of Westminster 59
38th parallel 175, 176–8

Adams, Gerry 139–40, 142
Afghanistan 168, 170
Albania 152
Alliance Party (APNI) 130, 142, 149
Anglo-Irish Agreement (1985) 140–5
Anglo-Irish Agreements (1938) 70–1
Anti-Semitism 44–6, *see also* Jews
Appeasement 51, 53–4, 68–9, 122
Atomic bomb 150, 151, 174, 177
Attlee, Clement 92, 98, 99, 150

Baltic States 172
Battle of Britain 79–80
Battle of the Bogside 117–18
Belfast Blitz 84–5, 89
Berlin Blockade 156–9
Berlin Wall 161–2, 173
Bismarck, Otto von 1–2
Bloody Friday 126–7
Bloody Sunday 123–5, 139
Boundary Commission 59, 60–1
Brezhnev, Leonid 163–64, 166, 168, 170, 171
Britain
    1974 general election 134
    appeasement approach to Germany 51–3, 54, 55, 68–9
    direct rule of Northern Ireland 125–6, 135–6
    economic war with Ireland 64–6
    events leading up to Second World War 54–5, 74
        involvement with Russian civil war 147
    invasion threat from Germany 55
    involvement in Suez 161
    Irish treaty ports 71–2
    reaction to Anglo-Irish Agreement 143
    relations with USSR 148, 151–2
    Treaty of Versailles 6–8, 10, 15, 50, 51
    Welfare State 92–3
    Yalta 149–50
    *see also* Battle of Britain
British Commonwealth 58, 80, 97–8
Brooke, Basil (Lord Brookeborough) 83, 86, 94, 98–9, 102
Brüning, Heinrich 19–22
Bulgaria 152, 163
*Bunreacht na hÉireann* 66–8
Burntollet 113–14
Bush, George H. 170

Carter, James E. (Jimmy) 168
Censorship in Nazi Germany 42–3
Chamberlain, Neville 51, 53, 54, 68–71, 72–3
Chiang Kai-shek 174, 177, 178
Chichester Clark, James 115, 118–19, 122
China
    establishment of the People's Republic of China 174
    relationship with USA 166–7, 174–5, 176, 177–8, 183, 184
    relationship with USSR 166, 167, 174
    student protests (Tiananmen Square) 172, 173
Churchill, Winston S. 71, 79–80, 87, 89, 92, 149–50, 151–2
Communist Party (Germany, KPD) 4–5, 18, 20, 22, 24, 28–29
Conscription 72–3, 80
Containment 153–4, 158, 175, 177, 178, 187
Craig, James (Lord Craigavon) 60, 67, 71, 72, 73, 81, 85, 87
Craig, William 112, 124, 129, 131
Cuban missile crisis 179–80
Czechoslovakia
    1968 uprising 163–5
    and Second World War 53, 54, 69
    post-Second World War 152, 155

Dawes Plan 12
De Valera, Éamon 57, 59, 62–67, 70–1, 74–5, 80, 86–90, 95–6
Democratic Unionist Party (DUP) 131, 144
Détente 164, 166–8, 169
Direct rule 125–6, 135–6
Domino theory 175, 176, 183
Downing Street Declaration 119–20

Ebert, Friedrich 3–6, 8–10, 12, 13
Economic War (Anglo-Irish) 64–6, 70
Eisenhower, Dwight D. 177–8, 183
Enabling Law (Act) 29, 32

Faulkner, Brian 102, 105, 106, 111, 114, 122–5, 126, 129, 130, 131, 132, 133–4, 135, 136
FitzGerald, Garrett 131, 140–1
First World War 2–5, 57
Five-point Reform Programme 111–12
France
    1923 invasion of the Ruhr 10–12, 13
    1968 student demonstrations 108
    appeasement approach to Germany 51–3, 54, 55
    events leading up to Second World War 54–5, 74
    failed alliance with USSR 148

invasion by Germany 77, 81
involvement with Russian civil war 147
involvement with Suez 161
involvement with Vietnam 183
Treaty of Versailles 6–7, 50, 51
Yalta 150
Free Corps (*Frei Korps*) 4–5, 8–10, 15

Germany
before First World War 1–2
Berlin Wall 161–2, 173
post-Second World War division 150–1, 153, 156–7
Gerrymandering 101, 108, 119
*Glasnost* 171–3
Goebbels, Josef 23, 37, 39, 42, 49
Gorbachev, Mikhail 169–73
Göring, Herman 16, 28, 30, 31, 34–5, 52, 80
Government of Ireland Act (1920) 58–9, 60, 101
Greece
part in Truman Doctrine 154

Heath, Edward 125, 126, 131
Heydrich, Reinhard 40, 41
Himmler, Heinrich 31, 40–1
Hindenburg, Paul von 8, 13, 20, 22, 24, 25–6, 28, 31, 32
Hitler, Adolf
early life 14–15
ideals 15, 18
involvement with Nazi Party 14–18
rise to power 24–6, 28–32
Hume, John 130, 139, 142
Hungary
1956 rebellion against Soviet rule 160–1
alliance with Germany 54, 55
USSR invasion 149, 152
Hunger strike 86, 137–39
Hyperinflation crisis in Germany 11, 20

Internment 81, 86, 122, 123, 125, 129
Irish Republican Army (IRA) 57, 62, 81, 86–8, 96, 102, 108, 109, 115, 118, 120–2, 123, 124, 125–6, 132, 136, 137–9, 140–1
Irish Free State Constitution 58–9, 66–7, 102
Irish neutrality 69, 70, 74–5, 81, 86, 87–9
Italy
alliance with Germany 51, 52, 53, 55, 68
Treaty of Versailles 6, 50
Japan
alliance with Germany 51
atomic bombing 151
communist threat 175, 178
involvement with Russian civil war 147
Jews 23, 29, 34, 40, 44–6
Kapp *Putsch* 8–9, 10

Kennedy, John F. 109, 161–2, 179–83
Khrushchev, Nikita 159–61, 163, 166, 178, 180, 181, 182
Korean War 175–8

League of Nations 13, 49, 69, 148
Lemass, Sean 65, 90, 104–5, 106
Locarno Treaties 13
Ludendorff, Erich 16–17
*Luftwaffe* 50, 51, 77, 78, 80, 84, 85, 90
Lynch, Jack 105, 118

Marshall Aid (Plan) 155–6, 157
Mao Zedong 167, 174, 177
Media, control in Nazi Germany 42
*Mein Kampf* 18
Munich *Putsch* 16–17
Mussolini, Benito 51, 52, 53, 54, 68

Nazi organisations
DAF (German Labour Front) 30, 33
*Gestapo* 40, 41
Hitler Youth 18, 23, 38
SA (*Sturmabteilung*) 15, 18, 22, 23, 28, 29, 30, 31–2, 40, 45
SS (*Schutzstaffel*) 18, 22, 29, 36, 40
Nazi Party
25-Point programme 15, 48
origins 15–16
police state 40–1
reasons for support 23
use of propaganda 42–3
Nazi policy towards:
churches 39–40
economy 33–5
education 37
foreign policy 48, 50–5
Jews 44–6
judiciary 40–1
opposition 28, 29–30
rearmament 50
security forces 40
women 36–7
young people 37–8
Night of the Long Knives 31–2
Nixon, Richard M. 167, 184, 186
North Atlantic Treaty Organisation (NATO) 158–9, 166, 178
Northern Ireland Civil Rights Association (NICRA) 108–14, 122, 124, 125

O'Neill, Terence 102–7, 108, 110–15, 122
Organisation European Economic Co-operation (OEEC) 155
Paisley, Rev. Ian 105, 114, 131, 142, 144

Papen, Franz von 22, 24, 25, 26, 28
People's Democracy 112–15
  March 112–14
*Perestroika* 171–3
Poland
  British–French military guarantees against German invasion 55, 69, 74
  collapse of USSR 172
  gain of German territory as a result of Treaty of Versailles 6
  German non-aggression pact 49–50
  Nazi–Soviet Pact 55
  post-Second World War borders 149, 150–1, 152
  protests against communist rule 160, 163
  *see also* Warsaw Pact
Potsdam 150–1, 156–7
Power-sharing executive in Northern Ireland 129–30, 131–2, 133–4, 135–6
Proportional representation 5, 58, 101, 129

Reagan, Ronald W. 169–70
Red Rising (Germany) 10
*Reichstag* fire 28
Rhineland 6–7, 13, 51, 69
Röhm, Ernst 31
Romania 152
Roosevelt, Franklin D. 88, 149, 150
Royal Air Force (RAF) 69, 77, 79–80, 89
Royal Ulster Constabulary (RUC) 80, 81, 108, 110, 113, 119, 125, 136, 145
Ruhr region of Germany 10–11, 12, 13

Saar region of Germany 6, 50
Sands, Bobby 138–9
Schleicher, Kurt von 22, 25–6, 31
Second World War 41, 51, 74–5, 77–90, 95, 154, 174, 183
South East Asian Treaty Organisation (SEATO) 166
Sinn Féin 57, 59, 139–40, 141, 142, 144, 145
Social Democratic and Labour Party (SDLP) 123, 125, 129, 130, 131, 132, 134, 135, 139–40, 142, 144, 145
Social Democratic Party (SPD) in post-First World War Germany 3
Spartacist *Putsch* 4
Special category status prisoners 136, 137–9
Special Powers Act 101, 108, 111, 112
Stalin, Joseph 55, 68, 148, 149–50, 151–2, 155, 157–8, 159, 161, 166, 174–5, 176, 188
Strategic Arms Limitation Talks (SALT) 167, 168
Strategic Defence Initiative in USA 169
Stresemann, Gustav 12, 13–14, 16, 19
Sudetenland 53
Sunningdale 131–2, 133, 134, 135

Taiwan 174
Thatcher, Margaret 138, 140, 141, 144
Tito, Josip 152
Treaty ports 59, 70–2, 81, 87
Truman Doctrine 154–6
Truman, Harry S. 150, 153, 154, 158, 174, 176, 177, 188
Turkey
  as US missile base 179, 180, 181, 182
  in First World War 2

Ulster Defence Association (UDA) 122, 123, 135
Ulster Special Constabulary (B Specials) 58, 81, 108, 119, 125
Ulster Vanguard, *see* Vanguard
Ulster Volunteer Force (UVF) 57, 101, 106, 122
Ulster Workers' Council (UWC) 135, 136
United Nations (UN) 149, 150, 155, 166, 167, 171, 174, 175, 176–7
United Ulster Unionist Council (UUUC) 129, 133, 134

Vanguard 124–5, 129, 131
Versailles, Treaty of 6–8, 10, 14, 15, 23, 48, 50, 51, 68
Vietnam 164, 166–7, 183–87

Wall Street Crash 19–20
Warsaw Pact 158, 160, 163–64, 170
Weimar Republic and
  Article 48: 5, 12, 20–1, 22, 25
  Constitution 5–6
Welfare State 92–4, 95, 101, 106
Wilson, Harold 111, 118–19, 134–6
Wilson, Woodrow 6
World War I, *see* First World War
World War II, *see* Second World War

Yalta 149–51, 156
Yeltsin, Boris 173
Young Plan 12
Yugoslavia
  relationship with USSR 152, 159